TALKING
TO
THE SPIRITS

"Filan and Kaldera have once again created an impressive and necessary work for the flourishing spirit-working Pagan community. In these pages you will find an immediate, earthy, social, and accessible way to approach this dangerous and risky alliance with the Spirits. This book touches on personal gnosis, historical gnosis, Neo-Pagan perspectives and sociologies, and discernment of messages in alluringly deepening ways. It also shares responsible and proactive ways of working with gnosis and revelation in groups and community to achieve whole and integrated spirituality with an ear to the ever interesting, ever bizarre Otherworld peopled with Endless Spirits. As a spirit-worker, I personally attest that this book is a must read!"

GEDE PARMA, WITCHCRAFT PRIEST AND TEACHER AND
AUTHOR OF *ECSTATIC WITCHCRAFT* AND *SPIRITED*

"In recent years there has been a greater desire for deeper connection with the Gods within a polytheistic pagan framework. *Talking to the Spirits* is a practical manual for such work, particularly for those relying on their own impressions—personal gnosis—to fill in the gaps left by mythology, history, and established religions. In the same way, this book fills a gaping niche in the practitioner's shelf. It is clear the authors have dealt with a variety of challenges in deeper spirit work as well as found suitable solutions, and the subject matter is covered in an impressively thorough manner."

LUPA, AUTHOR OF *NEW PATHS TO ANIMAL TOTEMS* AND
EDITOR OF THEGREENWOLF.COM

TALKING
TO
THE
SPIRITS

Personal Gnosis in
Pagan Religion

KENAZ FILAN and RAVEN KALDERA

Destiny Books
Rochester, Vermont • Toronto, Canada

Destiny Books
One Park Street
Rochester, Vermont 05767
www.DestinyBooks.com

Text stock is SFI certified

Destiny Books is a division of Inner Traditions International

Library of Congress Cataloging-in-Publication Data

Filan, Kenaz.
  Talking to the spirits : personal gnosis in pagan religion / Kenaz Filan and Raven
Kaldera.
     p. cm.
  Includes bibliographical references and index.
  Summary: "A guide to direct communication with the spirits and the Gods"—
Provided by publisher.
  ISBN 978-1-62055-083-0 (print) — ISBN 978-1-62055-150-9 (e-book)
  1. Neopaganism. 2. Gnosticism. 3. Spirituality. I. Kaldera, Raven. II. Title.
  BP605.N46F55 2013
  299'.94—dc23
                                                                            2012035958

Printed and bound in the United States by Lake Book Manufacturing, Inc.
The text stock is SFI certified. The Sustainable Forestry Initiative® program
promotes sustainable forest management.

10 9 8 7 6 5 4 3 2 1

Text design by Virginia Scott Bowman and layout by Brian Boynton
This book was typeset in Garamond Premier Pro with Golden Cockerel as the
display typeface

To send correspondence to the author of this book, mail a first-class letter to the
author c/o Inner Traditions • Bear & Company, One Park Street, Rochester, VT
05767, and we will forward the communication, or contact the authors directly at
www.kenazfilan.com for Kenaz Filan and **www.cauldronfarm.com** for Raven
Kaldera.

CONTENTS

INTRODUCTION

Reclaiming Our Gods, Reconstructing Our Faith

Of all the lies we have ever been told, this is the worst: that the Gods no longer speak to us. If they ever conversed with mere mortals, we are told, they have long since gone silent. And in any event, everything they had to say to us can be found in their holy book (although, alas, there's some dispute on exactly *which* book that is). For our ancestors, Divinity was immanent, bubbling forth from rivers and springs, and whispering in the breezes that rustled through the cities and the farms. Our spiritual world is much more circumscribed: an inaccessible sacred casts a faint, chilly glow upon our profane lives.

Stranded in that cold and lonely darkness, some seek to reestablish our ancestral relationships with the Divine. To that end, many have declared their allegiance to the Old Gods. But as these pioneers have sought to progress in their faith, they have often found themselves stymied by centuries of conditioning. To find our way back to that ancestral place where we walked with the Gods, we must relearn how to see the world as they did.

> *HEATHEN (n): A benighted creature who has the folly to worship something he can see and feel.*
>
> **—Ambrose Bierce**[1]

1

When you go back far enough, everyone, regardless of culture or geography, lived in a world that was more alive than ours. The ground underfoot, the stones, the fire that cooked the food and drove off the darkness, these all had spirits—not just spirits in some other dimension who were "in charge of them," but spirits in them, who could be spoken to and allied with. At the same time, larger powers existed who were in charge of their "children" and watched over them . . . and could add us to that flock, if we were willing. Gods weren't something far removed from the physical world of flesh and soil and desires; the hundred Gods were only one step farther away than the thousand spirits. Between those groups was no firm line but only a gray area that often shifted depending on how much attention they were paying you at the moment.

Before we can make the leap to understanding the hundred Gods, we must first understand the thousand spirits and develop a soul-deep feel for how spiritually alive our entire world really is. Once we have connected with the river spirit and the local city spirit and a few of our ancestors, and we understand how their existence is woven into everyday life—not a superstition but an easily accepted fact—we can then begin to understand how the Gods, too, are part of that everyday life.

For as long as there have been empires there have been Gods of empire. Conquered nations were expected to make obeisance to the conquerors' Deities, and the tributes of subject peoples enriched many a holy temple. These offerings and rituals were more akin to the American Pledge of Allegiance or Soviet military parades than to the Christian idea of worship. In honoring the empire's Gods you proclaimed your loyalty—or at least recognized their military superiority. In building a great monument to your patron Gods you acknowledged their blessings, but also displayed your city's wealth.

But while people went to these public temples for public functions, for most, their primary spiritual focus was on the Gods of hearth and home. Local and ancestral spirits were more directly connected to the lives of their devotees and more ready to intervene in their daily affairs. Artisans, criminals, and farmers might have a special devotion to the patrons of their trades: fishers and sailors might propitiate both Poseidon and the nymphs who ruled over a particularly treacherous inlet.

These spiritual arenas—the public and private—coexisted in relative comfort. You might fulfill civic duties at a local temple, drop a coin in the stream for a local spirit on your way home, then spend some quiet time with your ancestors before your hearth. So long as you posed no threat to the established order, you were free to believe as you chose. It was only with the establishment of Christendom—first as an effort to preserve the crumbling Roman Empire, then as a defensive coalition against the new threat of Islam—that the religious authorities set out to control private spiritual practice.

Laws against malevolent magic are not unique to Christianity or to monotheism. What is unique to these traditions is how they define all other spiritual practices as inherently evil or, at best, terminally flawed. The mystical experience is either carefully delimited or rejected outright as demonolatry (demon worship) and sorcery. The idea of local wights is treated as silly; sentience, like souls, is a human phenomenon; and one should worship the Creator, not the Creation. It's easy to assume that all religions see their Gods as equally distant and detached—but that is not the case at all. Consider Japan, where Shinto spirits can be found in the heavens, on the sea, and in your family's outhouse! Dr. Gabi Greve, an art historian living in Okayama, Japan, writes about her experience with a toilet God.

When we remodeled our old farmhouse, we had to do something about grandfather's toilet. It was just a small pond in the ground, with two beams over it where you had to balance real hard while performing your job. Below you was the open sewer.

The local carpenter decided to drain the sewage water, fill the hole up with earth and level it with the rest of the ground. But before doing anything to this smelling place, we were informed, we had to pacify the Suijinsama [water God] living in this pond.

With plenty of ricewine (for the God and the humans) and purifying salt and a lot of mumbling prayers, the God was informed that
his palace was to go and he would be relocated in a wet rice field
further down. After the water was drained, a pipe was stuck in the
hole before it was filled up, so that the Suijinsama who might have
been left in the place would find their way out. This pipe is still
sticking out to this day.[2]

The polytheistic world features a plethora of Gods and spirits struggling with and against each other; there is no place where Divinity is
absent. Within a monotheistic world, there is only the One. That which
he declares holy is holy; all else is cast to the winds like chaff. If he is
not to be found in bejeweled idols or verdant sacred groves, he certainly
won't deign to be found in a septic tank, a whorehouse, or a rotting pile
of trash. And as the Creator grows ever more distant from Creation,
those who grew up hearing there was only one God find it just as easy
to believe there is none at all.

This is the place many modern seekers after Divinity find themselves. They have rejected the monotheistic religion of their upbringing and many of its outdated rules. They have replaced the concept of
the judgmental Father God with kinder, gentler divine parental models,
but they have not yet questioned the prejudices and preconceptions that
come with the teachings of a monotheistic faith.

For some, their Deities remain so distant as to be nonexistent.
Many replace the void left by God & Son with "archetypes" and other
equally nebulous terms that add up to "symbols for psychodrama." The
idea that their imaginary friends might actually exist outside their own
crania seems to them alternately silly and terrifying. Describing his own
flirtation with this sort of idealism at Oxford, C. S. Lewis said:

> The emotion that went with all this was certainly religious. But this
> was a religion that cost nothing. We could talk about the Absolute,
> but there was no danger of Its doing anything about us. It was
> "there"; safely and immovably "there." It would never come "here,"

never (to be blunt) make a nuisance of Itself. . . . There was nothing to fear; better still, nothing to obey.[3]

Others take a Newtonian approach: they seek to reduce a complex spiritual reality to its underlying equations. This has been going on at least since the Victorian era. Helena Petrovna Blavatsky sought the "Secret Doctrine" behind all modern religions. Aleister Crowley created tables of correspondence that mixed and matched Deities on Kabbalistic paths, stating "when a Japanese thinks of Hachiman, and a Boer of the Lord of Hosts, they are not two thoughts, but one."[4]

There are many good reasons why scholars and practitioners alike might want to examine commonalities of religious practice among different cultures. But this approach is quite different from the animistic worldview of pre-Christian polytheism. Scientific reductionism seeks to reduce the mysteries to recipes and rational explanations. Animism, by contrast, seeks a direct and personal engagement with the material world. The botanist may know that tree's genus, species, and approximate age; the shaman knows that it favors offerings of yellow ribbons, tells great dirty jokes, and readily shares gossip about the goings-on within this particular patch of land.

Many academic efforts to understand indigenous religions have fallen afoul of this. Mircea Eliade (and later Michael Harner) approached shamanism in a scientific fashion. They looked for the underlying mechanics of the religion, for things they could catalogue, measure, and reproduce. To a certain extent they (and others who have followed in their footsteps) succeeded. They introduced Western culture to iboga, ayahuasca, peyote, and other substances that can reproduce what feels very much like classical descriptions of a mystical experience; they explored the ways fasting, dancing, drumbeats, and other techniques could cause shifts in perception; and they sorted through reams of data to identify the most effective means by which these altered states could be induced.

Yet this approach points to a great disjunction between the worldviews of the shaman and neoshaman. The shaman is an entity within a living world, a being defined by interactions with other sentient beings both human and nonhuman. The neoshaman lives within a material universe, one that is essentially inert and where sentience is an exclusively human trait—or where, at best, human intelligence is seen as the apex of evolution to date. Tribal shamans are mediators and diplomats. They seek to protect the interests of their clan in a world filled with allies, enemies, and neutral parties. Many neoshamans, by contrast, come as colonists and conquistadors. The oil driller delves deep into Mother Earth in search of profit, while the neoshaman meditates on Mother Earth in search of wisdom, abundance, prosperity, healing, or other polite euphemisms for "personal gain." The interior and exterior worlds are treated not as complex interdependent ecosystems but as resources to be exploited.

Today's modern neoshamanism is largely a celebration of the primitive. By taking on the titles and ceremonial rites of hunter-gatherers or subsistence farmers, neoshamans hope to rid themselves of civilization's blinders and break through modern conditioning. Entheogens free them from logic while revelry frees them from inhibition. This evokes Friedrich Nietzsche's description of the Dionysian influence.

> He has forgotten how to walk and talk and is on the verge of flying up into the air as he dances. The enchantment speaks out in his gestures. Just as the animals now speak and the earth gives milk and honey, so something supernatural also echoes out of him: he feels himself a god; he himself now moves in as lofty and ecstatic a way as he saw the gods move in his dream. The man is no longer an artist; he has become a work of art: the artistic power of all of nature, to the highest rhapsodic satisfaction of the primordial unity, reveals itself here in the transports of intoxication.[5]

This view of shamanism often has more to do with romantic fantasy than reality. Those looking for "noble savages" living in peaceful harmony with nature are likely to be disappointed when they actually encounter indigenous peoples. The lives of nomadic, hunter-gatherer, or subsistence agriculture societies are anything but delightful and idyllic. They do not live in a happy world where cherubic animals perform Busby Berkeley routines and dispense homespun wisdom. They recognize their surroundings as animate and sentient, yes—but they are also well aware that those surroundings can turn on them with little notice. In their capacity as intercessors and messengers, the shamans of these cultures deal with enemies as often as friends, and the stakes are frequently life and death for shaman and tribe alike.

More important, the Dionysian viewpoint fundamentally misstates the role traditional shamans play in their community. One undertakes the spirit journey not for intoxication but for clarity. The shaman's world is not a free and unbounded one. On the contrary, it is constrained on all sides by restrictions and taboos. Their practices are not a "return to nature." Rather, they attempt to make sense of nature, to intercede with the shadowy and frequently hostile forces threatening them and their community. Far from escaping order and rule, shamans help to establish them; they escape their society only so they can work for it as intercessors and arbitrators between the various realms.

In our culture the Priests of Science and Lords of the Grove of Academe fill the roles the shaman fulfills in an indigenous society. Like our historians and intellectuals, shamans provide a framework by which their community members can understand the various phenomena that shape their lives. Their stories preserve ancestral knowledge and help ensure the survival of the next generation; they serve as boundary markers between the village and the wild places, between the tribe and the outlanders, between the living and the dead. While they may seem charming and primitive to us more civilized types, we might do well to consider another observation by Nietzsche.

> Wherever we encounter the "naive" in art, we have to recognize the highest effect of Apollonian culture, which always first has to overthrow the kingdom of the Titans and to kill monsters and, through

powerfully deluding images and joyful illusions, has to emerge victorious over the horrific depth of what we observe in the world and the most sensitive capacity for suffering.[6]

If we are to honor the Gods as they once were honored, we must not be deceived. We must understand that they have never turned away from us; rather, we turned away from them. We must know them not only in the dim distant echoes of their long-ago words and deeds, but also in the minutiae of our daily lives. It is not enough to know the ancient stories; we must also hear and participate in the stories they are writing in the Here and the Now . . . and, most important, we must understand how to listen for their whispers once again.

1

WHY PERSONAL GNOSIS?

I think religion/spirituality without personal gnosis is uninspired, boring, and desiccated, like a cracker. A really tasteless cracker. A very disappointing cracker. However, I happen to also think that personal gnosis without religion (some semblance of structure, tradition, method, ritual), is like peanut butter without the cracker—it's ridiculously messy, difficult to hold on to, and can get kind of icky. Balancing personal gnosis with tradition is a critical task in order to maintain a living spiritual tradition.

—Ruby Sara, U.S. Neo-Pagan

This is the first question that needs asking, because some people suggest that the safest form of religion is simply following the rules, activities, and beliefs currently set down in writing, and going no further than this. With this worldview, there is usually room for discussing existing accepted dogma with an eye to putting it aside if it proves to be outdated, and for dissecting the finer points of how to apply the existing dogma to one's life in a personally satisfying way, but there is little to no room for additional spiritual information. Is it safer? Definitely. However, we would argue that the goal of religion is not to be safe, but to facilitate a connection with the Holy Powers, and the Holy Powers are by definition not safe. They do not conform to our ideas and desires, and they have their own agenda that may not include our convenience and emotional comfort. Indeed, most renowned spiritual leaders have made it clear that if you're too spiritually comfortable, you're missing the point.

We, the authors of this book, clearly acknowledge our bias that personal gnosis is an important and integral part of not only personal spirituality, but group religion as well. Any religion that does not recognize and acknowledge any contemporary gnosis is a dead religion; its rituals are skeletons preserved in museums, and its priests are grave keepers. Sooner or later, any spiritual practice followed sincerely will lead to personal gnosis. Seekers will recite the Qur'an until they find themselves transfixed before the presence of the Almighty; acolytes will look for Aphrodite or Ochun or Freya until she appears in some form. This gnosis may not be a literal vision or a voice (although we suspect those are more common than many imagine), but it will be a Knowing that will transform their lives. That Knowing, when it comes, will be impossible to describe and just as impossible to ignore. It will be shaped by the individual's experience and what he or she brings to the table, but it will clearly come from something that is outside of and much larger than the individual.

GODS AND THEIR SIDE EFFECTS

Personal gnosis is the end result of asking your guides for assistance, or the answer to a problem, or a push in the right direction. It is the spiritual awakening that comes when you realize that this might be a two-way communication—you address the ceiling (or the Moon, or a candle, or a statue) and somewhere in the galaxy, Something hears. Not only did it hear, but it is talking back. It may not be words, like a conversation. You may have to be more alert than that. You may see a well-timed commercial on television, or find a friend calling you to ask about the very thing you seek, or

the means to achieve your goal will begin to manifest around
you. The words of a God are changing your reality, your
perception, and your very soul.

I encourage my students and clients to seek out gnosis. I
give them exercises and experiences in hopes of provoking the
cosmic "aha" that will help bring their spiritual lives into
better focus. Gods deal with humans very personally, and they
know your soul better than you do. They will twang the right
string and get it to vibrate on such a level that it cannot be
ignored for long.

—**Del, U.S. Pagan**

It's been said that personal gnosis is the side effect of having a relationship with actual Gods. In Abrahamic religions, a personal devotional
relationship with one's Deity may or may not be encouraged depending
on the sect in question—some sects prefer that all religious activity be
mediated through clergy; others are more comfortable with people having a "personal relationship with Jesus" or whoever is most accessible to
them. Even so, there is often an assumption—spoken or unspoken—
that it's not possible to make it a two-way conversation. The snide comment is often bandied about that "if you talk to the angels, that's prayer;
if the angels talk back, that's insanity." If questioned, some people will
say that while certain special human beings were once able to hear God,
that doesn't happen anymore for a number of reasons (mostly having to
do with how much more sinful humans are these days).

That attitude has worked its way into modern Paganism, in that
some claim that the Gods no longer speak to us for a number of reasons
(mostly having to do with how technologically based and detached our
culture has become). In spite of this, however, some people find that
when they go to the trouble of creating a regular spiritual discipline
that involves quality time spent with their Gods, they start noticing
a sense of presence, and perhaps become aware of subtle guiding messages as well. Throughout the ages, one possible side effect of prayer
has always been the potential for those prayers being answered in some

way—which in turn leads to a deeper relationship, which in turn leads to more two-way connection with the Holy Powers.

> *Personal gnosis has been crucial to my spiritual journey: it has often turned me round quite abruptly from the path I thought I was following and directed my steps in a different direction— repeating the process several times if I am too timid or too skeptical to make the change. As the years have gone by, I have learned to trust these experiences because they have always been proved, either in the short or the long term, to be important to my personal evolution, and to my relationship with the Deity I serve. Because of this, I am usually disposed to respect other people's accounts of personal gnosis, unless I have good reason to mistrust either the circumstances or the individual.*
>
> **—Rose Alba, U.K. Pagan**

BUT ISN'T PERSONAL GNOSIS SOMETIMES WRONG?

> *I believe that personal gnosis is a vital component of a mystical religious practice. Where there exist lacunae in our source materials, it is necessary to seek gnosis to repair our damaged understanding, but even if this were not the case, personal gnosis is still indispensible. One cannot have a sincere, living relationship with one's Gods or spirits unless one is open to receiving personal gnosis in some form or another. However, no one has the right to demand uncritical acceptance of their personal gnosis as divine truth by the wider community. Certain messages are tailored for certain heads; not every being that shows up claiming to be a God actually is one; and even the best spirit worker will get their wires crossed some of the time.*
>
> **—Mordant Carnival, U.K. Pagan**

On the other hand, the big problem is, of course, how to determine whether a given person's gnosis should be considered to any extent by any other human being in the world. This is where religious doctrine steps in, because one of its purposes is to give people guidelines when it comes to accepting the gnosis of a lone stranger or a different group. This is not a bad thing. It's appropriate for people to look to their religious group (assuming they belong to one) for information about these things. In general, they don't expect that source to be unbiased. What they do expect is that the group will have given careful thought and serious consideration to those questions. While one may disagree with the answers posed by the mainstream religion that one left, one may also have little respect for a religion that hasn't come up with any answers to those questions or that brushes off inquiries as being the job of one's personal spiritual discernment. That's unsatisfying for seekers, and they will generally go elsewhere to find the answers they want to study. (Not to believe in an unqualified way, but to study and to compare with other answers. We'll get further into that question when we discuss the problems of seekers.)

Pagans spread themselves across the whole spectrum of the personal gnosis question, from the ones who feel that it should be given free rein everywhere and the ones who don't trust it at all. Most are in the middle, acknowledging its benefits but worried about the drawbacks of discernment, as the following Pagans point out.

The line between personal gnosis and delusion is a thin one. In my opinion, this is the reason that the branch of Zen Buddhism I have been reading about does not recommend active participation in the faith without a guide (someone who knows the pitfalls and can point out when you're being delusional). It may also be the reason that the various traditional mystery religions still existing in Paganism are not fond of the way in which Paganism is commercialized for public consumption. Religion by and large teaches us to reach for God, however we define God. Our own ego will complicate this process in a variety of ways, and we may confuse the constructs it creates for actual spiritual experience. On a much more personal level, I feel that personal gnosis is a vital component of a variety of spiritual traditions, so long as it is balanced by a rational, skeptical eye. It is through personal gnosis that one reaches an understanding with an immanent, personal Deity. It is through personal gnosis that the individual accepts or rejects the various dogmatic parts of his or her faith, or forms new beliefs.

—Raenshadoe, U.S. Pagan

I feel that personal gnosis can be very important to personal practice, and even sometimes to communities, but that caution is necessary in approaching it. We as individuals, and as communities, need to have ways of discerning genuine spiritual knowledge from self-delusion so that our practices don't become pure fantasy. Not everything that we get is going to be either true or useful, and it's best to acknowledge that up front rather than kidding ourselves about how we're special little snowflakes whose every subconscious whim has to be followed.

—Erynn Rowan Laurie,
U.S. Celtic Reconstructionist Pagan

We also believe that discernment is important, and especially discernment regarding whether a given gnosis is relevant to anyone else, even if it's true. That's what much of this book will be dedicated to discussing. However, it's crucial that Pagans understand the reality of the equation, which is that having Gods means having personal gnosis . . . sooner or later, for most people, anyway.

Much of my opinion on the matter depends on the context and the manner in which any statements of personal gnosis are shared or discussed with others. On the one hand, people will have different experiences, different interpretations of the same materials, and a variety of other things that distinguish them from everyone else. This wondrous diversity is something that should be encouraged and celebrated whenever and wherever possible, and I believe this can be done in relation to a variety of matters in a respectful and mutually productive way. I also think that when certain individuals or communities tackle a particular issue and come up with answers that work for them through various channels of personal gnosis, this actually builds practice and sustains a spiritual community, so I think this is a necessary and even desirable process that should be encouraged.

On the other hand, I have a very big problem with people who will not admit that something is their own personal gnosis rather than a thing that is part of a religious tradition, and they often suggest that it is in fact a part of some tradition rather than simply their interpretation of it. Almost as bad is the idea that any interpretation of a religious tradition is a valid one, and therefore any idea is as good as any other and is immune to critique. A further item of irritation in this category is the assertion that all religions, at some point, were "made up" based on an authority that wasn't anything other than an individual's whim, ultimately; and while this may also be true, it isn't necessarily helpful or useful to say when attempting to justify why one's opinion on a matter should be trusted.

So, for me a great deal of my reaction to discussions of personal gnosis in general, and to specific items of personal gnosis in particular, very much depends on the manner in which something is presented and discussed. If the words "but that's just my opinion/experience/thought/interpretation/ suggestion; yours may differ" is not a part of the statement at some stage, then I'm likely to be at the very least suspicious, and probably less inclined to trust or put any credibility in the opinions and information that are subsequently offered.

—**Philip Bernhardt-House,**
U.S. Celtic Reconstructionist Pagan

2

DEFINITIONS

If we are going to have theological discussions, we must first agree on our terms. Unfortunately this is often more easily said than done; consider the radical differences between the Jewish and Christian use of the term *Messiah* or the Catholic and Protestant definitions of the *Eucharist*. But despite these difficulties we must make the effort if we are going to address the serious but long-neglected conundrums at the heart of our subject matter.

To that end, we are attempting to define and use terms as objectively as possible, rather than utilize them to insult someone else's viewpoint. By speaking with various correspondents and comparing and contrasting their use of the terms with historical use, we hope to create a basic lexicon for current and future travelers on this path.

Our definitions are not set in stone and should not be taken as the final word on the subject. As we reestablish the lines of contact with the Old Gods, we will inevitably face new questions and find ourselves examining once again our prejudices and preconceptions. And ultimately, as always happens with mystical experiences, we will find ourselves tasked with describing the indescribable and putting into speech that which transcends all language. Considering the many wars and conflicts that have arisen over abstruse points of doctrine, we should keep these linguistic limitations in mind.

GNOSIS

Simply knowing. Understandings gleaned by direct experience of the Divine in whatever form. These can be very dramatic and fill in large gaps in our knowledge, or they can be more subtle, simply enabling one to relate better to a known Deity or spirit.

—Mordant Carnival, U.K. Pagan

Gnosis is revealed knowledge, by intuition or contact with a Higher Power. Gnosis is not book learning; it's another, equally valid way of knowing.

—Jordsvin, U.S. Heathen

Gnosis: spiritual knowledge, usually gleaned through experiential or meditative means. Gnosis is when you ask the Universe a question, and you receive an undeniable answer— even if you rationalize it away as being "your own inner voice" or "cementing a decision"—the moment you accept the inspiration you seek, you have achieved some form of gnosis.

—Del, U.S. Pagan

My definition of gnosis is, simply, spiritual or ritual knowledge and insight. This knowledge or insight may be about the self, the nature of spirit/Deity, the world, ritual, or other topics within the purview of one's personal or group spirituality and practices.

**—Erynn Rowan Laurie,
U.S. Celtic Reconstructionist Pagan**

During the early days of Christianity, followers of various beliefs within the community squabbled among themselves for primacy of position. One popular movement took its lead from the mystery cults that were popular at Eleusis, at Delphi, and throughout the eastern

Roman Empire. Instead of *pistis* (πίστις), or faith, they relied on *gnosis* (γνῶσις)—knowledge based on experience of the Divine. They sought salvation not from sin but from ignorance, and redemption came not from mere belief but from direct personal revelation. But, alas, those who favored faith won the backing of Constantine and his successors. By the end of the fifth century, their Gnostic competition had largely been reduced to a heretical footnote in the history of the True Religion.

Near the end of the nineteenth century, a number of occultists became interested in the Gnostics. The most important occult thinker of the period, Helena Petrovna Blavatsky, was particularly enamored of Gnosticism, believing it a direct link to the "ancient wisdom" that had been preserved since time immemorial by the "Secret Chiefs." Her devotees and detractors alike followed her lead: G. R. S. Mead translated numerous Gnostic texts, while Aleister Crowley named the central ritual of his Ordo Templi Orientis the Gnostic Mass. Swiss psychotherapist Carl Jung devoted particular study to Gnosticism, recasting its doctrines and rituals as techniques for analytical psychology and self-integration. And this interest only grew stronger with the 1945 discovery of many long-lost Gnostic texts at Nag Hammadi and their subsequent translation.

The various Gnostic sects had little in the way of dogma—indeed, dogma was shunned as a device of the evil "demiurge," who was responsible for creating the material world and who closely resembled the Old Testament's Jehovah. But they were united in believing that humankind contained a spark of Divinity, which, when they awakened, would be freed from its prison. In being awakened, they would return to the Oneness of the Godhead. This awakening could take place neither through reason nor faith, but only by a direct revelatory experience that transforms the Gnostic. This experience would free them from the constraints of time and space. The mundane world we perceive through our five senses was not something to be worshipped or even honored, but rather a trap from which only a select few might escape.

But while the Gnostics saw the world of the senses as a pitfall keeping us from reality, most modern philosophy sees it as the only thing worthy of consideration. The idea of a "higher reality" is so much silliness and superstition, in their view. That which is Beyond All Words is beyond all meaning; that which cannot be weighed, measured, and quantified directly or through its impact on our world is of no importance.

Using the materialist and/or scientific approach, one can describe the various sensations one has during a mystical experience and measure its effects on the mystic's life through various tests. One can discuss how this mystic's experience is shaped by various sociocultural and historical factors. One can give the mystic a thorough physical examination to check for signs of disease and examine electroencephalograms in search of any aberrations from the norm. But one cannot answer (or even ask) the most important question of all: During this experience, who is communicating with the mystic?

Our usage of *gnosis* draws upon these various definitions but seeks to avoid some of their errors. We recognize the value of the Scientific Revolution and the scientific method; we are not Luddites seeking a return to some romanticized pretechnological Eden. However, we also recognize the limitations of science and reject the idea that it should be the sole method by which we seek meaning in our lives. But unlike the Gnostics of late antiquity, we do not believe that the material world is inherently evil. We do not believe that enlightenment, however one might define that term, is an escape into a blissful spirit world. Rather, we believe that suffering is the price we—humans and Gods alike—pay for sentience; if we want relief from pain and injustice, it's up to us to make things better, with or without divine assistance. Above all else, we reject the idea that the Gods are inaccessible to us. Rather, we believe that they are immanent in this world and that they regularly communicate with the beings who reside therein.

PERSONAL GNOSIS

This is one person's individual revelations, specific to that person and his or her relationship with personal Gods. Personal gnosis could consist of stories about the Gods and details about their characters, enmities, and familial relationships; it could be appropriate items for a harrow or altar; it could be a preferred offering. Sometimes guidance about one's life path can come in the form of personal gnosis, such as suggestions for a course of study or a career change.

—**Mordant Carnival, U.K. Pagan**

Personal gnosis is spiritual knowledge that applies directly to one's life and one's own spiritual practice. Others may find it interesting, helpful, or informative, but unless they too have undergone some form of journey to hear said wisdom, it will remain an outsider's perspective. I can explain how a certain shamanic journey taught me that all goods and services must be bartered rather than bought, and make a personal oath to live my life in accordance with my personal gnosis. Others who hear of this may do it too, but it will have a different meaning to them, and the experience will seem devoid of the drive that makes it easier for the gnostic to engage in it.

The Universe, your Gods, your guides, and spirits all have different shards of information that pertain to myriad people. There is no promise that every person who goes looking finds his or her own little instruction booklet on how to manifest desires and always be happy, but more often than not a sincere request for information or assistance from the Universe (Gods, guides, spirits) will at least meet with some form of gnosis.

—**Del, U.S. Pagan**

Divine messages aren't always intended for public consumption; most communications between Deity and the individual are strictly personal. While these messages may change your life and be of immeasurable benefit to you, they are not intended as directives to the community.

So what might a God say to a mortal? Lots of things, including:

Complaints: If you have been raised on a steady diet of positive reinforcement, you may not be ready for the experience of a God calling you out on your darkest secrets, or even just telling you that your present behavior is unacceptable. Alas, the Gods are often more quick to criticize than praise . . . and the fact that they are right only makes their words sting more. But once you get past your initial defensive instincts, you'll find that they generally offer advice on how you can correct your failings.

Declarations of Love: These are hardly so uncommon as you might think. There are many myths of Gods falling in love with mortals. Zeus, for instance, enjoyed his various paramours, and the Japanese royal family traces their descent from the Sun Goddess Ameratsu. You may not feel you're worthy of such divine attention, but the Divine may beg to differ. These love affairs can be as complicated, ecstatic, and exasperating as relationships between mortals.

Encouragement and Advice: Just when you've reached your breaking point, when you're convinced you can't go on, you may hear a voice telling you not to give up hope. You may suddenly see a solution to what you thought was an insurmountable problem. The Gods, spirits, and ancestors frequently intervene in our lives; it's just that we often take credit for the ideas they inspired.

Marching Orders: They may come to inform you that "you must do this" or "you must not do that." Western culture places a premium on free will and freedom of choice. The idea of losing autonomy, even to a God, makes many uncomfortable. We have found the Gods are often less concerned with getting consent than with getting things done. We've also found that they will not infrequently place taboos or restrictions on their chosen ones. Both Raven and Kenaz have various "thou shalt nots" laid upon them by their spirits, as do most other spirit workers they know.

Stories: The Age of Legends never ended; the Gods continue to craft myths today. They still use parables to get their points across, and they still regale us with tales of their past and present adventures and misadventures. These stories may be for our ears only, or they may be intended for public consumption. They may be mind-numbingly complicated or deceptively simple. They may be heartbreaking tragedies or side-splitting comedies. They may be told with flowery prose or with scatological obscenities. But they are every bit as important and relevant as any of the stories they told us in the past.

Etcetera: The Gods and spirits are individuals with their own personalities. Our interactions with them can be as varied and unpredictable as our interactions with our fellow human beings—if not more so! We have a tendency to pigeonhole Deity into convenient categories—X is a "Love Goddess," Y is a "Fertility God," Z is a "Sacred King." When you begin interacting with the Divine up close and personal, you will find they are far more complex and nuanced than that; they are neither archetypes nor stereotypes, but distinct and fully formed beings.

UNVERIFIED PERSONAL GNOSIS (UPG)

Unverified personal gnosis is personal gnosis not substantiated by other reliable sources, such as historical information, extant lore, or competent spirit workers.

—Mordant Carnival, U.K. Pagan

Unverified personal gnosis is when someone shares the information or assistance that person received from guides or guardians with others, especially when it pertains to the guide in question. If one were to shamanically journey to meet with a particular God and share information about such things as where the God was found, what he was doing, what he talked about, and what stories he told, since (presumably) only one person was on the journey (or several were but all were within one altered state of consciousness at the time), there is no immediate clear way to check the information for accuracy when it steps outside the published and known lore of a guide. Is Loki's favorite meal macaroni and cheese? Does Hanuman feel uncomfortable being on an altar that has no space for or representation of Rama? The answers to these questions are considered UPG until more people have the same experience with the same guide.

—Del, U.S. Pagan

Unverified personal gnosis would tend to be something informational that is usually introduced, without the qualification of "my experience tells me" or "my research tells me" given beforehand (though sometimes it may), to indicate someone's idea about a particular subject of contention or question. People do often say "my UPG on this is . . . ," but they rarely (if ever) say "my UPG, based on my meditations and my research, is . . . ," which gives me great cause for skepticism on many occasions. How it is possible to discern, if no such information is given, whether that person didn't come up with a thought on the matter two seconds before he or she said the statement or typed it? While inspiration can strike that quickly, and such inspirations can be valid and useful, nonetheless the tendency I've found is that UPG is in the territory of "If I say this, then don't even try to contradict me, because it's my experience, and you can't tell me whether that's right or wrong, so shove off." While I agree with that sentiment to an extent, at the same time, there's an immense amount of preemptive posturing and statements of individual infallible authority often involved in making such statements, which I don't think are always particularly useful in then having reasonable or rational dialogue. (And I would disagree vehemently with anyone who might suggest that reason and rationality have nothing to do with religious experience.)

—Philip Bernhardt-House,
U.S. Celtic Reconstructionist Pagan

Unverified personal gnosis is the moment after the prophetic vision, when you're still trying to digest what you've just experienced. Is that voice in your head a contact from the Divine or a sign of incipient insanity? (This is a big problem in a culture that equates nontraditional expressions of spirituality with thought disorders, and an even bigger problem for those living with mental illness.) Are you a prophet on fire with love for the Divine or just another fanatic convinced you have found the Truth with a capital T? Are you hearing the Gods or just listening to wish-fulfilling affirmations bubbling up from your subconscious?

When dealing with spiritual communications, there are several ways of distinguishing between signal and noise. Divination is one particularly good method; it's so important that we have devoted two entire chapters to it (see chapters 10 and 15). Casting yarrow stalks, reading tarot cards, exploring the flight of birds, or searching for other omens— all these can provide a neutral voice that affirms or contradicts your experience. And it is vitally important that you be open to disagreement. If you're in contact with the Gods, their message will survive honest questioning and sincere doubt. Be very wary of any entities— Gods, spirits, or clergypeople—who caution you against verifying their statements for yourself.

As you become more experienced, you will become familiar with your spirit contacts. You will be able to recognize the voice of your local landwight or Divinity just as you can pick out a friend amid a crowd of people. It will become more difficult for an imposter spirit to trick you and increasingly easy to distinguish between genuine messages and subconscious noise. This is the way possessions are verified in Vodou; if you know Zaka, Ghede, Ogou, or other lwa by meeting them at a few different parties, you'll be able to spot a phony possession even if you're totally head-blind.

Familiarity with the person presenting gnosis can also be helpful. If we know a person is generally functional and trustworthy, and is also a real priest or priestess of Deity X, we are inclined to believe that individual's claims about a message from X. This, alas, can be both good and bad. With enough research and determination, a skillful con artist or ardent but deluded person can put on a very convincing show. If we are truly skeptical, it hurts to have to say, "I don't think that is a genuine conversation with X"—and I'm sure it hurts to hear it as well. It's tempting to smile and nod politely instead, thereby reinforcing the delusion. Nor is any spirit worker infallible; it's not unheard of for two priests of Deity X to disagree, sometimes vehemently, about the content of a message.

Another way of testing the message is applying it to your daily life: try it out and see whether you achieve results. If Herne tells you to go to a hunting site and you bag an eight-point buck fifteen minutes after you get there, it's a pretty good bet that you've had a genuine gnosis. If you don't, that's not necessarily a red flag—it could be that you learned some valuable lesson by sitting alone in the woods—but it's not going to be as convincing to the masses. (And this may not be a bad thing. It could well be that this message was for you alone and didn't need to be shared with the community.)

One common rule of thumb used in many contemporary spiritual circles is "if the gnosis was good for you, it was real." This can certainly be helpful in spotting spiritual parasites, impostors, and self-destructive delusions. But it may not be particularly reliable when dealing with actual contact with the Divine. The idea that all contacts with the Gods must be personally empowering to the individual is a modern one. A discouraging number of prophets and mystics have been martyred for their faith; many others have had their lives tossed into upheaval.

When the Gods come into your life, they can be ruthless about getting rid of clutter. Sometimes the items they consider unimportant are among your most cherished possessions. People and things that you feel are an integral part of your identity may be ripped away from you suddenly and painfully. You may be tempted to label this process as spiritual parasitism, mental illness, or personal failure. It may be any or all of these things—but it may also be verification that you have been chosen by Deity. Those who have lived through this generally find themselves in a better place after it is completed, but that can be cold comfort as your comfortable existence is turned upside down.

PEER-CORROBORATED
PERSONAL GNOSIS (PCPG)

Knowledge and understanding gained from personal experience of the Divine independently verified by several competent spirit workers.

—Mordant Carnival, U.K. Pagan

There are, believe it or not, quite a few people out there who have found ways to communicate with their guides. Some of them may have even talked to the same guides as you have. After a while, a pattern may emerge in which several astral journeyers return with similar or identical information with regard to matters ethereal. So although it may start out as a piece of information you have no way to prove, the more others agree with it and experience it for themselves, the more it moves from being UPG to PCPG.

—Del, U.S. Pagan

PCPG is UPG that is shared between several different people and/or corroborated with written documents. It is still functionally UPG, but gives more of a basis for saying, "I've experienced this; you may as well," and for indicating the direction of a group.

—Hrafn, U.S. Heathen

PCPG would simply be the same UPG that another person or persons have arrived at independently. That "independently" part is important—sharing one's UPG with someone else doesn't mean it's peer-corroborated, necessarily, though that person may accept it as his or her own UPG.

—Elizabeth Vongvisith,
U.S. Northern Tradition Pagan

I would define it as personal gnosis that has been discussed with other members of the religious community to which the individual belongs and, while not necessarily accepted by the whole community, at least validated as authentic by a number of them. I would even go so far as to suggest that peer corroboration of personal gnosis can be a method by which change is accomplished in a religious community or different branches of a religion formed. As an example, consider the Reformation split of Lutheranism from the Catholic Church and the current Episcopal schism over gay ordained priests.

—Raenshadoe, U.S. Pagan

Peer-corroborated personal gnosis (relatively rare, but certainly not unheard of) is when two people's individual and subjective experiences agree on a particular point of practice, detail of imagery, or basis for belief. This is very different from someone agreeing with someone else's idea—that can and does occur all the time. Usually the discerning of PCPG is accompanied in my experience with a sort of resonance or feeling of deep and numinous connection, not only with the original experience itself, but also the individuals, community, and Deities with whom the particular matter of PCPG is connected.

**—Philip Bernhardt-House,
U.S. Celtic Reconstructionist Pagan**

Peer-corroborated personal gnosis may be a message or vision received by numerous people at geographical or social divides. It may also be a message or vision that is received by one person but found resonant or applicable by the community. The prophet has been honored; the words have been recognized as divinely inspired; the Gods have spoken to multiple followers to make sure the communication is received. While most instances of UPG are aimed at the individual, PCPG is a message for the faithful—or at least for those faithful who are ready for it.

You will note the use of "corroborated" rather than "verified." Gnosis cannot be verified like a mathematical proof or a scientific theory. Evidence that seems utterly convincing to you and your friends may garner only scorn from those outside your faith community—and from those inside it as well. Even those communications that are accepted as divine by large numbers of people are subject to skeptical questioning. More than a billion people recognize the New Testament as divinely inspired; an equal number believe the Qur'an to be a direct message from Allah via the angel Jiv'reel. After centuries of armed and unarmed missionary activity from both camps, there is still no universal agreement as to whether Jesus was a prophet or the Son of God. Given that track record, you can hardly expect your message to meet with universal acceptance.

Indeed, this can be one of the greatest challenges for those who have made contact with their Gods. Their message seems so clear, so direct and to the point; it's hard to imagine how anyone could doubt it. And yet when you share your good news, you are met with skepticism, scorn, and hostility. We've provided some pointers for dealing with that in the next chapter. For now, the most important thing is to understand that you are going to meet with detractors. If you fancy yourself a prophet come to lead the adoring masses, you're likely to be sorely disappointed. (Those who doubt this should explore the life stories of those prophets who actually succeeded in founding world religions.)

We should also remember that peer corroboration is not infallible. Communities frequently follow misguided but charismatic leaders and reject sincere messengers. Delusions can spread as quickly as any other disease. In January 1692, nine-year-old Betty Paris and her eleven-year-old cousin, Abigail Williams, began falling into "fits" wherein they claimed they were being pinched, prodded, and tormented by "witches." Soon other girls in their small village of Salem, Massachusetts, were afflicted with the same malady. To root out this evil, a Court of Oyer and Terminer was convened. By the time it was dissolved in May of 1693, nineteen people (fourteen women and five men) had been hanged, one had been pressed to death under heavy stones, and at least five more had died in prison.

Dealing with personal gnosis requires us to walk on the razor's edge of skepticism and faith. Blind obedience to every voice that pops into your head—or every claim of "divine inspiration" from a leader—will not help your religious development and may well get you into serious trouble. Yet sneering stubborn disbelief will prove no more useful when you find yourself the focal point of the meeting place between humanity and Divinity. Learning to trust the Gods enough to listen to them can be a Herculean task. Learning to trust yourself enough to reject an inauthentic message, from whatever source, can be equally difficult.

3

DIVINE DOWNLOADS

What Personal Gnosis Feels Like

It's the beating heart of my spiritual practice. Through personal gnosis I come to know my ancestors, the land spirits, the Gods. I learn things I could not know any other way. I sometimes get direct communication, but my signal clarity is poor, so I don't rely solely on that. Information seems to come in a rush of synesthetic data; sometimes there are spoken words, but more often there'll be a jumble of words, images, and sensations. Sometimes the initial inspiration will come to me out of the blue, a sort of "Aha!" moment, and then I'll go to my Gods and ask for confirmation. Sometimes I get messages through coincidences or random events. I do a lot of urban magic, city magic, and I find that the city will often pass on messages from the Gods in various ways.

—Mordant Carnival, U.K. Pagan

Obviously, personal gnosis is going to be a little different for each person. The image that people usually get is of the heavens opening and a great voice speaking to them, as in a waking full-sensory hallucination.

While this does happen to some people, it's much more subtle for the majority of individuals. Sometimes it can be subtle enough to be more like a trail of breadcrumbs than a divine phone call, as Hellenic Pagan P. Sufenas Virius Lupus points out.

> *If I get direct words or a "message from the Gods," I tend to be somewhat suspicious. In my own experience, the Gods rarely speak directly to me; they often slowly and subtly nudge one in particular directions, or "show" rather than "tell," but then these showings must be interpreted, and such interpretation can go right or wrong. I've had several visionary experiences of different Deities that have been beneficial to me in later practice. I've also had occasions when I was researching a particular question in libraries and other academic settings, and it seemed that the Deities in question subtly directed me to certain resources, often quite at random, which ended up being useful—opening a random volume in a twelve-volume set of books, for example, and then opening directly to the page that was necessary. (Very rare, but it has occurred on a few occasions!)*
>
> *I did have an experience once in April of 2005, when after my weekly Antinoan devotions, and after finishing the last syllable of the singing I was doing, there was a (literal) flash of lightning outside the window, followed by thunder. I took this as a good sign, but then was on extra alert thereafter for further "signs" that might lead in a useful (but entirely unknown) direction. I went into a bookshop, found a book that sounded interesting, and flipped through the index to see if Antinous was in it, and he was. I soon found out about a particular bit of information on some ancient devotees to Antinous in his holy city of Antinoöpolis that was entirely unknown to me or my colleagues and coreligionists at the time. I had occasion the next day to follow this up further at the British Library, and a particular date (May 10)*

emerged as a date of significance for these particular devotees. Because that date was only about a week and a half away at that stage, I was able to share this new information with my coreligionists on the relevant date, and it was greeted with appreciation and enjoyment.

Personal gnosis can emerge in almost any situation, but for me, research, dreams, and discussion are excellent places to make such connections, which can then be tested and refined through a number of methods including experimentation, further contemplation, and additional research.

—P. Sufenas Virius Lupus, Hellenic Pagan

PERSONAL AND IMPERSONAL MESSAGES

Information doesn't always necessarily have to come as a personal message from Gods in order to be valid. Most ancient traditions have some sort of conception of a great transpersonal collection of information held on some otherworldly plane that could be tapped in to. Whether referred to as the Akashic Records or the Well of Wyrd (or even in its later limited and nonspiritual explanation as the collective unconscious), there have always been people who have claimed to tap in to it for knowledge of what has been, what is, and what could be. Poets, writers, and musicians are said to have a semi-direct line to it, especially when they are able to create particularly inspired masterpieces. Sometimes it can be difficult to figure out whether inspiration comes from the Gods, the Great Library, or some combination of the two, which is not impossible. U.S. Heathen Jordsvin comments, "I've gotten spells and answers to personal questions. Sometimes it comes directly from the Gods, sometimes from Great Dreams, as opposed to the ordinary ones, sometimes just quietly 'knowing' in a way that has to be experienced and really isn't describable."

My Gods rarely speak directly to me. The few times they have, it hasn't been in an instructional fashion. The fact that I believe they have spoken to me at all, of course, could be my ego speaking to me. However, the full sensory immersion of "hearing" them in those moments leads me to believe otherwise. The times I am most certain of having experienced my Gods have been in dreams. This likely comes from my personal belief that my lack of control in dreams makes it easier for them to communicate with me. The experiences have been much more real, and much more vivid than the dreams I usually have. I scrutinize the experiences I have in the course of meditation much more aggressively, but I believe in the validity of some of those experiences as well. The experiences I consider to be direct experiences with Deity I tend not to share, however.

I do believe that the Gods, the Earth Mother, the Sky Father, my ancestors, and the various spirits speak through elements of the world around me. I do believe I can feel them around me even if I cannot always interpret what they are trying to communicate, when and if they are trying to communicate. The wind in the trees can be the Earth Mother reaching out to touch me at just the right moment. The multitude of ravens following me about all day a sign that Odhinn is trying to get something across, and I should pay more attention. A great deal of what I consider my own personal gnosis is the adoption of ideas into my system of belief. This is a reasonably rational process for me, but new ideas don't get adopted until I have thoroughly felt them out on an emotional level and found them to be true. Occasionally, newly-arrived-at truths conflict with existing truths, and this creates a problem. This process, though not directly involving the Gods, is about as personal gnosis as you can get, in my opinion.

—Raenshadoe, U.S. Pagan

The most common form of personal gnosis seems to be a deep "feeling in the gut" that something is right. People fumble for good language for this concept—"It pings!" "My inner bell strikes when I hear that!" "It's a deep-down knowing!" Indeed, it seems like one of the telltale signs of that feeling is how difficult it is to describe the moment of gnosis. One of the words often associated with it is *clarity,* as if the veil of uncertainty or mystery has, for one moment, been lifted and a clear external concept comes through. It makes us draw in our breath—in fact, the word inspiration comes from *in-spire,* or to breathe in. These moments of inspiration may appear to us through chance conversations, glances at random writing, even radio and television. The Gods have always been said to work their messages through our everyday surroundings; just because those surroundings now include technology not available to our ancestors doesn't mean that it can't be a yet another synchronous medium for the Gods to manipulate in order to get through our thick heads.

Although I work as a full-time spirit worker, I also maintain a healthy amount of cynicism about my practice. This means that sometimes my UPG comes as a whisper in the night, or a voice in the head, or having a moment of clarity when presented with something the Gods want—like seeing a woman on the street wearing a traditional head covering and thinking, "Oh, I'm supposed to do that too!" If I try to dismiss the subtler forms of communication (or downright ignore them because I don't like what is said), then the strange coincidences start. I'll hear songs that refer to whatever it is they're trying to communicate, followed by a Law & Order episode that deals with the subject. Then I'll have a friend bring it up in conversation, followed by my mother sending me some silly e-mail forward that mentions it. Usually it takes three or more strikes before I stop everything and use divination to clarify if I'm just trapped in a synchronicity loop or if there's an actual message I'm not getting.

—Del, U.S. Pagan

What personal gnosis doesn't seem to do for anyone is to provide all the answers to everything, on demand. Even spiritually advanced teachers throughout history have been caught out by circumstances that they did not see coming or stumped by problems that seemed unsolvable. Most professional diviners who do their fortune-telling as part of a spiritual practice will admit that they run up against a wall on a regular basis, and that wall seems to be about the Holy Powers saying, "No, they must figure this one out on their own. It will not mean as much to them coming out of some seer's mouth as it would when they learn the lesson from experience." Rather than seeing personal gnosis as the easy answer book we all long for, it may be more useful to view it as a series of clues, trail signs pointing us in the right direction so that we can find those answers on our own. Thousands of years of anecdotal evidence suggest that the Gods want us to search and find rather than just be spoon-fed all our lessons—or it may be that some things can only be shared and learned through experience, whether we like it or not.

What we can be sure of is that none of us can claim to be the only one who gets led down any particular road by the Gods. Wherever we are led, it's probable that thousands of footprints lie in the dust around us, even if we can't see them. That's the truth that we face when we find our own gnosis echoed by the voices of the ancients, or by our peers . . . but that's a story for another chapter.

> *I was intuitively drawn to all things connected with Astarte, and was bowled over to find confirmation of my intuitive worship in the ancient texts. I have another more recent experience of this: each day for more than ten years now I have been reciting my "Invocation to Astarte, Queen of Heaven," which is my integration of various offices, titles, and salutations applied in the past to the Goddess under several of her names. A couple of years ago I was suddenly inspired (at a time when I did need extra help!) to add the following at the end: "May my eyes be open each day to behold your beauty, my ears open to hear your voice, and my heart open to receive*

your blessings with gratitude." A few months ago whilst doing my occasional and ongoing research, I came across the following prayer to Qadashu, "the Holy One," a Canaanite epithet applied to Asherah, Anat, and Astarte: "Mayest thou grant that I behold thy beauty daily." It was definitely the first time I had come across it, and I was so pleased to have my inspiration validated in this way.

Another example is when I was a single mother of two daughter's, ages twelve and nine, delighted to be a mother of course, but very lonely and desperate for love. I joined a dating agency in desperation, but I knew in my heart of hearts that it didn't feel right. On the journey to and from the girls' school, I used to pass a Waitrose supermarket, and (this is divine revelation at its most practical!) every day those words would jump out at me—Wait, Rose!—and I knew I was being told not to try and make things happen before their time . . . but I was so impatient. Well, as the months went by a strong mutual attraction developed between me and a local shopkeeper, one Leslie Robert Bunker. He had been there all the time when I used to bring the girls from across town to visit the park, because I knew it was a place where I would one day be happy. And now we've been married for more than six years, and I've no regrets or doubts whatsoever, except to wish that I'd taken the supermarket's Goddess-given advice and not made my life so needlessly complicated all that time ago!

—Rose Alba, U.K. Pagan

LEGENDS, LORE, AND LIVING FAITH

On Primary Sources and Holy Writ

I find the ancient stories to be sources of inspiration and education, and a good base of knowledge. In my personal tradition, I find the authors of our primary sources did a good job of trying to illustrate the character and personality of the Gods and spirits in question for the time period they were known best. However, I also believe strongly that the Gods are alive and magic is afoot (to steal an overused phrase) and that as humanity grows, evolves, and changes, so too the Gods become more than what they were so many years ago. One of the primary reasons for personal gnosis, in my opinion, is to fill in the gaps where the primary sources leave off, or to extend the stories to what happened after "happily ever after."

Yes, sometimes I am given personal gnosis that directly contradicts a widely accepted primary source. History is written by those with the literacy and the ink, not necessary by all parties involved. I listen to the modern stories and allow my own bullshit monitor to filter out that which doesn't work for me. In general, though, I have found that reading the personal gnosis of others has deepened and expanded my knowledge and understanding of my Gods and my tradition, which is based on and rooted in primary sources.

—Del, U.S. Pagan

Every language must have an underlying grammar, a structure upon which sounds, characters, and gestures are combined in certain constrained and predictable ways. Mystics may experience the Divine in a lightning flash that transcends all language, but in its aftermath, they must try to incorporate the vision into their daily life. To describe it to themselves—and later to others—they will use the words and symbols of their culture. Of course, this incorporates a chance for error. It also offers a way of communicating, however imperfectly, the vision of the ineffable.

Since Freud and Jung, we have concentrated on personal interpretations of dreams; we focus on what the symbols mean to the dreamer. A similar focus prevails in many contemporary spiritual and theological circles. Faced with the immanence of the Gods, we ask what impact their presence has on the seer. Their role as protectors and progenitors of the clan, the city, or the people is subjugated to their new role as therapist: the Gods and spirit allies become a resource to be tapped for self-improvement, something to be exploited rather than worshipped.

Tradition provides a different lens for viewing our experience and a different language for communicating it. It gives us access to the teachings of others who have been touched by the Gods, to their techniques and their coping mechanisms; it provides information that has been vetted by centuries of profitable use; and it gives us goals and guideposts against which we may measure our visions. This can help us to separate the spiritual experience from wish fulfillment and to navigate the fine line between enlightenment and self-delusion.

Orthodoxy forces us to deal with uncomfortable issues in its taboos, restrictions, and moral requirements. We may approach its strictures as reformers or as reactionaries, and we may follow its rules with varying degrees of adherence, but we must engage with and be shaped by them nonetheless; we must allow its worldview to color our own. We must address problems we would rather avoid and account for transgressions we might prefer to bury. In a self-led spiritual quest, we may never find our way outside our comfort zones and may never face the difficult questions.

This is a particular challenge for those who seek to reconstruct the religious practices that existed prior to the triumph of monotheism. While many have attempted to re-create modernized versions of the ancient Deities, the results have been a decidedly mixed bag. Sometimes these reinterpretations have been colored by political agendas; the co-opting of many Nordic and Germanic symbols and myths by white supremacists is one particularly egregious example. In other cases, the Old Gods have been reduced to window dressing for various feel-good ideologies and psychodramas. Those who have sought to bring them back in all their majesty and terror face a great obstacle. We do not have a large body of tradition to draw upon; instead, we must rely on fragments and scraps to piece together the beliefs of our distant ancestors.

This great shortage of information means that any surviving snippets are particularly cherished. *Lore*—verifiable information about the lives and religious practices of ancient cultures—becomes the standard by which contemporary approaches to the Old Gods are judged. In many cases this knowledge is used not as a jumping off point but as a delineator that separates believers from heretics. Ancient poems and reports are sometimes treated with the respect fundamentalist Christians grant to the Bible: as inerrant, inflexible guides to the One True Way of pleasing Divinity. But while this approach provides the spiritual seeker with an orthodox framework for worship, it also has many potential pitfalls.

PRESERVING THE LORE,
TRANSMITTING THE LORE

I think that the trustworthiness of primary sources depends
greatly upon the individual text or source and its provenance.
I certainly do not regard any written source from the Irish

tradition as infallible. I'm not a literalist in any sense when it comes to medieval pseudohistories or the mythologies. Everything within the Gaelic literary tradition was written down after the conversion of the Gaels to Christianity and must be viewed through that lens at the very least. All written sources need to be regarded with some skepticism and examined thoroughly for their biases, the influences on them from other cultures, and their assumptions.

With this said, I do think that a thorough knowledge of the major texts is important in any tradition possessing a literary corpus. Lore should be regarded as an important guide, and one with potential veto power, but not as defining the absolute limits of all knowledge regarding personal practice within any given tradition. Given the vast amount of territory and time-depth that Celtic encompasses, what holds true in County Mayo in the fifth century may have nothing whatsoever to do with Celtiberian practices on the Portuguese coast seven hundred years earlier.

It's important to recognize regional differences and to acknowledge that they will develop within modern Reconstructionist paths just as they did in the original cultures. Celtic Reconstructionist practice in New England is going to be very different from Celtic Reconstructionist practice in the Pacific Northwest, for reasons ranging from land spirits and weather patterns to the temperament of the inhabitants of those regions. Emphases on different Deities will arise, holy days will be celebrated somewhat differently due to seasonal changes and local vegetation, and the flavor of ritual will depend on the cultural preferences of individual groups. All of these factors are also going to influence the nature of the personal gnosis experienced by individuals living in these diverse places.

—**Erynn Rowan Laurie,**
U.S. Celtic Reconstructionist Pagan

They're as valid as any ancient source and must be taken with the same grains of salt. Historians are useless if they do not consider the biases of their source as well as how many times that source may have been hand copied as time went on. Religion and spirituality do not excuse bad scholarship. Additionally, one must consider translation; many sources that are today considered "primary" really aren't. Caesar is not a reliable "primary" source on Druidic religions of Gaul. He is a reliable source on Roman observations of Druidic religions. A primary source on Druidic religions of Gaul would have been written by a Druid from Gaul.

If you want to read primary sources, learn the primary source language—and in particular, become knowledgeable about the primary source language of the era. Modern Russian is quite different from medieval Russian and even more different from Slavonic, which is the language many "primary" source materials are written in. Even the meanings of extant words have changed over time. Groznyi (terrible) did not have exactly the same meaning when it was applied to Ivan the Terrible as it has today. That being said, the best source of information is the one closest to the point of origin—in time, in context, in form, and in distance. And sometimes, the best primary sources are not historical texts at all.

—Aleksa, U.S. Pagan

As a phenomenologist of religion (with a master's degree in religious studies, in addition to my other advanced degrees), I have to accept, at least in principle, that the records of religious experiences that have been left to us from the past have some validity, if not in actually telling us what people thought or experienced, then in telling us about their cultural context and the milieu in which they existed, and which may have given rise to particular ideas of Divinity. One of the realities that is inherent in such a conception is the recognition that, in ancient times as much as today, time, place, individual personhood, and those persons' individual motivations have a great deal of influence upon what is written and recorded, and can possibly encompass a great deal of variation on a particular matter.

It is also a good and useful (and, I'd suggest, necessary) thing to take into account these same factors of (as the exegetes say) tempus, locus, persona, et causa scribendi in examining the contribution of any ancient text to our understanding and practice of a particular religion. If it is a matter of mythology, then infinite variation and diversity are to be expected and encouraged—and, most important, appreciated. If something is a record of a personal devotion, such as a votive inscription, then it is often a demonstration (at whatever distance) of a personal encounter with or understanding of a Deity and should be appreciated as such. However, due to the durability of some of these matters, or even the very fact that they were recorded, one can assume that many eyes have passed over them before and understood them, and that in some way these understandings ultimately shaped what came after them for that particular Deity or religious tradition. So, no matter how minor something might seem, it may in fact be very important to pay attention to it and respect it as a record of the past and of someone's experience, and as part of the widest and most encompassing content of one's religious tradition.

Of course, certain things are no longer desirable or in many cases even possible when it comes to what is described in ancient texts. However, when this is the case, the texts in question should still be accounted for and understood before being entirely dismissed or downplayed, and specific reasons should be given (even if it seems obvious, or should seem obvious) for why the particular texts in question are not followed in terms of a particular matter of debate. If the dismissal amounts to "because I don't like it," then that should be said, so that others can be free to have a different interpretation and possible liking of the material under scrutiny.

—Philip Bernhardt-House,
U.S. Celtic Reconstructionist Pagan

Because we are a highly literate culture, we tend to learn things from text. Books—and now e-readers, tablets, and the Internet—are our preferred media for the storage and transmission of information. Our religious beliefs were shaped by the Reformation, when the printing press took scripture and its interpretation from the hands of an educated clergy and turned it over to the individual. Given that, it's not surprising that we equate "lore" with stories we can read. Nor is this entirely a modern phenomenon. Many religions have holy books, not just the big monotheist faiths. Consider the Hindu *Vedas,* the Zoroastrian *Avesta,* and similar texts.

Sacred books can preserve a great deal of ancient knowledge and provide a framework upon which we can build sociocultural institutions and identities. After the Temple's destruction, the rabbis preserved Jewish identity and culture through their veneration of Torah and Talmud; they allowed the Jews to survive as a people when many peoples were consigned to the dustbins of history. We cannot minimize the value of the written word. But neither should we minimize other ways of preserving information that are perfectly functional and that even have advantages over the literary approach. Some alternatives include the following.

Songs and Recitations

Singers and bards have long memorized lengthy passages. The *Iliad* and *Odyssey* were transmitted orally before being preserved in writing. Even today the Kirghiz preserve their ancestral history in the *Manas* saga, an epic of more than 236,000 lines—almost nine times the length of the *Iliad* and *Odyssey* combined! (And yes, there are *manaschi*—trained performers of the saga—who know every line.) These songs and stories are more flexible than the written word. The poet-singer is given room to improvise, to alter the text to address contemporary problems. Current events can be incorporated into the tribe's collective memory and become a part of their mythology.

Oral epics grow within a well-established culture, yet are less subject to official censorship and control. Controlling printing presses and libraries is one thing; controlling the songs the grandparents sing to the children at night is a far more difficult matter. The *chante lwa* (lwa songs) of Haitian Vodou come out of a society in which dictatorial government by force has been the rule. They feature many double entendres, allusions, and sly winks that are clear to the poor peasant singers but that a wealthy spectator would likely miss. In a land where expressing one's grievances can be fatal, the chante lwa allow believers to communicate safely with their peers and with their spirits.

And while the written word can convey information with great accuracy, some emotional nuances can better be transmitted by music. Rhythms can induce altered states of consciousness and even full-on trance possessions. Marching songs can gear up an army for war; love songs can put an audience in a romantic mood. Sufi mystic Syed Mumtaz Ali said their devotional Sama songs were

> a means of increasing the brightening light of the burning flame of the love of Allah and it has a tremendous spiritual effect on the listeners. Many a Sufi undergoes a state of unveiling of spiritual divine mysteries. When such states coming from the world of the unseen thus become overwhelming, the Sufis experience a particular kind of spiritual state of transformation which is called "wajd" or spiritual ecstasy.
>
> . . . Sama which moves and activates this mystical element in man in such a way that it makes the listener totally unaware of his surroundings in this phenomenal world to some other reality. The man thus becomes completely unaware of this world, its surroundings and the effects of the corporeal universe. Sometimes the effect of

Sama becomes so intense and severe that all the energy and strength of the listener's limbs becomes suspended and he loses his consciousness. One who remains intact and manages to stay on his original position even after passing through such a state of deep ecstasy reaches and attains to very high spiritual positions indeed![1]

Art

In cultures in which only a privileged few are literate—that is to say, most cultures throughout history—the masses must get their religious education through other means. The decorations in temples and cathedrals were not just for show. They were also a means by which stories could be passed down to spectators. Murals told the story of a people's noble triumphs and heroic defeats. Statues gave concrete form to abstract ideas and provided a tangible representation of intangible beings. By meditating upon those images, postulants could gain an understanding beyond a merely intellectual apprehension. Standing before an enormous marble sculpture of Poseidon, they could feel both the sea king's grandness and his personality. The *Netjer* (Egyptian Deities) could be symbolized with hieroglyphs but came to vivid life in wall paintings and brightly colored statues.

Idols were a nexus between the sacred and mundane worlds, a literal embodiment of spirit. In creating images of the Gods, craftspeople brought them into their place and their time. The Renaissance artists who painted saints in contemporary clothing and who surrounded Jesus with European shopkeepers and peasants were bringing his mystery into their era. They were focusing on the Crucifixion and Resurrection not as historical curiosities but as eternally recurring mysteries.

Monotheists condemned idolatry because they felt that it limited the infinity of the One God, that it focused on the Creation rather than the Creator. But few who venerated idols were so foolish as to believe that their God could only be found in a particular image. Rather, they recognized that their shrines were both wholly statue and wholly God: the Divine was infinite yet also present within the confines of the sacred image. (Christianity preserved some of this line of thought in their Mysteries of the Incarnation and the transubstantiation of the Eucharist.) Hindu scholar Shukavak N. Dasa explains:

> Hindus worship specific images that are described in scripture (shastra). The technical name for these sacred images of God is *arcya-vigraha*. Arcya means "worship-able" and vigraha means "form" and so arcya-vigraha is the "form to be worshipped." We can also say that God agrees to appear in these special forms that can be understood by human beings in order to allow Himself to be worshipped.[2]

Drama

Greek drama began as rituals to Dionysus. Comedies celebrated joyous stories during the green spring and summer, while tragedies honored sad events in his mythos during the cold fall and winter months when nature mourned. Through watching the downfall of heroes, audiences could experience pity and terror, resulting in a *catharsis* (purification) of negative emotions. The broadly drawn burlesques of comedies allowed them to laugh at human frailties. Often these "satyr plays" were ribald observations on love and lust wherein even the Gods could be subjected to gentle lampooning.

Ritual drama was hardly confined to the Pagan world. Medieval mystery plays like *Everyman* provided moral guidance and edifying allegory to the peasant crowds. Passion plays brought the arrest and crucifixion of Jesus to vivid life. (Alas, the audiences frequently became so engrossed in the action that they later took to the streets en masse to punish any "Christ-killing" Jews they could find.) On the Day of Ashura, Shi'ite Muslims commemorate the martyrdom of Husayn ibn Ali with parades of flagellants lamenting his death and wounding themselves to bleed as he bled. And Yiddish theater, which influenced American dramatic forms from Vaudeville to Hollywood, has roots in *Purimshpil,* comedic improvisations performed in synagogues during the Feast of Purim.[3]

Although it sometimes results in possession, dramatic reenactments need not draw down the Gods directly. More often they bring the audience to the Gods or to the events being celebrated. Whether as spectators or participants, they experience the past as present. This can become a powerful means by which community is created—especially when these dramas are performed for a strictly limited audience and serve as initiation ceremonies. Then they can serve both to enlighten and to mark the participants as a people set apart.

THE LIMITS OF ANCIENT KNOWLEDGE

Every source has to be viewed with a mind toward the era in which it was written as well as toward the author. Individuals view ideas and information through the lens of the culture in which they are immersed, and that will color any truths they have to express. And, of course, the older the text, the more likely it is to have been corrupted over time, whether intentionally or not. So long as these things are remembered, ancient texts and primary sources are a wonderful tool. For an interesting look at primary texts (namely, letters and the like), I recommend Missionary Conquest: The Gospel and Native American Cultural Genocide, *by George Tinker. Outside of being an interesting read, the author's dissection of a missionary's recollections versus his opinion of what more likely occurred relate to the topic of the trustworthiness of primary sources.*

—Raenshadoe, U.S. Pagan

Not even those practicing more or less unbroken traditions can claim that they know what their scriptures absolutely mean and say, so why on earth would we be able to, those of us reconstructing a broken tradition from folklore and ancient historical documents? So it's about as give and take as revelatory gnosis, truthfully—positive and negative.

—Ruby Sara, U.S. Neo-Pagan

We have a few statues and temple ruins, along with fragments of the prayers with which the priests petitioned and honored the Gods. But we have lost forever the music they played, the sacred dances they performed, and the elaborate details of the ceremonies that marked their holy days. Most of our knowledge of the ancient past comes from surviving written accounts, and therefore almost all of our lore is textual. While these words are very useful in establishing communication with and understanding the Gods, there are certain limits we should keep in mind.

Text can have a greater exactness than other forms of communication. It is easier to convey specific facts and precise numbers in writing than through interpretative dance or musical numbers. (We should keep in mind, though, that capturing the emotional impact of events was long considered more important than strict adherence to the objective details.) But the written word often preserves events in much the same way embalming fluid preserves a corpse. We can pay our respects to the Gods and ancestors and remember their deeds. But we cannot bring them into our time and place to create new stories for and with us. The creation of canonical works by definition makes all but a select few tales noncanonical. Instead of engaging with the Gods directly, we read their stories in books and on web pages.

The writers of many of the works presented as holy texts were not believers. Icelandic historian and poet Snorri Sturlson's *Prose Edda* is the source of much of our knowledge of pre-Christian Scandinavian spirituality. Yet Sturlson was a Christian talking about worship practices that had long been extinct. Ovid's *Metamorphoses* was not written for devotional purposes but to entertain wealthy patrons. When we treat their work as sacred scriptures, we give it a role its creators never intended. This, of course, leads us to a conundrum: must the authors of inspired texts be aware that they are acting as mouthpieces for the Gods? Can infidels be drafted into divine service without their consent or even their knowledge?

But this leads us to other conundrums. Why are the Gods not inspiring new poets and scribes to carry their message? If they could inspire nonbelievers then, why can they not do so now? Could it be that today's craftspeople might be unwittingly transmitting messages and creating new myths in their work?

MYTHS ANCIENT AND MODERN

I see Samael most strikingly evoked in a recent video game series: Assassin's Creed *by Ubisoft. Set mainly in 1500s Rome,* Assassin's Creed *follows Ezio Auditore da Firenze. In the second game of the series, Ezio seeks to uncover the plot that led to the hanging of his father and brothers. He trains to become an assassin, learning tricks of the trade from society's outsiders: prostitutes, thieves, and strange visionaries (da Vinci!). Ezio's quest for truth, freedom, and vengeance pits him against political and religious authorities, all of which are depicted as irredeemably corrupt. The only justice available to him is that which he can enact with his own hands. In his training as an assassin, however, he becomes a master craftsman, not merely a brute killer. There is an art and a skill to his work as he moves through Rome, bringing death to tyrants. Perhaps he's Rome's patron after all.*

—Anya Kless, priestess of Samael and Lilith[4]

The initial concept of a supposedly "fictional" paradigm and/or cosmology having partial or complete basis in an alternative reality is not uncommon among otherkin. Sections of the community accept as reasonable extrapolations of fact Tolkienesque elves and fae, Pernian dragons, and other entities resembling or derived from fictional sources. There are numerous theories behind the acceptance of such a concept, ranging from the creators of such fiction's unconscious "tapping" of these alternate realities to repeated "imprinting" on the collective unconscious (dreaming, astral plane, etc.), lending energy and therefore reality to said paradigms. I find either equally potentially valid, as well as many other related and offshoot theories that are too numerous and complex to list here with any hope of being accurate or comprehensive.

Suffice to say that anime, manga, live action [films], video games, and other creations that draw heavily upon Japanese, Chinese, and Eastern mythology, cosmology, and mysticism appear to have one way or another made their "imprint" known upon the metaphysical world. I've come to accept this through my own personal experiences with these paradigms, as well as an increasing number of unsolicited encounters and external confirmations by and with otherkin experiencing similar influences and shifts.

—Kinjou Ten[5]

We are Tië eldaliéva, meaning the Elven Path, or the Path of the Star-people. Our founders met online at Middle-earth Reunion (MeR) to create, or rather re-create, as closely as possible the original spirituality and way of the Elves, and in particular of the "Quendi," or the Elves described in J. R. R. Tolkien's collective Arda (Middle Earth) writings, also known as the legendarium. We came together to expand our understanding of the innate wisdom of the Elves—a wisdom that is so clear and well portrayed in these stories—as well as to integrate, and even practice, this wisdom in our everyday lives. This is not a role-playing game (RPG) or a work of fiction, but rather an actual spiritual path for anyone who wishes to travel it, and experience it, on a very practical level. . . .

We feel that J. R. R. Tolkien's legendarium is in fact a valid mythology, in that mythology itself is well-told and well-repeated STORIES! J. R. R. Tolkien, being an expert linguist and master storyteller, was the perfect medium. He invested fifty-six years of his life to create this gorgeous mythological "tapestry" by unraveling the time-tattered threads of the oldest stories of our ancestors, and reweaving the threads of these mythological "truths" from known and unknown legendary sources—filling in any empty spots with great care not to disturb the essence of the work but rather support it—and then arriving at a deep and profound result that strikes our collective spiritual chords, allowing us to do the ultimate: CONNECT with the One, the Source, or All That Is, even if only for a glimpse—and then we feel so alive and are mesmerized!

—L. Allen (Calantirniel)[6]

Batman and the Joker; Harry Potter and his classmates at Hogwarts; Frodo Baggins and Samwise Gamgee—all have become an integral part of our modern mythology. We may not know the details of our downstairs neighbors' lives, but chances are we know the Skywalker family history. Sherlock Holmes and Mr. Spock are as familiar to us as Odysseus and Jason were to the Greeks and Cú Chulainn to the Irish. And while only a few could rattle off more than a handful of praise names for Odin or Dionysus, just about everybody knows who's faster than a speeding bullet, more powerful than a locomotive, and able to leap tall buildings in a single bound. When seeking meaning in historical facts, it may behoove us to study our own stories and storytellers.

The influence of the printing press on the Protestant Reformation has been well documented. Many of our modern myths have been transferred through books. C. S. Lewis's *Chronicles of Narnia* and J. R. R. Tolkien's *Lord of the Rings* have had an enormous influence on Neo-Pagan thought and aesthetics, even though both authors were devout Christians. Anne Rice's *Vampire Chronicles* have inspired a whole generation of vampires who look to Armand, Lestat, and company not as monsters but as role models. And Alan Moore's graphic novel *V for Vendetta* (and the subsequent film) has been enormously influential on Anonymous, the shadowy group of hackers and activists connected with everything from anti-Scientology protests to Occupy Wall Street.

Do you think werewolves transform during a Full Moon and can only be killed by silver? That "ancient superstition" comes from Curt

Siodmak, who wrote the 1941 screenplay for *The Wolf Man*. Vampires disintegrate if exposed to sunlight? F. W. Murnau came up with that one for 1922's *Nosferatu*. Flesh-eating zombies come from Haiti? Try Pittsburgh, courtesy of George Romero and his 1968 *Night of the Living Dead*. And as they shape our myths, films also influence our vision of history. Our views of the nineteenth-century American West are still working their way out of John Wayne's long shadow. Our images of the ancient world are filtered through sword-and-sandal epics, from *Ben-Hur* and *The Ten Commandments* to *300* and *Conan the Barbarian*. And gay men may be on to something with their adulation of larger-than-life "goddesses" like Marilyn Monroe. Colin Clark's *My Week with Marilyn* gives us some insight into the process by which Norma Jean Baker achieved her apotheosis.

> When we got back to the main gate, a crowd had gathered. Despite Roger's protests, the two policemen had told their friends who the visitor was, and they had told their friends, etc. At first I thought Marilyn would be nervous, but she was clearly thrilled. She must have been feeling a bit unhappy at being incognito to her public for so long.
>
> "Shall I be '*her*,'?" she asked.
>
> Without waiting for an answer, she jumped on a step and struck a pose. Her hip went out, her shoulders went back, her famous bosom was thrust forward. She pouted her lips and opened her eyes very wide and there, suddenly, was the image the whole world knew. Instinctively the audience started to applaud.[7]

Once scorned as the idiot box, television served as a babysitter for generations of children. And our adults watch as much television as our children. Medieval troubadours entertained peasants with stories of kings and queens; soap operas bring us the lives and loves of tycoons, supermodels, and ruthless billionaires. Situation comedies of the 1950s, like *Leave It to Beaver,* celebrated our new suburban lifestyle, while *All in the Family* brought the generation gap and the social unrest of the

1970s into hilarious and often painful focus. And while charioteers and gladiators could receive a certain degree of fame and wealth in Rome, they'd look with envy at the accolades heaped upon our professional athletes.

TV's influence is not confined to the Western world. Located in the South Pacific and consisting of 92.7 square miles (240 kilometers) of land spread out over 2.2 million square kilometers of ocean, the Cook Islands are remote and isolated. Yet a 1990 Cook Islands enquiry into education concluded that on the main island of Rarotonga (population approximately fifteen thousand), video was "more influential than the church, the family and the school put together and was in the process of redefining the habits, customs, attitudes, values and lifestyle of Rarotonga youth."[8] Village subchief Dorice Reid complains, "Families are now spending more time sitting in front of the box instead of communicating with each other at the family home situation. . . . Whereas before at the end of the day you might go over to a friend's house after work and have a good old chat—or go down the road and see a friend, now there's none of that because you're sitting home watching television."[9] In India the TV industry is twice as large as the more well-known Bollywood film sector. More than 105 million Indian homes had televisions in 2007, with a crowded field of domestic and global media companies, including the News Corporation, Sony Entertainment, and Walt Disney, offering hundreds of channels.[10]

While mass media entertainment has traditionally been one of America's greatest exports, the balance of trade is shifting. Many of the twentieth century's most influential cartoons were animated in Japan for Western audiences. Today there is a large and growing interest in indigenous Japanese art forms like *anime* (animated films) and *manga* (graphic novels). Many of these deal explicitly with Japanese mythology: the Death Note series features the *shinigami* (Japanese death spirits), while a strong Shintoist strain of nature veneration and interaction with local *kami* (spirits) can be seen in Hayao Miyazaki's films, such as *Princess Mononoke* and *Spirited Away*. Much as Helena Blavatsky's Theosophy spurred Western interest in Hinduism, these art forms have introduced Japanese spirituality to a worldwide audience. Readers and viewers may well internalize many Shintoist ideas and reinterpret them for their own spirituality, much as the West has redefined terms like *karma* and *the wheel of death and rebirth*.

The late twentieth and early twenty-first centuries saw the rise of the Internet and the World Wide Web. Media consumption became not just passive viewing but an interactive experience. Fan forums discuss the hows, whys, and wherefores of their favorite forms of entertainment. Tolkien communities ponder eternal questions like "do Balrogs have wings?" while authors of *fanfic*—fan-written fiction—create new tales of Harry Potter, the Star Wars saga, and what some call "fictional universes" and others call "new pantheons." Many practitioners of alternative spirituality get much or all of their spiritual social interaction in chat rooms and online forums. Sociologist Helen A. Berger has suggested that modern Paganism provides

> a new image of what religion can be in a postmodern world; one without churches or clear boundaries, based on books and the Internet and individuals gathering together and interacting and then returning to practice what they see as their own eclectic religion.[11]

We may find it difficult to swallow the idea that today's entertainment may be tomorrow's scripture or that the Gods might speak through comic books or video games. But if we accept that there is continuing contact between the sacred and mundane worlds, is it illogical to accept that their communications would come using contemporary media and contemporary language? The idea that the best artists catch and transmit a spark of divine fire is an ancient one appearing in many cultures. We do ourselves and our Gods a disservice when we assume those holy flames no longer burn today.

> *Primary sources are trustworthy as nothing more or less than what they are: records of ideas expressed by people in those times and places. Beyond that, we must keep our wits about*

us when we read such texts. For one thing, those people were no less susceptible to bias than we are today. For another, there is no good reason why living Deities cannot change over the years (thus making ancient texts no longer the best source for today).

—Brandon, U.S. Ár nDraíocht Féin (ADF) Pagan

5

DELUSIONS, LIES, AND SKEPTICISM

For nonbelievers, it is easy enough to deal with people who claim they speak to Gods and spirits: they are either lying or deluded. There is no reason to give much consideration to the messages they claim to be receiving. A psychiatrist might determine an appropriate course of treatment for them; a law enforcement officer might seek a fraud indictment; and a sociologist might think them a rather interesting reaction to environment, family, or culture. But none would find it necessary or even useful to consider whether their messages came from some Higher Power.

For those of us who believe in Gods and spirits, the question is considerably more complicated. Not even the most ardent believers would argue that every purported message from the Gods is of divine origin, nor would they dispute that sometimes even genuine messages are misinterpreted or misused by people with their own agendas. Accepting the possibility of divine communication does not free us from considering any of the explanations set forth by atheists, materialists, and skeptics. Indeed, it makes them that much more pressing. If we take God-messages seriously, we must be certain we are actually dealing with the Gods and that we are following their instructions correctly.

LIES FROM THE HUMAN SIDE

We've all heard the stories of well-meaning people scammed by swindlers claiming divine inspiration. Many of them have a basis in fact. *Affinity fraud*—confidence schemes preying upon members of the grifter's own religious affiliation—is common. In 2001 five former leaders of the Greater Ministries International Church (GMIC) were sentenced to terms ranging from twelve to twenty-seven years after bilking at least $500 million from eighteen thousand Christian investors who were told that God would double their money.[1] Persuading people you speak for Deity is a good way to gain access to their money—and to shrug off investigators and skeptics as people doing the Devil's work.

There is certainly financial malfeasance to be found in the various alternative spirituality communities. The fortune-teller who divines dire curses requiring expensive ceremonies is probably the most notorious example of this misbehavior. But by and large, Neo-Pagans are skeptical of, if not openly hostile to, people who seek money for spiritual work. Gerald Gardner's rules against charging for initiations are in many cases taken as a blanket proscription against selling any sort of service. But while this might serve as some protection against those seeking to line their pockets at the expense of the gullible, it does little to stop other types of abuse.

Neo-Paganism is generally a sex-positive religious movement. Doreen Valiente's popular poem "Charge of the Goddess" proclaims "all acts of love and pleasure are my rituals."[2] Alas, some have used this as an excuse to foist unwanted attention on nubile newcomers. In many traditions of witchcraft the Great Rite involves ritual sex between priest and priestess. This is the holiest of their rituals and is generally treated with the appropriate respect and reverence; the vast majority of Great Rites take place between consenting, typically partnered, adults. However, there have been distressing cases in which members have been bullied or pressured into participating with claims such as "the Gods want you to do this, and it's just your Christian conditioning that is making you so reluctant." This is unacceptable behavior, and everyone should know that and not be taken in. If you find yourself being cajoled into bed by someone who claims, "It is not my libido that compels me; it is the power of [insert Deity here] that compels me," run, don't walk, away.

Personal gnosis can also become an excuse for bad behavior. Serial infidelity is met with "What do you expect? I'm a child of Chango." A devotion to Dionysus can be presented as a reason to continue drinking and avoid dealing with the issues caused by substance addiction. Extensive credit card debts and compulsive shopping become a sign that one is close to luxury-loving Lakshmi. Some blame the Devil for their failings; these folks want to give the credit to their Gods. In both cases it's an abdication of personal responsibility masked in spiritual trappings. Devotees can certainly, at times, express the shortcomings of their Deities as well as their strengths. The goal, however, is not to wallow in these weaknesses, but rather to overcome them and incorporate them into a productive and meaningful life.

One of the most common types of fraudulent gnosis in the Neo-Pagan demographic is motivated not by greed or lust but by a need for attention. Magical religions tend to attract people with large egos and overweening insecurities. They enjoy the status that comes with being recognized as a powerful sorcerer who has a hotline to the Gods. By setting themselves up as a divine mouthpiece, they gain the adulation they so desperately crave. Some of these efforts are clumsy and easy to see through—the "prophet" whose messages invariably proclaim his greatness and demand the unquestioning obedience of everyone within earshot is easy enough to mock or ignore as the situation requires. However, more sophisticated actors capable of more subtlety may be harder to spot. One useful rule of thumb is that mystics who appear more interested in themselves than in their message—and self-righteous and overly showy "humility" can be part of that act—should be treated with caution and suspicion.

Generally, the best response to this kind of "look at me!" playacting is to ignore it. These wannabe mystics are seeking attention—and if you are expending effort trying to debunk their claims, you are giving them that attention. (You are also providing them with a convenient "enemy" to pump up their sense of self-importance. They must be significant religious leaders if so many people are trying to silence them.) Refusing to reinforce their antics may cause them to behave in more appropriate ways and become useful members of the spiritual community. (We've all embarrassed ourselves on occasion, but most of us learn from our mistakes and move on.) It may also cause them to act out in ever more spectacular ways in an effort to prove they really are mighty magicians. This also works in your favor: the louder and prouder their idiotic behavior, the less likely they are to trick naïve newcomers.

We must also beware of "white lies." In the name of providing good advice, some will pretend it originates with the Gods. Their motivations may be good; they sincerely think their friend should break up with her abusive partner and think an order from Deity may be taken more seriously than a friendly suggestion. There are also times when gnosis is harsh and likely to lead to hard feelings or conflict. In those cases it can be very tempting to sugarcoat the message or ignore it altogether. Unfortunately, these difficult messages are frequently the most important. If you get the sense you're not hearing everything the Gods want you to know, or that you're being sold a bill of goods by someone with an agenda, be sure to press further or take whatever steps are necessary to get to the truth. (And if you're tempted to give "spiritual" advice without an actual message from spirit or to gloss over tough truths, no matter how noble your reasons, don't. Acting as a mouthpiece for the Gods is a serious responsibility, and one that requires absolute dedication. If you begin embellishing or censoring their messages, they are likely to turn away from you in favor of a more reliable prophet.)

LIES FROM THE SPIRIT SIDE

The previous section describes ways of dealing with someone else's gnosis. You might think that dealing with your own gnosis would be much easier. After all, you presumably know the difference between your own thoughts and voices and ideas coming in from outside. (That, alas, is not always the case, as we'll see in the next section. Sorting out divine messages from wish fulfillment can be a challenge for even the most skilled spirit worker.) But even if you have established a genuine contact, you must now determine whether your new friend is telling you the truth.

Many believe the spirit world is an utterly beneficent place, where Enlightened Beings sit patiently waiting to pass on wisdom to anybody who comes along. They have forgotten the old Hermetic axiom, "as above, so below." We don't place unquestioning trust in every stranger we meet. We don't assume that everyone has our best interests at heart and is concerned only with our highest and greatest good; we accept that people may act in ways inimical to our well-being. Yet many spiritual workers ignore these lessons. They open themselves up to any spirit that approaches and take every contact at its word without question.

A spirit might lie for a number of reasons. They may be idle tricksters motivated by boredom, for example—and many of these spirits are responsible for the horror stories connected to Ouija boards and amateur séances. Generally, they are neither particularly smart nor particularly powerful; spooky parlor tricks are about as much as they can do. But if you take one of them on as a guide or mistake it for your patron Deity, you may find yourself dealing with the spirit world's version of Bart Simpson making prank calls. Not only does this make you look like an idiot, it is also a waste of valuable time. The hours you spend communicating with some random astral moron are hours that you are not spending engaged in productive spiritual work.

This is not to say that one cannot have a useful relationship with a trickster. The Ghede are notorious for their foul-mouthed humor, while those who work with Loki, Coyote, or similar prankster Gods will not infrequently find themselves the butt of their jokes. The best way to distinguish between tricksters and low-level jokers is to look for "crazy wisdom." Is there a method behind the constant stream of seemingly inane comment? Can lessons be learned from their antics? When in doubt, it's always best to check with a diviner or with a priest of the purported Deity, lest you find yourself taking messages for Hugh G. Rection or Michael Hunt.

More troubling than spirits looking for entertainment are those looking for a meal. The spirit world is home to many parasitic entities that gain their sustenance draining energy from other beings. Some of these psychic leeches have little more sophistication or intelligence than a mosquito or tapeworm. Others are highly skilled predators who will happily talk you into letting down your defenses and giving them access to your tasty bits. One of the most feared spirits in Haitian Vodou is a *mo* (Kreyol for *mort*, or dead spirit). These revenants can latch onto living people and live vicariously through them. Hosts may find themselves reliving the malevolent spirit's death; their behavior may change, and they may experience fugues and memory lapses as the mo takes over their body. One of the most common ways of attracting a mo is visiting sites where violent deaths took place; ghost hunters are advised to take proper precautions or find a new, less dangerous hobby.

If you find yourself dealing with fatigue, unexplained weight loss, or general malaise after making contact with a spirit, you may have attracted one of these parasites. Baths of saltwater and rue can help drive away an unwanted dead guest, while calling on your Gods and your ancestors can help you with other energy-sapping entities. But as in most situations, the best measure is to avoid infestation altogether. Treat an unknown spirit with the same caution you would show to any other stranger, and be on the lookout for signs the spirit is not what it claims to be or symptoms that it is doing you more harm than good. Keeping a harmful spirit out of your life is generally much easier than getting rid of it once it has latched on to you.

DELUSIONS

We must start this section by drawing an important distinction: there is a difference between *deluded* and *delusional*. Deluded people have come to an erroneous conclusion. Those who are delusional are suffering from an underlying condition that makes it difficult or impossible for them to distinguish between fantasy and reality. (We should also distinguish *delusional* from *mentally ill*. Many people suffering from mental illness have worked out coping strategies. There are many more whose illness has an impact upon their life but does not critically impair their logical or cognitive functions. We'll address the issues of actual mental illness later in the book.) Many people who are generally sane and functional have nonetheless come to conclusions that others would consider bizarre or even ridiculous.

> *Hang in there, Shabbir. I admit, I was sad the rapture didn't happen, but think of it this way. Our unsaved loved ones will not be suffering five months, but instead will be able to have a nice life until October 21. What a merciful God we have! Most likely, salvation is over and we are living in a dead, desolate world, but still we should pray to God for our loved ones. The October 21 message has spread like wildfire! It reminds me of when Jehoshaphat was to fight a battle, but God told him to sit back while he did all the work. The same thing about October 21. We don't need to witness with this date. God is doing it all by himself. Just type October 21, 2011, into Google and look under the news section, and you'll see what I mean. How many media people were there during the May 23 Open Forum, when Mr. Camping proclaimed the October 21 date? That was God doing it! Trust me, October 21 will be here before you know it. Five months will go quickly. At least it's not five years. We are being tested! God is further separating the wheat from the tares. True, believing in this date doesn't mean someone is saved, but we know we are in a major testing and trial period. God bless you!*
>
> *Judgment Day Part II—October 21, 2011*
> *The Bible guarantees it.*
>
> **—Jason R. Cohen, May 25, 2011,**
> **four days after Harold Camping's May 21, 2011, doomsday**
> **prediction failed to materialize[3]**

*People ask: "Why would they do that?" It doesn't make sense
to give up everything. Unless . . . you know. Unless you know
what they knew. And what I know. That DO [Marshall
Applewhite, founder] was the second coming of Jesus Christ.
That's what I'm here to help people understand.*
> **—Rio DiAngelo, Heaven's Gate member, 2007,**
> **discussing the suicide of thirty-nine fellow**
> **members ten years earlier[4]**

In 634 BCE, 120 years after the founding of Rome, many Romans were
convinced the city would be destroyed; a similar panic took place in
389 BCE. Apocalyptic panic broke out throughout Christendom in
the year 1000; when Christ failed to make an appearance, some mystics
speculated the end was coming in 1033, the one-thousandth anniver-
sary of his crucifixion. In the seventeenth century, Sabbati Tzvi claimed
to be the Messiah and promised to take the throne in 1648 and later
in 1666.[5] The modern world is no less susceptible to promises that a
brave new world will rise atop the ashes of the old. As this manuscript is
being written, many are looking to December 21, 2012, and the "end of
the Mayan calendar." By the time you're reading this, chances are there
will be a new doomsayer and a new group awaiting salvation.

You might think that a failed End Times prediction would discredit a prophet utterly, but history suggests otherwise. Charles Taze
Russell taught that Christ would establish the Kingdom of God on
Earth in 1914; later, his followers predicted the End would come in
1918, 1925, 1932, 1941, and 1975. Since that time, his organization, the
Watchtower Society (Jehovah's Witnesses), has stopped setting absolute dates.[6] Yet in 2010 they reported 7,508,050 practicing members
and 18,706,895 attendees at their annual Memorial of Christ's Death.[7]
The more invested you become in a revelation—and you can't get much
more invested than preparing for the end of the world—the harder it is
for you to walk away from it. What looks to outsiders like a complete
failure can be spun as a simple misunderstanding, and indeed, persecution and ridicule can bring remaining believers closer together.

Social scientists Hugo Mercier and Dan Sperber have suggested that reasoning did not evolve to help us make better decisions and find the truth, but to win arguments. "It was a purely social phenomenon. It evolved to help us convince others and to be careful when others try to convince us."[8] Confirmation bias—the tendency to interpret information in a way that confirms our preconceptions and to minimize data that contradicts them, especially when dealing with emotionally charged issues—is a well-known cognitive phenomenon. Given that, it's not hard to see how a group might rally around its mystics in the face of clear evidence that they are dead wrong.

It's also easy to see how aspiring mystics might mistake their preconceptions for actual gnosis. If you want to talk to your Gods (and most worshippers do), you're going to be inclined to believe your hunches come from them; you're likely to interpret ambiguous signs as positive omens and dismiss negative omens as mere coincidence. In time, you might well be able to persuade yourself that those strong feelings are presenting as voices in your head, and to have lengthy conversations with a projection of your Deity that you created.

This may not be entirely a bad thing; this projection can, in time, become a form within which your God may take up habitation. But it can also become a block that keeps you from experiencing Divinity. Many of these God-projections are idealized mirror images of their worshippers. Instead of getting in touch with the Deities of myth, adherents create star players in what fan-fiction writers call "Mary Sue stories." In a Mary Sue story, a stand-in for the writer engages in all sorts of exciting adventures and promotes the author's favorite agendas. A tale written by a mousy librarian named Joanne in which Joan the beautiful librarian and heiress saves Buffy the Vampire Slayer from certain doom, seduces Harry Potter, and then helps Ayn Rand become president is a Mary Sue story. The people who regularly have conversations with Republican Jesus wherein he expresses his support for free markets, segregated schools, and the Second Amendment are engaging in Mary Sue mythologizing. So, too, are many of the New Agers who talk to dolphin-riding archangels who tell them of the vital role they play in manifesting the Unconditional Reddish Violet Light of the Fifteenth Harmonic Dimension.

The deluded mystic may well find these Mary Sue myths convincing. After all, their "Deities" behave exactly as they would expect and support appropriately "godly" causes. Should they begin acting in unexpected ways, their words are dismissed as fantasy or as "the Devil coming as an angel of light," or the equivalent in their worldview. The projection becomes a cocoon within which the worshipper can stay safe and warm and morally comfortable, but one that insulates against any kind of outside spiritual influence.

But let us say that you are indeed dealing with a true spirit contact, one that is not the product of your imagination and one that is not lying to you. Surely now your problems are solved and all you need do is act as divine amanuensis. Ah, if only things were that simple . . .

GETTING THE MESSAGE— AND GETTING IT WRONG

Cross-cultural communications can be a challenge. Wars have been started over misunderstood comments and inadvertent insults. Given that, it's not surprising that spirits and humans sometimes have difficulty getting their points across. A Deity last served in late antiquity Europe or in Pharaonic Egypt may have a very different point of reference than mortals incarnated in early twenty-first-century America. Their definitions of words like *success, duty, loyalty,* and *love* may be quite different from ours. They may use analogies and metaphors that are perfectly clear to them but that have long since been lost to history. And, being Gods, they may find it difficult to put their ideas in a form that humans can understand. (Imagine trying to teach your cat about existentialism or your goldfish about economics, and you'll get some concept of the difficulty.)

Another complication arises when we consider that spirits are not embodied in this world and have difficulties with pinning predictions down to exact times, dates, and places. They see things before they happen and can describe the proceedings in chillingly accurate detail. But they may not be able to say that these things will be happening next Thursday three doors down the street from your apartment at 7:37 p.m. Those who expect that kind of exact detail—meaning, largely, skeptics who are more interested in debunking precognition than in doing an unbiased study of it—will likely see this as "proof" that all these predictions are false. The same confirmation bias that plagues mystics affects scientists and materialists as well.

They can be very specific, direct, and to the point when they are telling you something you need to know that affects your personal life. They can tell you that you need to break up with your partner, that you need to leave your job, that you need to follow through on a laundry list of things that Need to Be Done in a precise order. But that level of detail is generally reserved for personal gnosis, not for messages that are to be shared with the world at large. The world is a complex system; while they can safely become more directly involved with a single entity, it is difficult to project the long-term ramifications of hands-on interference with large groups. Their engagement with our world is careful and cautious. Where we often overestimate our capabilities, the Gods are well aware of their limitations.

The Gods often speak in parables and riddles. This forces us to engage with their words, to interpret them, and to apply them to our lives and our situation. It makes us participants in the act of creation, not mere automatons following marching orders from on high. It allows us to take their ideas in ways they might not have imagined and adds yet another layer of depth and complexity to their work. Sometimes we get their messages wrong, but sometimes we get them more right than even they could have hoped. They may correct us if we get too far off point, or they may give us room to create something that our children and our children's children will reinterpret according to their needs. An evocative myth that resonates through the ages and that provides inspiration for millennia may be more true than a straightforward and detailed command. It will certainly, in the long run, prove more useful.

All this is to say that you may never entirely understand the full meaning of the messages you get from the Gods. Centuries from now people may still be debating how those passages should be applied to their current situation. The point may not be to know, but to trust—and that includes trusting yourself to follow them even if you don't get their message entirely right. Like musicians performing from a score, we should follow their notes to the best of our ability while at the same time making them part of our personal performance. Slavish adherence to the letter of their words may be far less useful, to you and to them, than doing your best to capture their spirit.

6

SO WHO CAN BE A MYSTIC?

While the ability to experience mystical states is more common than the ability to horse (be possessed by) spirits, it is by no means a universal talent. The techniques given here may help you to establish a better instinctive feeling (what Vodouisants call *konesans*) for the spirit world, but there's also a certain element of innate ability. Not everyone can carry a tune; of those who can, not everyone can become a professional opera singer. Many devoted worshippers will have to content themselves with bathing in the warm glow (or ice-cold aura) of a God's presence. If they are fortunate, they may encounter their patrons or guardians through an occasional dream or an omen sent in their direction. While they may reap all sorts of psychological and spiritual rewards from their devotion, they will never experience their Gods up close and personal. As spirit worker Linda Demissy puts it:

> *I'm so not a mystic. I'm in my spirituality like I am in my work as a therapist: "Great One, is there something to do, something to fix, something to work on, something to learn? No? Okay, let me know when there is."*
>
> *The closest I come to devotions is doing things to entertain the Gods. I'll play music and sing, dance, organize group*

rituals, or go shopping with them. To me, relationships mean mutual sharing of what's going on in our lives and doing activities together. With Gods, the sharing is mostly one sided, and the activities are pretty limited, so it's not a full relationship. Doing things for them when I know what they want is as close as I get.

Nor will all with the gift actually become mystics. A talent for mysticism is rather like innate athletic ability; it rarely bears fruit unless combined with long hours of training and practice. Just as there is no way to become a world-class gymnast or powerlifter in ten easy lessons, there is no way to make yourself a mystic without working at it. Those with a vocation for mysticism often find themselves driven to arduous, painful disciplines in an effort to improve their connection to the Divine. Whether they chose the path or were pushed down it, once they are well ensconced on the road, everything else in their life either becomes subsumed into the mystical path or falls away altogether.

This may seem horribly unfair. Why, we may wonder, do the Gods hide themselves? Wouldn't it make things so much simpler if we could ask the Divine for answers rather than rely on scriptures and religious leaders? As the main character in C. S. Lewis's book *Till We Have Faces* cries out:

I say the Gods deal very unrightly with us. For they will neither (which would be best of all) go away and leave us to live our own short days to ourselves, nor will they show themselves openly and tell us what they would have us do. For that too would be endurable. But to hint and hover, to draw near us in dreams and oracles, or in a waking vision that vanishes as soon as seen, to be dead silent when we question them and then glide back and whisper words we cannot understand in our ears when we most wish to be free of them, and to show to one what they hide from another; what is all this but cat-and-mouse play, blindman's buff, and mere jugglery? Why must holy places be dark places?[1]

These questions have troubled humanity since time immemorial. Many creation myths speak of a fall from grace. India's Vedic texts speak of a *Satya Yuga* (perfect age), when humans were ruled by the Gods, and contrast it with the confusion and immorality of our present *Kali Yuga*. The Hellenic peoples spoke of a departed Golden Age when Gods and humans conversed freely, while the Abrahamic faiths have the disobedience of Adam and Eve in the Garden of Eden.

A more prosaic answer may be that too much of the Divine is hazardous to a human being's mental and physical health. The myth of Semele being incinerated by a glimpse of Zeus has some basis in truth. Our nervous systems aren't built to handle direct contact with the Gods; constant contact with them can cause a number of serious physical and psychological problems. The Gods may keep their distance for the same reason we try to limit our involvement with fragile ecosystems: they know their presence will do us more harm than good. Those who have to interpret their messages must prepare for their job through extensive training—and even then they have a distressingly high rate of illness, madness, and death.

But despite this, there are still many who would see the Divine in all its beauty and terror. Those who love the Gods may think that seeing them is worth any sacrifice. If you want to be a mystic, or if you feel that you may be called to the position, here are some indicators that you might have the mystic's talent.

THIN BOUNDARIES

Psychiatrist Ernest Hartmann observes a distinction between people with "thick boundaries" and "thin boundaries." People with thicker boundaries make clear distinctions between "self" and "not-self." They tend to think in a more linear fashion, separate logical and emotional considerations, and have greater difficulty with free association. By contrast, people with thinner boundaries are much more prone to free association and are more responsive to hypnosis.[2] Their daydreams and reveries are more vivid than those with thick boundaries, and they may have difficulty distinguishing between these experiences and "reality."

Those who have thinner boundaries tend to make better mystics. A study of the students at Ramtha's School of Enlightenment in Yelm, Washington, found they had extraordinarily thin boundaries; only music students and people suffering from frequent nightmares tended to score higher.[3] Psychologists also note a correlation between ecstatic and nightmarish visions; the Hindu mystic Ramakrishna spoke of terrifying demonic hallucinations and their attendant physical effects:

> I would spit on the ground when I saw them. But they would follow me and obsess me like ghosts. On the day after such a vision I would have a severe attack of diarrhea and all these ecstasies would pass out through my bowels.[4]

Those with thin boundaries are also significantly more empathic than others. When navigating through a crowded world while dealing with the emotions of those around them, this can become a decidedly mixed blessing. June, an empath from an early age, describes her childhood:

> *I became a loner. I didn't understand why at the time. I was naturally tuning in to so many things, and I didn't know what I was tuning in to or what to do with it, and I became a very moody child. I don't know why I picked up all different people's feelings, but I did. Plenty of times I would be down and I didn't understand why, and then I'd realize I was picking up other people's moods. My escape was sleep. I would sleep long hours to keep away from all those feelings. I didn't know what else to do.[5]*

Those with thicker boundaries often see thin-boundaried people as vague, fuzzy, and unworldly. When living in a materialistic society like our own, they may meet with skepticism, ridicule, and even persecution. Thin boundaries can also lead to romantic difficulties; those with very thin boundaries often feel immediately attracted to others and find themselves in numerous intense but short-lived relationships. (Some respond by forming defensive mechanisms like projection, a tendency toward paranoia, and "splitting" people into entirely good or entirely bad categories—hallmarks of what is often diagnosed as borderline personality disorder.)[6]

This is not to say that all mystics are incapable of taking care of themselves. Thin and thick boundaries are ends of a spectrum, not an either/or choice. Dr. Hartmann defines them as a state rather than a trait. Our boundaries will become thicker when we are focused on a mathematical task or other activity requiring intense concentration, and thinner when we are engaged in reverie or dreaming. A perceived external threat will also cause our boundaries to thicken. Hartmann gives the example of America's post-9/11 tendency to see the world in terms of good vs. evil and right vs. wrong.[7] It should also be noted that flaky, irresponsible behavior is not a sign of mystical ability but rather of flakiness and irresponsibility.

SINGLE-MINDED PURPOSE

Indeed, mystics generally are driven in a way that would give Wall Street executives pause. The word *enthusiasm* comes from the Greek *enthusiasmos*, inspiration in the presence of a God—and mystics are nothing if not enthusiastic. But while Freud (and many psychologists who have followed in his footsteps) tried to equate mysticism with hysteria, British scholar Evelyn Underhill points out:

> Both mysticism and hysteria have to do with the domination of consciousness by one fixed and intense idea or intuition, which rules the life and is able to produce amazing physical and psychical results. In the hysteric patient this idea is often trivial or morbid but has become—thanks to the self's unstable mental condition—an obsession. In the mystic the dominant idea is a great one: so great in fact,

that when it is received in its completeness by the human consciousness, almost of necessity it ousts all else.[8]

Many rationalists have presented mysticism as the antithesis to
direct action; they claim that logical thinkers get things done, while
mystics contemplate their navels. But when they need to accomplish
something, mystics typically attack the problem at hand with an awe-
inspiring zeal. Joan of Arc led an army; Siddhartha turned his back on
his kingdom and family in search of enlightenment. The Lakota medicine man and visionary Black Elk believed that "everything that I did
not do for my people—it would be my fault—if my people should per-
ish it seemed that it would be my fault."[9]

Their intensely focused will allows mystics to get things done without troubling themselves about the dangers or details. They are able to
accomplish the impossible because they never stop to think that they
can't. As Sufi mystic Hazrat Inayat Khan observes:

> The mystic can readily jump into anything and come out of it again;
> into the water, into the fire, whatever it may be. If the mystic thinks
> that he must go to the south or he feels he must go to the north, he
> will not trouble his brain by asking himself why he should go. He
> only knows that there is a call for him to go, and he goes; perhaps he
> finds the reason there.[10]

This selfless devotion to duty is also an important job skill for a mystic. If the Gods choose to talk to you, there's some reason for their conversation. Typically they want you to accomplish some task or send some
message, and this may not jibe with your best interests. Many prophets
have been ordered to chastise their local religious or political leaders, and
a disproportionate number have wound up martyrs for their faith. Given
that, and the other difficulties attendant upon the mystical life, it may be
that only the most driven even attempt to follow that difficult path. Or
it may be that the Gods have high standards when choosing their messengers; after all, would you trust just anybody for an important assignment?

Whatever the reason, it is clear that mysticism demands powerful discipline . . . but it also requires something more.

The focused passion of the mystic also tempers the boundaries problem, which has a tendency to make someone into a reactive drifter when it is not alleviated by something stronger. True mystics display as much implacable drive as otherworldliness, while people who merely have inadequate boundaries but no divinely given drive will not accomplish much, and will be continually blown aside from their compass until they wash up on the shore.

PASSIONATE LOVE FOR THE DIVINE

Among books liable to awaken erotic ideas, I do not hesitate to include works of mystical devotion, in which the love of God is assimilated to human love. . . . Extravagant mysticism, like romantic sentimentalism, contains a great deal of latent sensuality.

—**Louis Proal**[11]

The pious are devoted to their Gods: they follow their commandments, offer them sacrifices, and meditate on their teachings. Mystics often take that devotion to an almost unseemly level. Their love for the Gods is not a bloodless and proper respect; it's an intense, lusty, and sometimes erotic passion. And the Gods reciprocate: mystical encounters can have a decidedly sexual character. Saint Teresa of Avila described one of her ecstatic experiences:

This angel . . . was not tall, but short, and very beautiful. In his hands I saw a long golden spear and at the end of the iron tip I seemed to see a point of fire. With this he seemed to pierce my heart several times so that it penetrated to my entrails. When he drew it out, I thought he was drawing them out with it and he left me completely afire with a great love for God. The pain was so sharp that it made me utter

several moans; and so excessive was the sweetness caused me
by this intense pain that one can never wish to lose it, nor will
one's soul be content with anything less than God.[12]

Magicians and psychologists alike have long recognized the power
of sexual energy. By channeling their libido for spiritual causes, mystics
can have intense direct experiences of their beloved Gods. This is not a
simple "sex with Gods"; rather, it is a sublimation of the erotic instinct
for a religious cause. Thista, a devotee of Artemis, describes her relationship with her patron.

> *I keep a lot of journals, and one is an Artemis Journal. It's*
> *different from the others because each of the entries is written*
> *to her, almost like a letter. What kinda shocked me about it*
> *looking back on some of them is that they read like love letters.*
> *In fact, if someone read it who didn't know me or anything*
> *else about my relationship with her, they might assume that*
> *there's a romantic or sexual element to our relationship*
> *. . . but there's not. When I stopped to think about how our*
> *relationship might look to someone on the outside . . . it really*
> *does resemble a romantic relationship in many ways . . . and*
> *yet there's absolutely nothing romantic about it. Love and*
> *devotion are at the root of my relationship with her, and yet*
> *sex has absolutely nothing to do with it. She's not like a lover,*
> *spouse, or dominatrix to me. It's . . . something else entirely,*
> *ecstatic yet aware, enamored yet neither romantic nor sexual.*

In some cases this relationship with Deity can be an exclusive one.
Many sects of Christianity expect celibacy from their clergy. While it
is fashionable to scorn this as "sex negativity," there can be good spiritual and magical reasons for turning our attentions away from physical gratification. While sexual frustration can lead to many neuroses
(for further information, see Sigmund Freud, Wilhelm Reich, and the
"pedophile priest" scandals that have rocked the Catholic Church),

sublimated and redirected sexual energy can lead to powerful transformative experiences. A small but growing subset of Pagan mystics have discovered this; they live celibate lives as God-spouses, eschewing physical relationships in exchange for a closer connection to their Deities. Elizabeth, a Northern Tradition Pagan nun, writes:

> *I'm a consort of Loki, and the monastic role I have is not unlike that of a Christian nun who is seen as a "bride of Christ." My personal gnosis for that role is much more flexible and personal, and pertains largely to my relationship with Loki, who is my God, my patron, and my guardian, but also my husband and lover. I don't share a lot of that with other people, so I don't think about whether it'd be accepted. However, it's a matter of public record that I consider myself married to Loki and that my main job is being a priestess and nun dedicated to him. That wasn't my decision; it was Loki's, and Hela's, and it means everything to me.*

Even those mystics who are not committed to celibacy often find it difficult to maintain outside relationships. This can be particularly challenging when dealing with a less devout partner. Interfaith relationships can be challenging enough, but when your significant other has a noncorporeal primary partner, they can be well-nigh impossible.

BEING CHOSEN FOR THE JOB

Those who lack one or more of these qualities may still find themselves called to a mystical path. The Gods can be capricious: they will appear to whom they will, when they will. A near-death experience, serious illness, or other trauma may trigger changes in someone's psychological structure and energy body, opening up mystical abilities, or the Gods may decide to start talking to a particularly devout follower for their own reasons, just as they may never contact someone who would appear to be a perfect candidate. Mysticism is a two-way street; if the Divine doesn't cooperate for whatever reason, the mystical experience won't happen.

This can lead to two very different problems. Those who are unable to contact the Gods despite their best efforts may rail against the injustice of the spiritual universe and the Deities who don't recognize their genius. They may become resentful of the group's mystical members, or they may even try making up visionary experiences in an effort to gain their moment in the limelight. Meanwhile, those who have a knack for mysticism may be tempted to think of themselves as special and important. This is an especially grievous temptation for mystics who have never found a niche in the "real world." Going from being the class weirdo to being the One Who Speaks with the Gods can be a head-swelling experience. Should their contacts with the Gods slow down or cease altogether, they may have a hard time readjusting to life without the Divine. Both cases can be dealt with using the same answer: it's not about you.

As we have already seen, mysticism is not about ego stroking but about ego dissolution. Being a mystic is about contact with the Divine, not about prestige and power. When you begin functioning as a mystic, you need to check your need for approval and your emotional baggage at the door. If you don't, you may find the Gods reminding you of your place in the grand scheme of things—typically in a painful and humiliating way. (In any event, being a mystic is a singularly bad way to get positive attention. For further information, see the lives of various saints and martyrs.)

The idea that one must have a vocation before taking up a spiritual office may seem strange to someone raised in a culture that holds as one of its primary myths "you can be whatever you want to be if only you expend enough effort." But instead of seeking someone else's job, you would do better to learn your own strengths and discern the best ways to serve your Deity. A caring listener who can offer sympathy to those in need or a good cook who can feed a hungry congregation may be just as important to a God's plans as a dozen visionaries. Creating hierarchies and striving for the top of the ladder will only lead to dissension and disappointment.

JUDGING THE MESSAGE
BY YOURSELF

The Process of Discernment, Part 1

Stoics of the Greco-Roman period had a four-stage graduated method for accepting propositions as knowledge. This same method might make for a good way to evaluate personal gnosis. First, we begin with an impression. This might be a sensation, a thought that pops into one's head, a vision, or a feeling. At this point, it is pure experience. It is not yet personal gnosis because personal gnosis involves insight, and this has not reached a level of cognitive participation worthy of "insight."

Second, we come to the stage of assent. Everyone knows the senses can play tricks on the mind; eating the wrong thing can make you feel funny, and so forth, and consequently you are not necessarily required to give assent to an impression. If it seems suspect, you can simply deny or ignore it. But if you do assent to it, then you become involved in it, and insight may arise. At this point, it is totally unsupported by corroborating evidence, yet it might logically fulfill a definition of gnosis, and it might be powerful for you. So even at this early stage it could be valid in the sense of being efficacious for you.

Third, we reach a stage where the personal gnosis must be submitted to the scrutiny of reason. Note that religious experiences quite often involve the irrational, and so the personal gnosis would not necessarily be discounted at this stage if it included irrational aspects. Note also that reason depends on a person's worldview. If it is within your worldview that Gods can talk to us, then it is not unreasonable to conclude that a God did talk to you. If the personal gnosis passes the test of reason, as applied according to your worldview, then it becomes a conviction.

Finally, it must be compared with the experiences of past ages and sages, and generally win confirmation by the verdict of humankind. Only in this way can what began as an impression finally be considered knowledge. In the case of our personal gnosis, we might support it with relatively unbiased arguments, comparing it with facts, traditions, but also others' experiences. In this way, it can be considered well grounded and just, and therefore be "valid" in that sense as well. This stage is what I would probably equate with the term peer-corroborated personal gnosis.

—Brandon, U.S. ADF Pagan

There are two parts to successful personal gnosis: *discernment* and *signal clarity*. Discernment is a rational process; signal clarity is a condition created by superimposing a set of skills on top of a certain amount of talent. In this chapter, we'll focus on the process of discernment. Let's say that you have been working on listening to the Gods or spirits, and you think that you have something. A message came, whether in a waking vision or a dream or a voice or just a strong feeling. Perhaps an omen fell out in front of you. How do you know if it's real? Here are the steps to take, one at a time, to discern whether it's real, your own internal voice, or some combination of the two:

1. **Is it consistent with external reality as we know it?** Deciding this part could range from asking, "Is it really possible for me to levitate my actual body with my own will, as this spirit tells me I can?" to asking "Is that person really doing what the spirit says that person is doing, and is that consistent with what I know or can find out about the individual?" Be extremely skeptical if it does not pass this point. At the very least, check with other sources multiple times.

> *For instance, mental shapeshifting does not contradict well-supported scientific findings (and could possibly be explained or reinterpreted through some mechanisms of psychology), but full physical shapeshifting from a human into a wolf contradicts known biological possibility. Now, just because something isn't consistent with known science does not mean I discard it outright—what is scientifically "known" has been known to change, after all (we once "knew" the Sun revolved around the Earth), and could be inaccurate or misleading— but it does mean I am more skeptical and will subject the phenomenon to a harsher scrutiny.*
>
> **—Djeriwepwawet, U.S. Kemetic Pagan**

2. **Is it consistent with what is already written about that God or spirit?** If it's completely off from all written accounts, that's another strike against it. By "off," we don't mean "not written about," because certainly we don't know everything about all the Gods and spirits, and they might be telling you something that is not in the sources you can get hold of. We mean that there is explicit writing saying the exact opposite of the information you have—for example, saying that a Deity had no children when several written accounts refer to this well-known God over here with all these attributes being referred to as that Deity's child and no one else's. Be careful to look at multiple sources; Gods were often worshiped differently from one place and time to

another, and the information you've received may be congruent with a different tradition of that Deity.

The principal concern is always with relevance to the lives of those involved, an appeal (whether aesthetic, spiritual, intuitive, or whatever else may stimulate one's sense of something being appealing) that the practitioners feel toward a particular thing, and its ability to make their lives more meaningful and their engagement with the wider world (especially outside of specific ritual time) richer, smoother, and more loving whenever possible. If a particular item of personal gnosis does all these things, it should be accepted; if it does not, then it should be questioned at the very least, if not outright rejected. While researching ancient texts that have survived (which include specific cultic hymns, inscriptions, and other matters, as well as accounts of ancient historians, but also critiques from Christian church fathers) and the precedents presented in them is useful, it's not utterly necessary, and some of the matters in them may not be useful or appealing to do in today's world in any case.

—**P. Sufenas Virius Lupus, Hellenic Pagan**

3. **Is it consistent with what other devotees of that Deity or spirit say about the entity?** While we've stated that every God and Goddess treats every worshiper differently, if you interview a number of people who are devoted to or have worked closely with that Deity and they all say, "That really doesn't sound anything like him or her—actually, the Deity is very much the opposite of that," that's another strike against the message. If the reviews are mixed—if some people say that it sounds familiar while others don't—then you may be dealing with a different aspect of that entity or more than one of you may be wrong. Ask the Deity or spirit in question for more clarification.

As far as my own UPG goes, I judge it by three things: whether it might be motivated by some subconscious wish of mine, whether it makes sense according to the logic of previous UPG and primary sources, and divination. If it's UPG that I might find myself writing about publicly, I also add second, third, and fourth opinions—in other words, I ask people I trust who work in the same tradition and are familiar with the Gods, cosmology, and so forth what they think. Sometimes we agree; sometimes we don't. Sometimes we find that now we have PCPG. If it's a minor point, I might concede that perhaps I'm wrong, but if it's something I feel is important and all signs point to "yes," I will go with what my own instincts tell me.

—Elizabeth Vongvisith,
U.S. Northern Tradition Pagan

The hair color of the Goddess Eir is irrelevant to me—I see it as black; other people see it as blonde or red; and it probably comes down to a difference in a purely subjective and trivial experience. It basically has no impact. That Odin and Freyja did some work with me on past relationships is something that I can warn other spirit workers might be coming because both I experienced it and my teacher experienced it. If it doesn't come, or if it comes in a different form, well, their experiences may be just what they need. Again, negligible impact. That Eir is not a Goddess of healing and a handmaid of Frigg? That has a more substantial impact and is worth considering in more depth. It contradicts established lore and other people's experiences, including my own. This doesn't mean that someone who sees her as a Goddess of war is having an invalid experience per se, simply that that individual is probably not talking to the same "Eir" that I am. That said, it isn't the path I am on, and I will call it such.

—Hrafn, U.S. Heathen

4. **Does it contradict your own experience of that Deity or spirit?** If, up until now, you've experienced Deity X as wanting this and valuing that, and now you have something that is entirely different, be suspicious. It may just be that you're experiencing another aspect of that entity—Deities and spirits are not one-dimensional—or, in some cases, that your former experience of the entity was your own mental sock puppets and this is the real thing, but be careful anyway until you have better corroboration.

If I normally experience Bast as a bright warmth, and then suddenly one day some entity pokes at me claiming to be Bast but feels like prickling saltwater, I'm going to be suspicious, because it doesn't fit my past experiences of Bast. That doesn't mean there isn't an alternate explanation (i.e., a different spirit, or one of her messengers), or that it's not Bast, but I'm nonetheless going to be very careful in my interaction with said entity.

—Djeriwepwawet, U.S. Kemetic Pagan

5. **Is the tone and nature of the message consistent with itself and with the worldview of the cosmology it claims to be from?** Watch for internal inconsistencies to both the message and the nature of the creature. If a spirit claims to be the soul of a piece of wild natural land and then asks you to sacrifice a chemical-filled Twinkie to it, that's a problem. Djeriwepwawet points out that if a spirit presenting itself as Bast-Mut gets aggravated and changes demeanor suddenly before schooling its behavior back to its former manner, that's also an inconsistency and makes the message less believable.

6. **If this message came from another person but is specifically about me, do I trust the source?** How well do you know and trust the individual from whom it came? If you know that person well, you might know that he or she is solid and doesn't go

around throwing unconscious opinions out in the form of messages to others . . . or you might know that person well enough to
remember that he or she does have a tendency not to be so self-
aware. If you don't know the person well, what do other people
say about the person? (Don't take the opinion of someone who
only knows of the individual; go for friends and colleagues, or
at least people who have had multiple dealings with the person.)
Your gold mine would be finding others who have also been the
target of the individual's messages and asking about the results
of those pronouncements.

7. **Intuitively, does the message feel right on every level?** Does it
"ping"? If not, put it aside and look at it again in a few days. If it
still just doesn't feel right, discard it. If much of it doesn't feel right
but something in it somehow "pings," then it might have a kernel of
truth underneath the baggage. See if you can uncover that kernel,
either by a twenty-questions form of divination or by meditating on
each part of it to see what does feel right. It's fine to say, "I think
there's some truth in it, but I haven't figured out how much yet."

*I think that teaching people to have compassion for themselves
and each other is important. People sometimes take a very
rigid binary approach to their input: either every single
message is perfectly correct in every detail or I am mad or
stupid or a failure. It's important to learn to handle input
gently and to have a lot of different boxes to put received gnosis
in other than "true" or "false." People need to understand
that we're mortal, we're squishy, we're going to make squishy
mortal mistakes, and it's not a good idea to get too invested
in being right all the time. We also need to learn to agree to
differ on some things.*

—Mordant Carnival, U.K. Heathen

8. **Is it too gratifying?** One of the hallmarks of one's internal sock
monkeys is that the message always props up your ego in some

way. Even if it's a Great and Terrible Task, there's probably still a certain amount of "Oh no, I'm going to have to suffer for the Gods! How exciting!" This doesn't mean that every real message is guaranteed to make you miserable, but if it's too close to what you already hoped it would be, be suspicious.

Obviously, it's important to draw a distinction between personal gnosis and fantasy, especially as imagination can be a channel for revelation. In my experience there is often an element of surprise—not so much surprise at the content of the revelation as at the sudden appearance of it from somewhere outside your own mind, the conviction that you now know something you didn't know before. A personal gnosis usually shifts the points so you find yourself on a different set of tracks, rather than patting you on the back as you continue to wander your own sweet way. And then of course if you can find any historical or empirical verification for what you have been told, all the better— though sometimes you have to wait for that and take it on trust in the meantime.

—**Rose Alba, U.K. Pagan**

9. **If I'm not sure that it is 100 percent true, would it harm me to incorporate it into my worldview for the moment?** Sometimes the best test of a message is to give it a whirl on probation and see what happens. Obviously, this is not the right path for a message that will have severe consequences in your life, so if the spirits say that you should dump your spouse or move to Myanmar, hold off until you have a second, third, and fourth opinion (see chapters 10 and 15 for divination advice). However, if it won't hurt to insert it into your worldview on probation, as it were, and give it a try, go ahead. If it turns out to be less than workable, you'll find out soon enough.

The first and foremost criterion I apply to any form of gnosis is as follows: if it holds meaning for, and is spiritually significant to, the person for whom it was intended, than it's good enough for me. Even the cosmic kicks in the ass that some of us get can be meaningful to us, even if it's not the most positive experience. If the UPG (or PCPG) moves you to make positive changes in your life, meet your goals head on, and grow in your spirituality, I think it's valid.

If I feel something is significantly different from my own understanding of how X works (or how Deity Y feels about X), I will endeavor to "fare forth" myself and verify the information with the Deity in question, if that entity will discuss it with me. Most Deities I've encountered in this work find it tedious, but also honorable that you're willing to go so far to check the veracity of something. Finally, I trust my gut. If something feels hinky, it probably is. However, this is always superseded by the first and foremost criterion. If my intuition says that Deity X would never actually contact a certain person, but it has brought to that person joy, devotion, and spiritual bliss, then who am I to argue?

On the other hand, the problems I've had with personal gnosis occur when someone takes his or her interpretation of the message from the Gods as undeniable fact, against the better thoughts of safe and sane practice. The message you got might be that a rusty kitchen knife is the best thing to use for the ritual cutting, but you'd probably be happier using a sterile scalpel. The visual you had of the rite of passage may have looked like you took your client into the middle of the woods at night, alone; what you didn't see is the four people just off in the distance with their flashlights off prepared to help if anything goes awry.

It's too easy to accept a message from the Gods as the One True Way it has to be done, and I'm not denying that sometimes that's exactly what it is. However, if a dire,

*unintended result (like, say, death or serious physical harm)
is likely to occur, it may be worth asking a few questions or
getting some divinatory verification. Sometimes guides are
unaware of modern practices and can communicate only in
the terms they understand, even if you know a better way.
Sometimes the message can be misinterpreted. Do you really
need to learn decorative Japanese rope bondage for your God,
or do you just need to add some form of movement restriction
to a ritual? Do they need you to smoke that cigarette for
them, or is lighting some tobacco in a fire just as good?
These are examples I have run into when Gods are trying to
communicate through visions and when questioning would
not be untoward because it was a matter of clarification.*

—**Del, U.S. Pagan**

10. **Is it something I can afford to put aside for the moment?**
Sometimes sitting on a message for a week, or a month, or even
a year or more is the key to finding better discernment on the
matter. Emotions that have been clouding the issue may change
and fall away, and new information may come out to help verify
it. Unless the message includes immediate action, it might be
best to sit on it for a long time and then see how you feel about
it. If you're worried about what the Gods will think, you can
promise them a specific date on which you will ritually revisit
the information and ask them to help you gain better clarity in the meantime. As the Gods don't experience time in the
same way we do, if the message is real, it will probably still be
pertinent.

*On an individual level, I know many people who verify
their gnosis through a personal vetting process. They look
for signs, they ask for signs, to verify their revelations. If
they receive none, they move forward. If they receive obvious
signs, they may give that revelation some more consideration.*

For instance, in finding one's fetch [a spiritual contact] in traditional witchcraft, you may think your fetch is the black bear; maybe you have a great affinity for them and have had a dream or two about them. So you do some serious meditation, prayer, and ritual work, and you ask for signs. Suddenly you see black bears everywhere—in the news, in books you pick up at random. Best of all would be to randomly see a black bear or several in the wild. However, if you see none of these things, you might need to reconsider. It's a process that takes time. Often I think we are too hasty in accepting what we believe as personal gnosis—the process of weighing and making decisions about our practice should take time. It's a dance, a delightful and enriching process.

—Ruby Sara, U.S. Neo-Pagan

I learned from Isaac Bonewits, the founder of Ár nDraíócht Féin, that it's often easier to make a decision about spiritual matters by considering their mundane equivalent and using common sense. If I tell you we're having Bob over for supper, and you know almost nothing about him, how will you know what he likes? You can ask me or someone else who's met him. I can tell you I bought him a hot dog, and he seemed to like it. From that, you can guess that he's probably not vegetarian or allergic to gluten. It's not much, but it's better than nothing at all, and until you meet him or hear someone else's stories, you'll have to assume the information is accurate. I can't make it to supper that night, but you serve him roast beef, mashed potatoes, bread. If he says he doesn't eat meat, then either I lied or he's recently gone vegetarian. But if he praises your cooking, you'll be pretty sure my hot dog story was true. You have no reason to question it. A lot of personal gnosis is like that.

I could tell you a story about Bob wrestling a bear into submission. That might be a tall tale, an exaggeration, or an unlikely truth. Until you talk to Bob yourself, you'll just keep it in mind as "an interesting story about Bob" and not worry overly about whether it's true or not. It doesn't affect your life much either way. If I say Bob is a doctor and that he says you should take a specific herbal supplement to improve your mood, there's no reason not to try it. Either it works or it doesn't, and little is lost if it doesn't.

On the other hand, if Bob tells me to tell you that you must move to a more southern country to relieve your health issues, then that's a pretty big life change. You'd be a fool not to seek out advice from at least two more doctors before making such a big change. I could be lying for personal reasons, Bob might not be qualified to make such a prescription, or I may just have misheard him.

The point is, we lead our lives with insufficient, inaccurate, and incomplete information. We make educated guesses about what we don't know, based on what we believe to be true, have heard about, or can verify through experience. One week, onions are supposed to cause cancer. The next week, they're touted as a cure for cancer. It would be nice to know the Complete Truth about our Gods and what they want from us, but we have to make do with what we can get. If it's important, try to get independent confirmation. If it isn't, don't you have anything better to do than correct someone else's incorrect beliefs? Like, say, deal with your own problems first?

I've written down a few stories that I believe are inspired by my Gods. When I ask them how accurate these are, the answer I usually get is "Close enough!" I'm translating experiences of their world into something I and my peers can understand. If they think it's good enough, I'm not going to lose sleep over it.

—Linda Demissy, Canadian Pagan

WEAPONS IN THE BATTLE

When it comes to the process of discernment, there are two ways that you can arm yourself. Both are worthy of continuous effort. The first is self-knowledge—the more you know about the inside of your head, the better. (This can also help with signal clarity, which we'll touch on in the next chapter.) If you're really sure what the lying-to-yourself voice sounds like in your head, you can stomp it whenever it comes up and save yourself a lot of trouble. The second weapon is studying what has already been said—about your Gods, about *anyone's* Gods, about how this process has worked in the past—and what messages were sent.

> *I do not endeavor, O Lord, to penetrate thy sublimity, for in no wise do I compare my understanding with that; but I long to understand in some degree thy truth, which my heart believes and loves. For I do not seek to understand that I may believe, but I believe in order to understand. For this also I believe—that unless I believed, I should not understand.*
>
> —**Saint Anselm of Canterbury**[1]

> *Intellectual knowledge is the foundation—but not the entire edifice—of our relationship with God. The Torah is not telling us to reduce this vibrant connection to a sterile equation. Once a rational foundation is in place, the Torah says to "return it to your heart." We must then work on creating an intimate, deeply personal and satisfying relationship with God, assimilating what we know in our minds into our feelings. We need to use our intellect to guide our emotions. Emotions are powerful tools, but when they are in the driver's seat, we are taken into dangerous territory. Feelings can sweep us off our feet and carry us to a world of illusion.*
>
> —**Rabbi Nechemia Coopersmith**[2]

Mystics in various traditions draw a distinction between intellectual knowledge and the deep insight of spiritual awakening, but this does not mean that they have minimized the importance of study and scholarship. Without a firm intellectual foundation, mysticism can degenerate into escapism and self-deception. Unable to distinguish between the Divine Light and material bubbling forth from their subconscious, untrained mystics can find themselves entranced like Narcissus at various pretty images. Instead of bringing them closer to the Gods, these visions only send them wandering down blind alleys of delusion that draw them away from practical spiritual or material work.

Study, while not a method to attain altered states, is the Path of Sacred Scholarship in Dale Cannon's book *Six Ways of Being Religious*. The better you understand your patron Deity through study of the best available sources, the easier it will be for you to distinguish between divine contact and wish fulfillment. When you have internalized their tales, you will be better able to recognize their presence. You will be able to recognize them by their behavior and demeanor and to spot an imposter spirit or a dream that originates within your mind rather than outside it. Exploring the primary sources, or academic works on the culture in question, can teach you a great deal about the role your patron Deity played in the past and can be expected to play in the present.

Doing research will also make it easier for you to identify them by name. Instead of identifying a vague "Sun God," you will be able to distinguish between Sol Invictus, Amaterasu, and Apollo—or, for that matter, between Apollo and Helios, two distinct Gods whose stories are often conflated by people with a cursory knowledge of Hellenic mythology. Many popular books present sanitized and homogenized versions of a few well-known stories. With more research, you may discover little-known roles and images that will help you put a name on your spirit contact and get some idea of appropriate offerings.

Research can help you verify your UPG. Let's say you get a strong feeling that the pomegranate Persephone ate in the Underworld was somehow connected to sterility and barrenness. This may seem counterintuitive at first. Today, most people associate the pomegranate with fertility: its round shape resembles the swollen belly of a pregnant woman, and when it is opened it is filled with seeds. But a closer study reveals that the pomegranate was frequently prescribed in classical and medieval medicine as an abortifacient and contraceptive. Modern tests on rats and guinea pigs have found that adding pomegranate to the diet of female rats and guinea pigs results in a measurable decrease in pregnancies.[3] Armed with this information, you would have evidence that your hunch was indeed the product of divine inspiration.

Study can facilitate a religious experience. The very act of compiling information about your Deity can be its own prayer. It is a meditation constrained by facts and hard data, one that is less likely to go drifting off into flights of fantasy. And if finding information can be a form of prayer, making that information available to other worshippers can be a powerful offering. Artisans and religious writers throughout history have taken difficult concepts and put them in forms that the laity can understand. By digging out material from primary sources and dry academic texts and bringing them to a wider audience, you follow in their footsteps.

Like any spiritual technique, this approach can have its pitfalls. It is possible to use your learning and research to construct elaborately crafted, historically accurate delusions. Some people do make a fetish of research and scholarship; their path becomes less a direct encounter with Divinity than an effort at re-creating an ancient faith down to the smallest details. We also need to keep in mind that scholarship is not a static pursuit. Egyptology as it was practiced in Victorian times bears little resemblance to today's academic discipline; this century's brilliant professor may well be the next century's quaint curiosity. If our visions don't jibe with contemporary academic thought, it could be that they are wrong or it could be that our scholars are in error.

If we wish to reforge the old connections with the Gods, we would do well to understand the ways they were honored in the past. But we also need to understand that the world has changed, for better and for worse, in the long centuries since they were last honored. The trick is to create ways of veneration that are appropriate for our society and that meet the needs of both modern Gods and modern worshippers. An exclusive focus on their ancient glories runs the risk of placing them safely in a Golden Age and making them irrelevant to the here and now. Ultimately, we may do best to follow the lead of Reconstructionist Judaism and give the past a vote but not a veto.

MAD WISDOM

Mental Illness and Personal Gnosis

I learned early on to listen to my inner voice and not the cacophony of foolishness that is conventional "wisdom." I recognized that the experience some call "psychosis" was for me an attempt at spiritual transformation, and I sought out wise teachers who could help me. I was fortunate to find this help within Tibetan Buddhism, where the lamas taught me the spiritual nature of my mental states and instructed me in yogic disciplines to stabilize mind within body.

My experience with altered states of mind prepared me for the mental and physical changes of death and dying, which other people fear so much. For example, many people begin to experience depression as they grow older. But I have already, by necessity, learned to deal with depression. Over time, I learned to recognize depression as a kind of prayer. For me, it has become a stabilizing energy that enables me to absorb and accept the vicissitudes of life with calmness and patience.

—Sally Clay, who spent more than thirty years
in the American psychiatric system[1]

Historical evidence suggests an encounter with the Gods is often more frightening than enjoyable. The mind-shattering terror one felt in the presence of Pan inspired our English word *panic*. *Holy fools,* adepts driven mad by their close relationship with the Divine, can be found in Tibetan Buddhism, Zen, Sufism, Tantra, and Russian Orthodox Christianity, among other traditions. But today those experiencing "mad wisdom" are more likely to find themselves institutionalized than lauded as saints.

The very idea of personal gnosis is controversial enough in many quarters. Personal gnosis involving intense, disabling visions is often rejected out of hand. If the Gods want only the best for their followers, why would they inflict schizophrenia, bipolar disorder, or crippling psychosis on a devotee? Instead of dealing with this disquieting theological issue, it is easier to discredit the message and messenger. This is especially easy because of the stigma attached to mental illness. Revelations that fall outside your comfort zones can be safely ignored if they come from a "crazy" person.

This can be a difficult issue. We should not dismiss all bizarre behavior as "insanity," but neither should we pretend that insanity does not exist. Many mental illnesses can mimic the effects of a mystical experience. It can be difficult to distinguish between a psychological disorder and an encounter with the Gods—especially when you take into account that the two are not mutually exclusive. The Gods often find cracked or even broken vessels to be the most useful. But just as not every mystic is mentally ill, not every mentally ill person is a mystic. Joan of Arc and Francis of Assisi heard voices, but so did Charles Manson and John Hinckley.

Mentally ill shamans know that our brains aren't entirely reliable. We know we can't always rely on what we believe to be "reality." This gives us a certain advantage over spirit workers who have never had to question the evidence of their senses or their logic. For them, getting a message wrong can be embarrassing. For us it can mean a trip back to the hospital.

We tend to be more careful about our revelations and treat them with a healthy skepticism that is often lacking in the Neo-Pagan community.

Having a spiritual contact (what Spiritualists called a fetch) to sort out the real voices from the subconscious sock monkeys is very useful. Finding that contact can be the first step to recovery, or at least to making peace with your sickness. But taking that leap of faith and trusting one voice amidst the many can be a terrifying step, with huge consequences if you are mistaken. If at all possible you should get assistance from a qualified spirit worker who has experience dealing with mentally ill clients. And you should be ready to listen if that spirit worker tells you "I don't think that message comes from the Gods." A valid contact can help; a sock monkey will only lead you further into delusion and dysfunction.

**—Kohinoor Setora, spirit worker
living with mental illness**

Mental illness can be tremendously lonely and isolating. Reaching out to sick people with understanding—even if you must let them know that their "revelation" is just another symptom of their condition—can go a long way toward easing their suffering. We are not obligated to reinforce sick people's delusions, no matter how much they might want us to do so. But we do have a moral responsibility to treat them with kindness and respect. And those of us living with mental illness must understand that we too have responsibilities to ourselves, our community, and our Gods.

My primary tradition is Celtic Reconstructionist (CR) filidecht, the practice of sacred poetics within a CR framework. A fili is, at least in part, a sacred poet and nature mystic within the Gaelic spiritual and literary tradition. The filid have links with the draoi, or druids, though they are apparently not and never were identical with them. The emphasis in filidecht is on verbal magic, poetry, music, and inner work toward spiritual transformation and visionary insight. Animism and polytheism are both important strands within this path. Otherworld work, visionary practices, and mantic and divinatory work are all part of the thread.

I often describe myself as a professional madwoman, and I identify in large part with the geilta of Gaelic tradition—those who have been made "mad" by their experiences yet attempt to place their difficulties and challenges firmly within a spiritual context, using them to generate poetry and spiritual/mystical experience as ways of healing and of normalizing life after intense trauma. It could be said that one major difference between a fili and a geilt is that the fili usually works within society while a geilt is at its margins; one is socially sanctioned while the other is not.

—Erynn Rowan Laurie,
U.S. Celtic Reconstructionist Pagan

Of course, for many people, any kind of a belief in Gods and spirits is evidence of mental illness, and so is a belief in communication between corporeal and noncorporeal beings. Our premise in this book is that such things are possible and are not evidence of neurochemical problems. But a certain percentage of the population *does* suffer from mental illness, and thus a certain percentage of people claiming personal gnosis for a particular belief or behavior will also be mentally ill. The part that everyone needs to remember about people who present with a very unusual personal gnosis is that there are three possible options regarding their mental health: first, they are completely sane and the message is just an unusual one; second, the message is a product of their mental illness; or third (and probably most difficult), they are actually getting a valid message from an actual entity, but their mental illness is distorting it.

Actual mental delusions—magical thinking, "hearing voices," and various other conditions associated with psychosis—are not so prevalent as overactive imaginations. But that is cold comfort for those living with a brain that sometimes plays cruel tricks on them. If you suffer from a disorder that causes delusional thinking, you may well have a greater than average sensitivity to the spiritual world, but you are going to have to learn how to sort out those signals from your brain malfunctioning. Kohinoor Setora offers some observations on how she copes with her illness:

> *When I'm tired or overly stressed, background noises can begin to take on a pattern: it's like listening to a garbled conversation in a language I don't understand very well. Occasionally I will pick up words, but they are usually nonsensical or insulting. (Very few schizophrenics have voices telling them they are God; far, far more have a constant dialogue in their heads berating them for being stupid, horrible people.) There are few complete sentences and almost never a whole paragraph; they are just disjointed words floating in the aethyr.*
>
> *Spirit voices, by contrast, generally speak in complete sentences. Conversing with spirits is like conversing with people. Some are stupid, some are frighteningly smart, some are very nice, and some not so nice. But they have distinct and fully formed personalities, unlike the line noise. That doesn't mean you can trust all of them, any more than you can trust everyone you meet on the street. But once you've made a few friends on the Other Side, they can help sort out the ones you can trust from the ones you need to avoid—and let you know gently when your sanity tank is running on fumes.*

If you are a spiritual seeker living with mental illness, you may have to coordinate your spiritual work with your mental health care plan. This can be very challenging; while you'll find a few sympathetic professionals who are willing to treat your religion respectfully, many will write off any revelation you have as yet another sign of mental illness.

Perhaps the best thing to do is follow the AA approach: take what you need and leave the rest behind. You may find it useful to smile, nod, and be discreet about your spiritual work while discussing problems that can be treated by counseling and medication.

Whether you are the seeker with mental illness who is trying desperately to figure out how to tell one message from another or the spiritual practitioner faced with the rambling seeker who has either a crazy-sounding message or a crazy-sounding affect, it's important to take things slowly and not jump to conclusions. Every tool of discernment you have should be pressed into service. Del, a U.S. Pagan shaman who specializes in counseling the mentally ill (among other minority groups), sent us this advisory:

> *It would make for a nice and neat little world if people who experience unverifiable personal gnosis and people who "hear voices" as a manifestation of mental illness were two distinct categories of people. It's actually been my experience (as a shaman who works with mentally ill clients seeking to incorporate spirituality into their treatment) that once you're predisposed to "hearing voices," it may actually be easier for you to receive personal gnosis as well. However, once your friends, family, and community know that you have a mental illness, of which a symptom is "hearing voices," any gnosis that comes out of your mouth garners a heaping load of suspicion. So how do you handle that?*
>
> *First of all, it can be comforting to know that in most cases of illness in which auditory hallucinations are a symptom, the things your "voices" say tend to be fairly predictable. Many paranoid schizophrenics, for example, are inundated with messages about the ill wishes of the people they know or witness around them. Others may have intrusive thoughts (which can sometimes feel like "voices in the head") that a certain class of people belong to a secret society that means to do them harm. In any case, the first step for people*

with any auditory hallucinations who feel they may also be receiving UPG is to get acquainted with the regular content of their hallucinations. Although some people who experience UPG have heard things since they were children, it's not as common; so if you've been hearing the same thing over and over since you were a child, chances are good that it's your illness talking. Most divine communications carry a one-time, meaningful importance that you may be reminded of later, but they manifest only when it's relevant to you or the person the message is for. So think back to when your illness began to manifest, and compare the messages you've received. When you begin to compare your organic mental mumblings with the messages of the Gods, you should find a distinct difference in method, message, and meaning.

Usually, messages that tell you to harm yourself or other people, or that denigrate or humiliate you or your loved ones, or that induce memories of traumatic experiences in your past are manifestations of mental illness. It's pretty rare for a Deity to expend precious resources just to tell you what a worthless piece of crap you are. And when a Deity asks for a sacrifice or ordeal, that entity tends to show you the positive outcome as much as the details of the undertaking—so if you hear voices telling you to cut yourself or enact dangerous behavior, even if you think it might be the message of a God or Goddess, it can't hurt to talk it over with a professional. They're trained to recognize the regular pattern of mental illness. Professionals won't likely support your hypothesis that this is some sort of divine message, but they can at least sort out what a typical auditory hallucination for someone with your diagnosis is.

Please don't think that only schizophrenics hear voices. Auditory hallucinations are much more common manifestations of mental illness than you might think, especially if you include intrusive thoughts (that is, a thought or feeling that feels like it comes from an outside source, rather than your own self-conversation). People experiencing anything ranging from clinical depression to bipolar disorder to personality disorders, as well as people recovering from addiction, may hear "voices" from time to time. Even diabetics and hypoglycemics may experience auditory hallucinations when their blood sugar is very low; people having TIAs (transient ischemic attack, a kind of stroke) sometimes feel as though they've experienced some sort of divine manifestation.

Auditory hallucinations aren't always negative, either, in case we were starting to think this was pretty cut and dry. There are several disorders in which messages of inflated self-importance or delusions of grandeur are part of the diagnostic material. If you're hearing things tell you that you're radically more important than the rest of the human race or that you're the only special child of a God and everyone else is dung, I'm willing to bet that this is probably your mental illness speaking.

So how can you tell if it's an actual divine communication if you suffer from these sorts of things? Well, like I said, first and foremost, get to know the sound of your "voices." If the message seems to be more of the "same ol', same ol'," it's probably your mental illness talking to you. On the other hand, if the message seems to be uplifting and meaningful to your life or the lives around you, and the way it makes you feel is different from how you feel on a day-to-day basis, it could be UPG. If your revelation has to do with a Deity and nothing to do with you at all, it could be UPG. In fact, if a message has nothing to do with you, but seems to be a message to someone else about their relationship to a Deity, it could be UPG.

But how do you know for certain? Sometimes you can't. Sometimes you have to decide that if there is any room for error, it's best to keep what happens in your head to yourself, even if it might be divine communication. Not all UPG is meant for mass consumption. If you absolutely must know if something is UPG or your own invention, it's time to get other people involved. You may want to talk to your doctor or therapist about your situation, and see what a professional thinks, if you have one who seems knowledgeable and understanding on those subjects. You may also want to seek out a clergyperson, spirit worker, or shaman for clarification. Finding someone who can perform divination on your behalf might help, especially if the person doing the divination knows that you suffer from auditory hallucinations and you need outside discernment as to whether it's divine. (You should not read for yourself in this case.)

I'm not afraid to say that I hear voices, and yet I am a practicing shaman with a reliable sense of UPG. I got to know the timbre and inflection of my inner voices, the messages they typically send to me, and what triggers usually cause a bout of this chatter. When my Gods talk to me, it is a completely different experience—I feel their presence throughout my body, and my head feels full of light. I often cry when I experience a moment of divine communication, even if the message is happy or neutral. In the times when I had difficulty differentiating between my auditory hallucinations and my Gods, I said to the Gods with all respect, "You know I have challenges, and right now my challenges are making it hard for me to discern the truth. If this is a message you want me to hear, you need to send me an omen, or say it in a different way, or send it to me through another conduit." It's not that I don't trust my own sense of UPG, but sometimes it sure helps to hear the same thing come out of another person's mouth. It's my UPG that the Gods understand our human shortcomings and do not fault us for things that make us organically different from each other—in fact, that's one of the interesting things about not being divine!

I am also honest with others when I am unsure whether

a message has divine roots or not. If I feel like sharing the message is important, I will tell them that my signal clarity may be murky, and they are welcome to do their own research to see if what I have to say brings any meaning to their life. I know I do this, regardless of my mental illness, when a message has to do with something I'm emotionally invested in. So I take even more care when the message may have come about due to an unknown trigger or trauma flashback. It can be risky, because it may mean disclosing that I am mentally ill, or the nature of my illness, to someone I'd rather not tell. But that's part of the decision-making process when one faces these sorts of challenges; if you feel you absolutely cannot disclose your illness, then it's probably best that you not share your UPG either. After all, you have no idea if the recipient of your UPG will judge you "crazy" because you think you have some sort of divinely inspired insight. So you're already making that leap of faith; you might as well be completely honest about how far a leap it is.

If the problem you're facing is that someone you know (whether that person is a member of your ritual group, or a friend, or a community member) is sharing "messages" that you fear may actually be manifestations of a mental illness, there is, unfortunately, not much you can do besides ignore the source. If it is causing a disruption or causing strife within your community, I would talk to the person alone, in a safe and secure atmosphere, away from wherever the disruption happens. Speak directly to the disruptive behavior, if that's the issue. If the content of someone's UPG worries you, don't be afraid to tell that person so in a place and time that's conducive to actually focusing on what you have to say, and where that person can feel free to disclose if a mental illness may be in play. I feel most clergypeople should have a Pagan-friendly therapist on their "Rolodex" for all sorts of issues, and this one may be the most obvious.

If you are the clergyperson or spirit worker faced with the client with worrisome UPG, well, one way that clergypersons or spirit workers have approached this in the past has been to say something like, "I am glad you feel you can share these messages with me. However, I'm a bit troubled by some of what you've said; I think it might do us both a bit of good if you discuss it with [therapist], just to get another opinion on what you've been experiencing and make sure there aren't any health issues involved." Make sure to emphasize that you don't think the person is "crazy" or even necessarily "mentally ill"; you're just concerned with the content of the message and you think it would be helpful if he or she spoke to a professional about it. If the individual seems scared, offer to go along or to arrange a meeting with the three of you in a nonclinical setting, if that's possible.

—**Del, U.S. Pagan**

GNOSIS AND MEDS

In the next chapter, we discuss signal clarity and how chemicals can interfere with the ability to "tune in to" the spirit world. However, that risk is a necessary one when it comes to medications that are maintaining your health. We are not our ancestors, and many of us live with conditions that would simply have killed us had we lived in the distant past or would have forced us to live a (probably short) life of misery. If you need medication in order to function well and be physically and mentally healthy, that's the most important thing. First things first: get your life in order before you upset the applecart with spiritual seeking. We also advise treating "orders" or messages to quit taking your medication with extreme caution and skepticism. Raven has had visitors show up at his house declaring that the Gods had "cured" them of the need to take antipsychotics; this invariably has led to misery for all concerned. (He has also had clients come in to ask about their spiritual path and received the message: "Don't jump the gun. First you need to see to that health problem, or stop your recreational drug habit, or get a job and move out of your parents' basement. Then you can worry about your spiritual path." Spirituality is not supposed to be an alternative to personal responsibility.)

Still, some medications do have a dulling effect on the ability to communicate with the Gods and spirits. Del's further opinion on the matter, from long experience, is that "some experiential evidence shows that any med, taken long enough, will become absorbed by the system, and its antipsi effects will wear off over time. The more the body 'needs' the med in order to function correctly (and in this, I'm adding my experience working with people with seizure disorders, on heavy CNS [central nervous system] druggage) the quicker the body/mind/spirit adapts to it, and it ceases to be a problem. Specifically, it seems that neuroleptics like Topomax, Dilantin, Neurontin, and the like have a big effect of shutting down psi. However, as the body adjusts, the psi returns in slow doses. Usually I advise people that if the psi doesn't return, it's not the right drug for long-term usage."

Wintersong, another U.S. Pagan shaman, considers the difficult problem of inappropriate medications and offers advice for spiritual practitioners who see clients with these problems:

One issue that has come up recently as an ambivalent debate among spirit workers is the problem of psychiatric medications and their effect on the ability of psychically talented people to use those talents. This is one area in which divination is crucial, especially in the case of SSRIs [selective serotonin reuptake inhibitors], antipsychotic medications, and antiseizure medications. Psych meds are highly variable in how they affect someone's mind and spirit connection. The same medication can give one person the mental clarity to better access their spirit connection without blocking it in any way (and some of them learn to work around any psychic side effects of lifelong meds without much trouble), but giving it to another spirit worker can completely shut down the spirit connection, a situation that can anger the spirits and cause them to find ways to get that individual off of those medications. Some have even found that this blockage lasted for years after they went off of the medication; they report having to work for a long time to bring back what had been lost, and some claim that it was never the same again. Take great care, then, before making the decision to take any psych med. (I realize that this is easy for me to say; it may be the case that if someone is in such a state as to need psych meds, that person may not be using his or her best judgment. That's why divination, preferably from a neutral party, is a good thing.)

There are no easy answers in matters of neurochemistry and psychic powers. This is an area that most of us in the spirit-work community would do well to acquaint ourselves with. I should point out that I am a big believer in using as few medications as is possible while still being able to function and be safe. Witness that I have Tourette syndrome, and I am willing to go around barking like a dog rather than deal with the side effects of the few medications that have any effect at all on my tics. And yes, some of that is because the medication side effects hinder my ability to function as a spirit worker (or anything else for that matter), although I would point out that there is a real difference between saying that a medication interferes with spirit work and that the side effects of said medication do. On an individual medication basis, the difference is semantics, but knowing the difference can have a big influence on where you go next.

As spiritual mentors and teachers, it also behooves us to be aware of what the consequences of going off of different medications are, and what the proper procedures for doing so are. A full AHFS Drug Information resource (like the Physicians' Desk Reference, only put out by the national pharmacist organization instead of the drug companies) or even the AHFS DI Essentials or AHFS Drug Handbook should be something that those of us who work a lot with students or who use medication ourselves have available for finding out that sort of information. Plus, when a student comes to you saying that the Fae are trying to kill her, it is nice to be able to check and find out that paranoid delusions are a withdrawal side effect of the antipsychotic your student just went cold turkey on before you go starting shit with the Fae.

Still, even if all the signs point to it, be very careful before encouraging people to go off of their medication, or refuse psychiatric help. Keep in mind that you may open yourself up to blame—from them or from their attorney—if they change their mind in the future and decide that their time of misery was your fault. You might do well to spread the blame a bit and have more than one practitioner involved with the decision, including at least one who has positive experience both working with people on medication and working with those with unmedicated mental illness.

SIGNAL CLARITY

Hearing the Divine Voice

They have wept and fasted; they have danced themselves into drum-beat-driven frenzies; they have cloistered themselves away and devoted their lives to prayer and contemplation. Throughout history, people have used various methods to achieve divine contact. Some have sacrificed home, family, comfort, wealth, and position for those lightning flashes of clarity. They have endured scorn, torture, even martyrdom for the privilege of speaking to their Gods. They may worship different pantheons and use different means for opening the ways, but all have felt it worthwhile to expend enormous effort to bridge the gap between sacred and mundane.

What follows are some of the more popular and efficacious ways of hearing those holy voices and filtering out the things that might blur their message. They can be used singly or in combination, but they should be used with reverence, respect, and a good deal of caution. Some can be hazardous to your health, but all have been used at one time or another to get people in touch with the forces that shape and rule our world. To meet them face to face, in all their glory and terror, is not something one should undertake lightly.

There are generally two different kinds of cultural approaches to being better able to connect with Spirit, or the spirits, whichever you prefer. One could refer to them as the *shamanic approach* and the *yogic approach*. The shamanic approach is to use altered states of consciousness, but to learn to control them instead of simply being swept away by them. Ideally, with the shamanic approach, one learns to step in and out of altered states at will by skillfully using a variety of techniques and tools. The yogic approach is longer and slower—while shamanic practitioners may take years and classic shamans decades to learn their skills, yogis may think in terms of doing the same thing for the rest of their life. For the yogic approach, one concentrates on purifying the consciousness—physical, mental, spiritual, and moral purity—combined with a number of repetitive physical disciplines to achieve this. Over a long period of time, one transforms and evolves one's mind into an instrument that can connect to the Divine without the use of altered states. While the two approaches do have a certain amount of crossover with tools and skills, it is usually true that the yogic approach tends to be focused on personal connection with the Divine, and the shamanic approach tends to focus on finding ways to be of service to others.

THE YOGIC PATH: PURIFYING THE CONSCIOUSNESS

First, let's start with the simple things that get in the way of your subtler senses. Modern spirit workers refer to the relative ability to see, hear, and generally sense nonphysical presences as *signal clarity*. Some people are born with better-than-normal signal clarity; others gain it as a result of specific practices (or sometimes severe physical trauma such as a near-death experience). Many religions, especially in Asia, have codified elaborate long-term procedures in order to increase signal clarity. While modern Neo-Pagan subcultures tend to lean toward the explanation that we are all born with wonderful signal clarity and it's the modern world—and disbelieving parents—who suppress it, most Eastern religions tend to believe that most of us are born head-blind, and we need to work in order to develop our inner senses. Rather than get into that argument here, let's just say that the side effects of civilized life can have some signal-suppressing side effects and address what any person can do to help the problem.

What Goes into the Body

When spirit workers discuss the effects of diet on their signal clarity, there are a lot of disagreements as to what variety of food helped them. For some, animal products and grains dulled their signal clarity; for others, it helped. Some felt that the animal products and grains were grounding, but they needed that grounding or they'd be overwhelmed. It may well be that when it comes to food variety, the best choice is to figure out what sort of food your body is most healthy when eating— and in our experience, that will vary widely from person to person. Many religious traditions around the world have opinions on what food helps to purify the body and spirit, and what food does the opposite— and many of those traditions disagree with each other, so the seeker is best advised to try different things and listen to the body. Some shamanic traditions, for example, find meat to be grounding and useful for building up strength; those closer to the yogic model may disagree. Yoga teacher Joshua Tenpenny says of the yogic food view:

> *Many yogic traditions classify foods in three categories. "Heavy" foods such as meat, fish, eggs, root vegetables, starchy vegetables, mushrooms, and alcohol are said to draw the energy to the lower chakras and dull the subtle senses. Spicy or salty foods, strongly flavored vegetables, refined sugar, and any stimulants are said to promote an overactive and aggressive mindset. These two types of food are appropriate (maybe even beneficial) for some people under certain circumstances, but someone trying to refine the subtle sense is advise to eat primarily "pure" and easily digestible foods such as fruit; mild, well-cooked vegetables; most dairy products (milk, yogurt, and clarified butter, but not cheese); and mild*

herbs and spices. Yogic traditions disagree on the classification of grains, nuts, and legumes. They are generally considered to be sufficiently "pure" for the average person, especially if cooked into porridge with healing herbs, but this may still be too "heavy" for some spiritual aspirants, especially while engaged in a period of intensive practice.

While the jury may be out on which foods to eat, there is one piece of wisdom that comes up again and again when spirit workers discuss this issue, and it is one on which everyone from raw-food vegans and meat-eaters agree. Chemicals are always a psychic deadener, and most of our food is laden with chemicals from seed to stove. The first and best thing you can do for your signal clarity is to *lighten your chemical load.* This means eating organically grown food whenever it is even remotely feasible—especially if you eat meat, dairy, or soy. Eating organic food is more than just a practice that is good for your body, good for the Earth, and makes the Gods of agriculture happy—it is also the simplest first step to being better able to talk to the spirits and hear them talk back.

Chemicals come into the body in other ways as well. They can be in the water, especially in urban areas. They can be in the air there, as well. They can be in household chemicals that we come into contact with, such as bleaches and cleansers. They can be in soaps and shampoos. They can be present in industrial buildings, and even in new carpets and paint, at home or at your job. Some people also need to take pharmaceutical medications in order to maintain their health through diseases and disorders that would simply have killed them in our ancestors' day. We are not suggesting that people stop taking their medications or flee the city to live with cleaner air and water. However, if there are areas of your life where you *can* cut down on chemical exposure, you should try it—and if your life requires chemical contact in some areas, cut down in others to make up for it. Water purifiers and air cleaners can help, as can consuming and using more natural products.

It's also possible to do regular detoxing with the aid of herbs—but do this only under the eye of a professional herbalist, and don't expect it to compensate for extensive and unnecessary chemical exposure. A safer and (for many people) more pleasurable detoxing is purification by fire, in a sauna or sweat lodge at the very least. We know that the state of bodily purification from a good sweat can combine with the quiet and ritual of the sauna to purify the inner senses. (Sweats can also be used as an altered-state technique, and we will touch on that in the next section, the shamanic path.) More advanced forms of purification have been used as part of the yogic approach and can be found in many older yoga texts. These include enemas, sinus rinsing, and other fairly intense bodily cleansing routines, both to free the body of toxins and thus create a physiological condition that adds to overall signal clarity, and to enable a spiritual cleansing through the physical act—an "as above, so below" correspondence.

Sleep

Whatever is wrong with you, sleep deprivation makes it worse. While sleep deprivation has been associated (like fasting) with some spiritual practices, in our experience people get little enough sleep as it is, and most of us suffer from long-term mild sleep deprivation. This clouds signal clarity and makes us feel duller and less able to focus. One of the biggest complaints that we hear from people trying to meditate is "as soon as I start meditating, I just fall asleep!" This doesn't mean that they aren't spiritually evolved enough to meditate—it simply means that they aren't getting enough sleep on a regular basis. As soon as they let go of their physical tension enough to go into a mild altered state, the sleep-deprived body jumps in and seizes the helm. If this happens to you—if meditation, prayer, or other such practices make you sleepy—then your best bet is to reorganize your schedule to get more hours of sleep per night, and then try again to meditate after a month of doing this.

Stress Relief

Stress can also block signal clarity, especially when it is stored in the body. Many of us keep our stress in our shoulders, lower back, or elsewhere in our tense muscles. Regular massage can give temporary relief from physically retained stress, perhaps long enough to relax and open to messages from the Divine—but again, if you get a massage and fall asleep, that's another sign that you're not getting enough rest. The real key is to find ways to relieve stress. The obvious way is to remove unnecessary stresses from your life, but that doesn't get rid of the necessary ones like children, bills, or making a living.

Fortunately, it's been found that prayer and meditation do relieve stress. While it is not the main purposes of these practices, stress relief is a wonderful side effect. This means that having a regular practice of some kind of prayer or meditation will eventually help reduce your stresses to the point where signal clarity is improved. The key here is to begin—and keep up—the discipline or regimen of deliberate "quiet time with the Gods and spirits," but not to expect much in the beginning. It may take months for the practice to make enough impact on your stressed-out life to clear up your inner senses. That's all the more reason to start immediately.

For those who have a hard time sitting still—a common complaint we hear from people with too much rather than too little energy—we suggest a moving meditative technique such as t'ai chi or chi gong. If you do it long enough to gain "body memory" of the motions, you can keep the more hyperactive portions of your brain focused on the movements while the rest is freed up enough by the repetitive ritual to tune in to something less physical. Deliberate-motion exercises like the above practices, or yoga, or martial-arts katas also relieve stress stored in the body and the heart as well.

Right Living

It's important to get one's life in order, and especially to get one's actions completely square with one's code of living. How does this build signal clarity? It's a subtle thing, but being one with your code, living your life with complete integrity, creates a certain energy around your destiny. Various cultures have referred to the workings of destiny as *wyrd,* or *ananke,* or *heimarmene,* or karma. However you refer to it, building up that energy around it slowly adds to your ability to "get in tune" with the Universe, and thus get in tune with beings who are more in tune with it than we are. From our experience, it seems that the Gods are less concerned with what code you live by and more concerned with you actually following it, assuming that the code is lived with real mindfulness and is not one chosen for negative personal reasons such as denial or obvious self-indulgence. Integrity, not a particular set of rules, is what helps get you in tune with the Universe.

Clearing Out Your Personal Baggage

As we make reference to in divination sections, every piece of psychological damage you own is a hole in your signal clarity. So is every bit of your soul or personality that you ignore, repress, or otherwise do not know inside and out. Part of the reason that working on yourself goes hand in hand with talking to the spirits is that the more of your personal issues you can clear out, the clearer you'll be in that dimension as well. This is also why, as we'll discuss when we talk about some of the more extreme mind-altering techniques, your baggage comes up first when you dive onto those roads. It will keep coming up, again and again, until you've cleared enough of it out that the Universe feels that you can be allowed through that door. Even then, once you form relationships with Gods or spirits, they will often find ways to make sure that you continue that work. After all, it's in their best interests as well—if you are more whole as a person, you will be able to communicate better with them.

THE SHAMANIC PATH:
ALTERED STATE TECHNIQUES

Next we'll discuss active practices that have been used by people around the world and throughout time to improve their signal clarity, either temporarily or permanently. In Raven's shamanic tradition, methods of achieving altered states are divided into eight paths, like an eight-spoked wheel. Many (though not all) of the following practices fall onto that Eightfold Path (which is not to be confused with the Buddhist Eightfold Path). The shamanic Eightfold Path includes the Path of Breath (meditation and prayer), the Path of Ritual, the Path of Rhythm, the Ascetic's Path, the Path of the Flesh (sexual techniques), the Ordeal Path (pain and endurance), the Path of Sacred Plants, and the Path of the Horse (spirit possession). For an in-depth exploration of each of these paths through the lens of Northern Tradition shamanism, you can refer to Raven's book *Wightridden: Paths of Northern-Tradition Shamanism*. For the final path of spirit possession, which we will not be covering here, we refer you to our previous book, *Drawing Down the Spirits,* which focuses on that practice.

We should also stress that no one utilizes all of these techniques and that no one technique is right for everyone. Most people who use controlled altered states on a regular basis have one to a handful of these paths that work for them. No one that we know is experienced at every one. That's why it's so useful to have a variety of ways of opening one's head. Some of these paths have long, slow learning curves, but it's harder to hurt yourself with them. Some have short, violent learning curves and can injure or even (in the case of the Path of Sacred Plants or the Ordeal Path) kill you. While you should do what works, not what others tell you ought to work, we still suggest that you start out with the safer paths and take up the more dangerous ones only under the guidance of experienced spiritual practitioners who know what they are doing.

Prayer

Even the most formulaic of prayers, like the dancer's tendu and plié, form necessary building blocks to spiritual expression. In many respects, the comparison to the discipline of a dancer's daily practice is quite apt. Prayer, as any mystic knows, is a discipline that trains the mind, heart, and spirit in attentiveness, mindfulness, and devotion to the Gods. Anyone can move to music, but very few people if any, can suddenly, without any practice or training, put on a pair of pointe shoes and pull off a flawless Swan Lake (though watching the attempt might be amusing in a sick, sad sort of way)!

In many respects, it is the same with meditation and prayer—these things pattern the soul to the touch of the Gods in the same way daily ballet practice develops a kinetic memory in dancers. It provides structure and language, place, and an expansive vocabulary by which we can express those experiences of the spirit that often resist the clarification of language.

—Galina Krasskova, U.S. Heathen[1]

If you want the Gods to talk to you, you will first need to get into the habit of talking to them. Throughout history humanity has approached the Gods through prayer. Some prayers were complicated rituals performed by the priests as intercessions on behalf of the tribe or the people. Some were simple, heartfelt conversations like those a child might have with a loving but stern parent. All were a means by which the worshipper sought to understand and to be understood by the Divine.

The difference between prayer and meditation is a gray area, and some would say that there is no difference. Others would point out that prayer is actively pointing the consciousness at a specific presence, while meditation can be entirely inward-focused, ignoring external presences entirely. Either way, they require putting yourself into a focused, mild altered state, which has the potential to move into a much deeper state. Both are mainstays of the Path of Breath, also known as the Path of Meditation, on the Eightfold Path.

Personal conversations are an excellent way of developing a close, personal, and loving relationship with your Gods or spirit guides. Setting up a shrine or an altar can provide you with a place where you can meet them for a chat. If you can't set up a permanent altar, a temporary one can work as well. You can keep a few representative items— such as a picture and a sprig of mistletoe for Loki, or a raven feather and an eye patch for Odin—in a small box and bring them out when you are ready to pray. This provides a "trigger" that will put you in an appropriately reverent and receptive state of mind and help open the lines of communication. It also establishes sacred space and sends them a signal that a worshipper is offering them praise.

Some spiritual authorities caution against the rote repetition of words, encouraging worshippers instead to "speak from their hearts." But while it is certainly worthwhile to talk to the Gods in your own words, there can be great value in memorizing and repeating someone else's prayers. As you contemplate and recite a text, you internalize it. Through meditation it may unfold new layers of nuance and meaning, putting you in contact with aspects of Deity that you might otherwise miss. One notable example of this is the Orthodox Jesus Prayer. Devotees repeat over and over the phrase "Lord Jesus Christ, Son of God, have mercy on me, a sinner." When feasible the prayer is repeated aloud; when it is not, they strive to repeat it internally. In time this repetition becomes automatic, and the worshippers find themselves drawn toward repentance and a deep interior connection with God.[2] Prayer beads, used in many traditions, can be a great aid in repeating prayers and establishing a practice of regular worship.

Recitation of specific prayers can help you stay focused during meditation. Much as yogis enter altered states by concentrating diligently on their mantras, you can reach out to your Gods and keep your mind from wandering off into unproductive realms. Combined with active visualization—willful concentrated efforts to feel the presence of your Deity with all five senses—it can help you to achieve a powerful and direct experience of the Divine. If you are reciting the Homeric Hymn to Delian Apollo, imagine the taste of the golden nectar in the cup he is given by Zeus. Hear the dark wave beating against the shores of sea-girt Delos and the high wailing of the shrill wind. Smell the salt air, see the glowing light beaming about the baby Apollo and the flowers blooming, and listen to the song he plays on the curved lyre. As you do so you may find that the visions take on a life of their own. Certain lines within the text may leap out at you or provide you with an answer to some question that has been troubling you. Or you may even find that Apollo or one of the figures mentioned in the hymn have a message for you in their own words.

Not only can prayer help you to establish a personal relationship with your Deity, it can help you to experience what German theologian Rudolf Otto called the *mysterium tremendum* and the *mysterium fascinosum*. The mysterium tremendum is the moment when we recognize ourselves as infinitesimal before the Infinite, when we are seized with a soul-chilling dread and terror in the presence of the Holy. It is a profoundly humbling moment, yet it is also the moment when we move closest to our Gods. We become fully cognizant of our flaws and yet at the same time recognize that our redemption lies within them. Our fear combines with an equally powerful desire to be united with them, the impulse that Otto called the *mysterium fascinosum*.

Both recitation and communication are important aspects of prayer and invaluable tools in any aspiring mystic's kit. Like an exercise regimen, they will have the greatest benefit if you practice regularly. The more you pray, the closer you will grow with your Gods—and the closer they will grow to you.

Breathing

> *Let the yogi try constantly to concentrate his mind (on the Supreme Self) remaining in solitude and alone, self-controlled, free from desires and (longing for) possessions. He should set in a clean place his firm seat, neither too high nor too low, covered with sacred grass, a deerskin and a cloth, one over the other. There taking his place on the seat, making his mind one-pointed and controlling his thought and sense, let him practice yoga for the purification of the soul. Holding the body, head and neck, erect and still, looking fixedly at the tip of his nose, without looking around (without allowing his eyes to wander). Serene and fearless, firm in his vows, subdued in mind, let him sit, harmonized, his mind turned to Me and intent on Me alone.*
>
> **—Bhagavad Gita[3]**

The Path of Meditation is also called the Path of Breath because if you can control your breathing patterns, you can change the consciousness at will. Breath is the means by which we pump life force around our bodies, and by changing our breathing, we change its flow and change the way our mind is working in the moment.

If you really want to explore this possibility thoroughly, we recommend looking into the yogic practice of *pranayama*. The yogis have perfected more techniques of consciousness-changing breathing than anyone else in the world, and that information is easily available and has many teachers. However, if you want to start in your living room without further research, we suggest trying the fourfold breath. It's simple—breathe in for a slow count of four, hold for the same count, breathe out for the same count, hold for the same count. Continue doing this, focusing on your breathing, until your body is used to it and your consciousness turns inward. Don't be disappointed if it takes many repetitions of practice to get to that point—the Path of Breath is not a fast road. It has a long, slow learning curve, and it can take months or years to make permanent changes in your brain—but at the same time, you are very unlikely to be able to harm yourself with it, unlike faster but much more dangerous paths.

Chanting and singing also count as part of this path, although they overlap with the Paths of Rhythm and Ritual. Buddhist meditation practices use chanting as part of their tradition of altered states, as do some Hindu practices including the devotional chanting of *kirtan*. Trained singers have reported that the rhythmic diaphragmatic breathing required for sustained singing can create an altered state. The Saami practice of *joik,* or sacred shamanic singing, is traditionally performed with a very interesting circular breath-pattern—joik-singers sing literally until they run out of breath, stop at whatever point in the chant that happens, take a huge breath, and pick up where they left off. This breath pattern can, over a period of time, "open the head" and create an altered state. If the song is aimed at a particular Deity or spirit, the essence of that spirit is invited to come through the open door of the singer's being.

Ritual

> *I've done it so many times that I hardly pay attention to the*
> *act anymore, but it pays attention to me. I light the stick of*
> *dried mugwort, I wave it in the four directions and around in*
> *circles, I sing the song in the ancient tongue that purifies the*
> *space, and it is done. I'm clear and ready to open up, ready to*
> *hear what can be heard.*
>
> **—Seawalker, U.S. Northern Tradition Pagan**

The second spoke of the Eightfold Paths is the Path of Ritual. That word has more than one meaning; for some people it is synonymous with "ceremony," meaning a specific series of actions done for religious purposes, with spiritual symbolism involved. Another definition involves the concept of "ritual" as "repetition"—something that is done the same way every time, regardless of its purpose. We define ritual as a combination of these two things—a repetitive action done for spiritual purposes and with that symbolism.

Repetition is the key to making ritual work to improve signal clarity. This aspect of ritual can be summed up by the following steps: (1) Choose a symbol that has a strong spiritual connotation and invokes a strong emotional response. (2) Perform some physical action that embodies, uses, or otherwise invokes that symbol. (3) Allow yourself to experience the response you have to that action. (4) Repeat steps 2 and 3—again, and again, and again. They can be repeated multiple times as part of a single ceremony or singly over a long period of time, usually linked to another periodic activity—for instance, performing your ritual before you pray, or before undertaking divination, or before eating or sleeping or anything else.

Over time, the process of ritual creates a "groove" in our brains that makes it easier to access that state at will. If we condition ourselves to do this thing, feel this way, contemplate and experience this spiritual essence, and then go into a mild altered state, we can use it as a tool. Beginning the ritual then simply propels the brain down the road to openness, with a lot less effort on the part of the practitioner. Ritual is also the easiest and safest way to attempt to facilitate giving a whole group of people an experience of the Divine that they might not otherwise have had. That's why it's the first and foremost tool of group religious practices.

Rhythm

> *In the beginning there was noise. And noise begat rhythm. And rhythm begat everything else. This is the kind of cosmology a drummer can live with . . . If the rhythm is right, you feel it with all your senses; it's in your mind, your body, in both places. The head of the drum vibrates as it is struck. The physical feedback is almost instantaneous, rushing along your arms, filling your ears. A feeling not unlike trust settles over you as you give yourself to the rhythm. You don't fight it, but instead allow yourself to be propelled by this insistent but friendly feeling. All sense of the present moment disappears, the normal categories of time become meaningless. . . . Here is the mystery and I don't think it can be solved, certainly not with words or numbers.*
>
> **—Mickey Hart**[4]

Scientific studies have shown that rhythm definitely has an effect on the brain, and it is certainly one of the oldest paths to an altered state, to the point where the drum and rattle are symbols of shamans and spirit workers the world over. Drummer and author Mickey Hart points out that "where there is a shaman, there is also a drum."[5] Rhythm pervades us all the time, from the microrhythms of our body to the macrorhythms of the day, the cycles of the seasons, the changes of the Earth. Rhythm has been used to bring whole tribes of people into mild altered states since the first Paleolithic people began to bang on hollow pieces of wood with sticks.

To this day, music is one of the most obvious altered-state tools, and the one that is most frequently experienced in everyday life. People listen to music because they want to alter their mood in some way. Every part of music is rhythm, and not just the drumbeat. Each note is what it is because it vibrates on a particular frequency. While we know that certain rhythms and certain frequencies stimulate certain emotions, moods, and neurological reactions, we have a long way to go before we can explain what any musician knows: that careful manipulation of these rhythms can do things to your head, even without your conscious knowledge or consent.

They can also do things to your body. Drumming—or any kind of percussion—is one side of the coin; the other is dancing, letting the rhythm rule your physical motions. Both trance drumming and trance dancing are classic tools in the box of mind-opening tricks. Chanting, while also part of the Path of Breath, is a chant and not just a random song because it has rhythm—repetition and a cycle. It's not just shamans who have said that music is the voice of the Gods. This is something that we all know, on some level. It's just a matter of following the road. Start by using rhythm of some kind, preferably played in such a way that it reverberates through your body as well as your eardrums, as a prelude to meditation, or a background to it. If you find the right combination of rhythms for your particular neurology, it can help to open the door for you.

Fasting

When I was to be a shaman, I chose suffering through the two things that are most dangerous to us humans, suffering through hunger and suffering through cold. First I hungered five days and was then allowed to drink a mouthful of warm water; the old ones say that only if the water is warm will Pinga and Hila notice the novice and help him. Thereafter I went hungry another fifteen days, and again was given a mouthful of warm water. After that I hungered for ten days.

—Igjukarjuk, Inuit shaman[6]

We are a culture of abundance, especially when it comes to eating. In the 1950s, an average portion of French fries was 2.1 ounces (60 grams); an average fountain soda, 7 ounces (200 milliliter); and an average hamburger patty, 1.6 ounces (50 grams). In 2003, a 7.1 ounce (200 gram) serving of fries, an 8 ounce (250 gram) hamburger patty, and 12 to 64 ounce (250 milliliter to 1.9 liter) soda were more common.[7] It is little wonder that obesity has become epidemic, and growing attention has been placed on our eating habits and the benefits of changing them. For those afflicted with heart disease, type 2 diabetes, and other conditions that can come about as a result of bad eating habits, our culture's gluttony has become a truly deadly sin.

Fasting is a singularly ineffective technique for losing weight if it is part of a "yo-yo dieting" regime. But it can help us become more aware of our bodies and our response to hunger cues. Many of us have never known true hunger. We may have had to wait a bit for a meal or been presented with food that we found distasteful—but we've never been forced to spend days or even weeks without eating. Fasting can teach us the difference between wanting and needing, between being full and being stuffed. Those are lessons that can carry over into other areas of our lives as well, including our spirituality.

As the body is emptied of food and allowed to rid itself of toxins, fasters often find it easier to concentrate on spiritual affairs. The worst hunger pangs fade within a few days, replaced with a feeling of lightness and energy. In this state, many report visions, intense dreams, or a stronger sense of a divine presence. Many initiatory rituals begin with a period of fasting. During this time, the initiates are purged of the things of their earlier existence and reshaped into clean vessels for their new life. The fasting serves both as a signpost marking their transformation and as a technique by which they might become most receptive to spiritual influences.

Although fasting may seem like a solitary discipline, it can also be a way to strengthen a religious community. During the month of Ramadan, devout Muslims will neither eat nor drink from sunup to sundown. Observant Jews refrain from food and water during Yom

Kippur, the Day of Atonement, while many Christians will not eat on Good Friday in observance of the Crucifixion. But fast days are not confined to the monotheist traditions. Devout Hindus may refrain from food on certain days of each week, depending on the Gods they wish to honor: they fast on Monday for Shiva and Parvati, on Thursday for Lakshmi, on Saturday for Hanuman, and on Sunday for all the Goddesses.

While there are few marked "fast days" on most Neo-Pagan calendars, there's no reason certain somber events could not be so commemorated. A Heathen group might fast on July 29—the Feast of Saint Olaf—to mourn the enforced Christianization of Norway, while Hellenic worshippers might mark the abduction of Persephone or the death of Adonis with fasting and mourning. During this time members might refrain from food and drink or eat only sparingly of ceremonially important foods—pomegranate seeds and juice for the Hellenics on the Feast of Persephone, for example, or bitter bread and wine for the Heathens to symbolize the Eucharist that was forced on their ancestors. It's easy enough to be a community gathered together in celebration; the strongest bonds are often forged in shared sorrows.

When you want to accomplish a task and need to let the Universe know that you are serious, fasting can be a very effective way of sending a message. In ancient Ireland those who had been wronged could seek redress through the *troscad,* a ritual hunger strike. Should the person being fasted against not come to arbitration but allow the faster to die, he would be held in contempt by his fellows; this shame would persist even after death unless he made amends to the dead person's family. The troscad is very similar to the *acharitan,* a Hindu tradition of fasting to protest injustice—and one that worked very well for Mahatma Gandhi.[8] Today, instead of vowing to fast unto death, many set a specified time for their fast, often beginning it on a significant date and continuing it for some set number of days to prove their will.

Fasting need not be an all-or-nothing endeavor. You can refrain from certain foods or from eating before or after a set time, which increases mindfulness of your nourishment and where it came from. As an example, the Pagan monastic tradition of the Order of the Horae has an "ancestral fasting" that involves certain sacred foods dedicated to each part of the year, such as eggs for Ostara or grains for Lammas; one "fasts" from those foods for three days before the astronomical holiday and then celebrates by eating them on the marked day. You can also abstain from certain items as a sign of devotion. Mambo Zetwal Kleye (Kathy Latzoni) does not drink champagne because it is La Sirene's chosen drink; in Lukumi, Oshun's children will not eat pumpkin because it is one of their mother's favorite foods. What you do not eat can become as sacred as what you eat; your abstinence serves to mark you as a devotee and helps to cement your relationship with your Gods.

Although fasting can be a powerful spiritual tool, it is not for everyone. Those with a history of eating disorders should be very careful about fasting. So too should those who tend to get overly competitive in spiritual endeavors. Fasting is a means of purification and cleansing, not a contest to see who can get the most points for extended starvation. There are many good reasons to fast, but impressing people with your dedication and toughness is not one of them. If you suffer from hypoglycemia, diabetes, colitis, liver disease, or other serious medical conditions, you should check with your doctor before undertaking any kind of arduous fast or disrupting your regular eating schedule. Also, complete fasting should not be undertaken by anyone who is on oral medications that they cannot afford to stop suddenly. After a day or two of not eating, the digestive system can shut down entirely, which means that you won't digest your meds. This includes birth control, high blood pressure medication, and especially psychiatric medication. (However, you can still do a raw organic food fast, described further on.)

In addition, many of us consume diets loaded with chemicals, which build up in our system as toxins, often in our fatty tissue. When we fast for more than a day or so, the body begins to dump toxins into the bloodstream at a higher than normal rate, and we get physically sick. This illness can ruin a spiritually oriented fast, and going straight back to the chemical-laden food after days of not eating can cause problems as well. Unlike our ancestors who could just stop eating their organically grown food, modern humans on a "normal" Western diet need to prepare for fasts by clearing out their system, and then slowly introduce chemical-laden food afterward. We suggest a full week of 100 percent organic whole foods before any fast, and another week of them afterward. Toward the end of the first week of organic food, you can cut out cooked food and just eat raw organic fruits and vegetables, raw organic milk or yogurt made with it, raw fish, and a small amount of soaked grains. Begin the coming-off week in the same way, with very small amounts—don't shock the system with a huge meal or you'll throw it up—and toward the end, begin to introduce small amounts of "impure" food. This protocol should flank any fast of three days or longer.

As previously mentioned, individuals with no-fasting conditions can still do a fast that involves only raw organic vegetables, raw organic fruits, raw fish from a nonpolluted source, raw organic milk or raw-milk yogurt, and soaked (not cooked) grains. Organic herbs can be used for taste, but not salt or sugar. Drink only water and herbal tea. This is a safe fast that can be eaten for an indefinite period of time, but will not interfere with medications or blood sugar problems. If you have an intestinal condition in which you do not digest raw fiber well, steam (don't cook) the vegetables. If you have allergies or intolerances to dairy products, drop the milk; if you are vegan, you probably won't want the fish, but if you've got blood sugar problems, you are probably going to need one or the other in order to get enough protein. For most Westerners who eat a chemical-laden diet, even a change like this will create a significant difference in signal clarity. This kind of cleansing and purifying fasting can also be used safely by anyone as a prelude to any major personal ritual.

Silence

> One day, when Subhuti was sitting under a tree in a mood of
> sublime emptiness, flowers began to fall around him.
> "We are praising you for your discourse on emptiness," the
> gods whispered to him.

"But I have not spoken of emptiness," said Subhuti.
"You have not spoken of emptiness; we have not heard
emptiness," responded the gods. "This is true emptiness."
And the blossoms showered upon Subhuti like rain.

—**Zen koan**[9]

The seeker has to be silent, then god speaks. If you speak then
god remains silent. Only one can speak. If you want to listen
to the voice of existence itself then learn the art of being silent.
Then disappear completely. Then just be there, available,
open, receptive, and you will be flooded with truth, with light
and that light, that truth, will liberate you, will make you
what you are supposed to be, what you intrinsically need to
be. Your real destiny will be fulfilled. You will feel immense
gratefulness and tremendous contentment. But one has to
learn the art of being silent, then a dialogue with existence
happens.

—**Osho**[10]

Silence is at the heart of mysticism, and it is arguably the most important tool in the spirit worker's kit. This is one of the basic tools of the Ascetic's Path, which includes purification, discipline, and paring down. Silence is the paring down of the "monkey mind" and its ability to keep up its distracting chatter. If we want to commune with the denizens of the worlds seen and unseen, we must first learn to be still. Many mystical and magical techniques require the supplicant to seek out items and to take positive action. Silence requires only that you do and say nothing, that you put yourself away to stand quiet and empty in the presence of those who came before you and those who came before them.

Although it sounds simple, you may find this step very challenging. The hum of tires against asphalt, the ceaseless aspiration of our computer fans, the rumbling buzz of our air conditioners, the high-pitched electronic mosquito hum—our modern world is a very noisy place indeed. Because of this, we have grown accustomed to overstimulation.

When we are forced to spend time in silence, we find it uncomfortable. Boredom soon sets in, we think of more entertaining ways to spend our time, and what should be restorative becomes instead an ordeal.

The best approach to this problem is the same one you take when you're trying to get into shape: gradually working up to longer periods of silence. In time you will find yourself able to keep still well enough and long enough to strengthen your ancestral connection. You may even develop a taste for peace and quiet, and find yourself called to an increasingly contemplative lifestyle; many a reluctant beginning jogger has gone on to finish multiple marathons. For now, try to spend five minutes sitting quietly and thinking of nothing at all. If you fail at that, find a period within which you are able to enforce an internal radio silence. Try to repeat that period, increasing a little bit each time. Keep a chart of your efforts, just as you would for any exercise regimen.

Thoughts will arise while you are trying to maintain this quietude. Let them rise, then let them disintegrate back into the silence. The distractions and temptations that trouble you are only as important as you allow them to be. Once you learn to separate your thinking self from the chattering of the monkey mind, you will find yourself better able to concentrate in mundane life and better able to find your calm, still center in a crisis. Background noise and personal distractions will drift through you like smoke swirling through air.

You may also benefit from incorporating silence into your daily life. Vipassana, a school founded by Indo-Burmese guru S. N. Goenka, offers ten-day courses in their meditation technique. During that time, students are expected to observe "noble silence"—silence in speech, body, and mind—and refrain from communicating with their comeditators. Simon Holloway, an Australian student who went through a Vipassana retreat in 2010, was unimpressed with Goenka's philosophy but found that despite his misgivings about the dogma, "the ten days were a useful and rewarding break away from the busyness of existence."[11]

For ten days, in the bushland of Blackheath, I wandered in silence.
For ten days, with neither phone, nor email, nor printed matter of

any description, I sat in the bush and I walked through the trees. I observed a lizard hatching from an egg, an old bee grooming himself and dying, and life positively teeming all around me. As a long-time fan of Sir David Attenborough and his remarkable documentaries, it was a very pleasant surprise to discover just *how much* one can see, up close and personal, if only one takes the time to shut up and sit still.[12]

Ten days of uninterrupted silence may be impractical for those who are still living and working in the mundane world with all its obligations. But you may be able to perform a silence fast from the time you get home to the time you leave for work, and refrain from idle conversation while on the job. You may be able to dedicate a weekend to silent meditation: unplug the computer, let your calls go to voice mail, and spend the time in quiet contemplation. Done regularly, these fasts will help you understand how many extraneous words you use in each day. They will also make you better accustomed to your interior monologues and help you sort out the voices of the Gods and spirits from the background noise of your subconscious.

Sensory Deprivation

> *For the first hour, you'll feel silly. For the second hour, you'll feel silly and uncomfortable. For the third hour, you'll feel silly, uncomfortable, and irritated—"Why am I doing this?" During this time, all your internal issues will come up, and you'll have to deal with them, because you'll have nowhere to run from them. If you can get through that part, then during the following period you can start to get somewhere serious.*
>
> **—Lydia Helasdottir, Pagan in Germany**

A more extreme form of silence, practiced for short periods of time, is sensory deprivation. Actually, any kind of silence is a form of sensory deprivation, but it is possible to spend time with even less sensory input. Ancient mystics isolated themselves from other people and crawled into dark spaces to "incubate" (the original meaning of the term *incubus* referred to the spirit that came to you during your period of silence and darkness). The ears can be temporarily stopped in order to hear the heartbeat. The eyes can be blindfolded, or the room plunged into darkness. The body can be mummified, swathed in heavy cloth, to keep out the sensation of air currents on the skin. Some would-be mystics have even explored being suspended in a harness while wrapped, blinded, and deafened, so that they had no sense of where anything was in space around them.

Such a journey should not be undertaken without a support crew. Journeyers will want people to keep checking on them, making sure that they are breathing and not in distress. As Lydia Helasdottir points out, the process has to go on long enough to break through the hold of the monkey mind over the psyche.

In ancient northern Europe, this practice was called "going under the cloak"; mystics would actually wrap themselves in a large woolen cloak with a waterskin and nothing else for hours or even days at a time. The last documented public practice of going under the cloak was performed by Thorgeirr the Lawgiver in medieval Iceland, whose story we will tell later in this book. A more moderate form of sensory deprivation can be seen in the northern shamanic practice of *utiseta,* in which journeyers sit in some wild place wrapped in a hooded cloak, and bring the hood down over their face to block out stimuli and limit breathing. (We suggest combining this practice with the fourfold breath mentioned previously.)

Fire

> *Wondrous to relate, I saw the land of the Slavs, and while I was among them, I noticed their wooden bath-houses. They warm them to extreme heat, then undress, and after anointing themselves with tallow, take young reeds and lash their bodies. They actually lash themselves so violently that they barely escape alive. Then they drench themselves with*

cold water, and thus are revived. They think nothing of doing this every day and actually inflict such voluntary torture upon themselves. They make of the act not a mere washing but a veritable torment.

**—Brother Andreas, in the
Russian Primary Chronicle, 1113 CE**[13]

Earlier in this chapter we discussed the practice of the sauna as purifying and detoxing the body, but it can also be used to put one into a transcendent state. The Finnish sauna, *banya* in Russia and *stofa* in ancient Germany, was used so often as part of ancient spiritual rituals that it became associated with "wizardry" during medieval times, and its use was discouraged (much to the detriment of medieval hygiene). Herodotus wrote about the people of the Black Sea region making a felt-covered hut and throwing water onto red-hot stones inside, creating a vapor hotter than any Hellenic bath. (He also relates that hemp-seed was thrown onto the stones for purposes of visions and prophecy.) According to his accounts, this Slavic sweat lodge was used for ritual cleansing before marriage and after burying the dead. The concept of building an actual permanent structure, however, was unknown in the southern Slavic areas until the people of Novgorod moved south, as mentioned in *The Lay of Igor's Campaign*. Novgorod, a northern Slavic city, had been settled by the Norse-descended Rus tribes, and was the mercantile capital of trade between them and their Viking cousins. With archaeological evidence showing that the early Russian banya was basically identical to the Finnish sauna and the Norse equivalent, it is likely that it is an ancient import from the Rus settlers.

Some scholars speculate that the sauna, or banya, became the secret temple of pagan rites in some northern areas, as much for its effect as for its privacy. Some Native American traditions use the sweat lodge in the same way, as do the modern Pagans who copy them; these sweat rituals are usually run for a group, as this is one of the few techniques that can bring a group of people together into another state of consciousness. In Raven's shamanic tradition, each sauna ritual is about connecting with the powers of fire, water, and stone; the building itself is called the House of the Ancestors, and the steam that rises is said to be the ancestors' breath. This makes the sauna especially effective for calling on ancestors, or for seeking the ancient spirits that the ancestors called upon. In Finland, the folk saying is that "in the sauna one should behave as if one is in church." Sweating of any variety can also be used as a transcendent altered-state method, and it is also part of the Ascetic's Path, although it can cross over into the Ordeal Path, depending on how hot and lengthy the steaming may be. The key is that, like other processes on the Ordeal Path, one must stay beyond the point of physical discomfort in order to reap the benefits of the transcendent state.

Nearly all healthy individuals can safely use a sauna for at least half an hour, although ritual sweats often go on for some hours, sometimes while spirits and ancestors are called in turn. On the other hand, sweats are contraindicated for people with unstable heart conditions and for individuals who have consumed more than a tiny amount of alcohol. Children and those with uncontrolled hypertension should probably avoid very hot saunas. In addition, plenty of drinking water should be present in the sauna, as those who don't stay hydrated can pass out.

Ordeal

> *You can talk about connection to the Divine, about opening and stimulating the energy gates of the body, about purification, offering, and devotion—but in the end it all comes down to the War against Comfort. All growth is painful; comfort is stagnation. Our scars trace an alphabet of freedom and self-determination. The price of entry is nonnegotiable. There's no pretending to suspend, no cheats or liars here. But remember that Power is only Power when it is used for a Purpose. Without Purpose, Power is sterile. . . . As for me, I've been using the Ordeal Path for more than twenty years to enter a variety of altered states. Offering makes space*

*for the Divine. Purity can be achieved, and it's harder to fool
yourself when you're hanging by hooks. The results have been
bliss, simplification, removal of fear, lessening the hold of
horrors, recapitulating the past. Learning how to guide others
all the way to the Hells and bring them safely back out is key
to that progress also. A person older and wiser than I once
wrote, "I myself am the offering on the altar of sacrifice."*

—Lydia Helasdottir, Pagan in Germany

The Ordeal Path is one of the more advanced—meaning dangerous—
spokes of the Eightfold Path, perhaps second only to the Path of Sacred
Plants. It is achieved by the use of the body's own chemistry when carefully controlled, noninjurious pain is applied, or when the body is in a
state of extreme endurance. Examples of the Ordeal Path range from
runner's high, to the Lakota Sun Dance, in which ritualists hang on
hooks, to the Hindu kavadi ceremony, in which devotees carry shrines
held to their bodies by spears in their flesh. In Indonesia, sanctified
practitioners get spikes put through the skin of their cheeks, and in
India devotees dance with balls and fruit sewn to their flesh. The
Ordeal Path may well be even older than the use of entheogenic plants
as a means to achieve altered states, as it requires nothing more than
one's body and knowledge of how to make it achieve the right chemical
cocktail without endangering life.

The biggest danger of this path is, ironically, not the physical damage that can be done if the techniques are not performed safely by an
experienced individual, although that is serious enough on its own. It is
that the Ordeal Path first triggers the subconscious psychological baggage of the individual going through the ordeal, and those monsters
must be faced and purified first before the mind and spirit can pass
into connection with the Universe. This is why it generally takes more
than one single cathartic ordeal to get through. In this way, the Ordeal
Path is similar to the Path of the Flesh, which uses sexual ecstasy as a
way to achieve an altered state. Because they both go through the body,
and because the body stores past emotion in its energy, beginning these

paths means that all of one's personal issues come up first, demanding to be dealt with. The price that the Universe demands for opening these particular doors is to let go of some wound that you have been holding on to—even if that is excruciating. Over time, however, this can be an immensely cleansing spiritual practice, as well as a quite effective doorway to other realms for those who are "wired" for it.

Plant and Chemical Allies

Thirty minutes after my taking the mushrooms, the exterior world began to undergo a strange transformation. Everything assumed a Mexican character. As I was perfectly well aware that my knowledge of the Mexican origin of the mushroom would lead me to imagine only Mexican scenery, I tried deliberately to look on my environment as I knew it normally. But all voluntary efforts to look at things in their customary forms and colors proved ineffective. Whether my eyes were closed or open, I saw only Mexican motifs and colors. When the doctor supervising the experiment bent over me to check my blood pressure, he was transformed into an Aztec priest and I would not have been astonished if he had drawn an obsidian knife. In spite of the seriousness of the situation, it amused me to see how the Germanic face of my colleague had acquired a purely Indian expression. At the peak of the intoxication, about 1 1/2 hours after ingestion of the mushrooms, the rush of interior pictures, mostly abstract motifs rapidly changing in shape and color, reached such an alarming degree that I feared that I would be torn into this whirlpool of form and color and would dissolve. After about six hours the dream came to an end. Subjectively, I had no idea how long this condition had lasted. I felt my return to everyday reality to be a happy return from a strange, fantastic but quite real world to an old and familiar home.

—Albert Hofmann[14]

In 1967, Harvard psychologist Timothy Leary encouraged a generation to take LSD and "turn on, tune in, drop out." Twenty-five years later, their children explored PLUR (peace, love, unity, and respect) with the help of MDMA (ecstasy). Today, psychonauts can choose from a wide range of legal and quasilegal tryptamines, phenethylamines, and cathinones—or go to the black market for prohibited substances. Those of a more spiritual bent can find recipes for ayahuasca and other mind-altering potions online, then purchase the ingredients on any of a number of websites dedicated to "ethnobotany," "plant shamanism," or other fancy words for "legal hallucinogens."

Plant and chemical allies (most of which are derived from plants—LSD is produced from ergot fungus, while MDMA manufacture begins with sassafras oil) are powerful tools for blasting open the doors of perception. Given a sufficient dose, even the most head-blind can have what feel like out-of-body experiences and spiritual encounters. Taken with appropriate preparations in a proper set and setting, the "trip" can be as life-changing as any other mystical experience. Lacking those, it may be little more than a diversion that entertains or terrifies but that has little impact after sobriety returns. Even worse, it may have an ongoing negative effect. Hallucinogen persisting perception disorder (HPPD) is a recognized long-term visual disorder during which the *tracers*, color trails and geometric distortions common to a hallucinogenic experience, persist long after the experience is over. And while there is evidence that dissociatives like ketamine and PCP can help schizophrenics in a clinical setting, there is equally strong evidence that they can trigger or exacerbate psychotic episodes in predisposed individuals when taken recreationally.[15]

Those who use plant and chemical allies—even currently legal ones—risk becoming casualties of the "War on Drugs." On February 4, 2010, Bouncing Bear Botanicals, a Lawrence, Kansas, wholesaler of "legal highs" and entheogens, was raided. None of the items seized—San Pedro cactus, Colorado River toads, morning glory, Hawaiian wood rose seeds, and the like—were illegal. But Bouncing Bear's owner, Jon Clark Sloan, was charged with twenty counts, including unlawful cultivation and distribution of controlled substances like mescaline, bufotenine, dimethyltryptamine, and lysergic acid amide.[16] On August 8, 2011, a British court found Peter Aziz, a self-proclaimed "fully trained Shaman of 35 years training," guilty of producing and supplying Class A drugs in connection with several ayahuasca rituals.[17]

When choosing an ally for a plant journey, it's wise to consider that some are less benevolent than others. Those who approach datura or belladonna casually will live to regret it: the anticholinergic chemicals in these plants can produce a delirium in which the user cannot distinguish between hallucination and reality, along with serious spikes in body temperature, a racing heartbeat, and bizarre, violent behavior. Many who approach these plants wind up hospitalized or jailed, and some do not survive the experience. Those who experiment with *Amanita muscaria* (the famous "Little Red Man") may find him considerably more demanding than the more benign *Psilocybe* mushrooms, as one unfortunate aspiring shaman discovered:

> *I think I now know what people mean when they describe the void because that's all there was. It was like my whole previous life, with everyone, and everything, in it had been one long dream, and that I had woken up in the void where nothing existed, had ever existed, or would exist in the future. Nothing is more terrifying or crazy like a mind that has not only been cut off from everything else, but also realizes that they never existed, and were only a dream. Time stretched off so far into the future that it no longer existed; past, present, and futures were one. I pleaded to no one for death at this point, but being alone and immortal there was no escape. I longed for the dream to begin again. (Maybe that's why God, or the Tao or whatever, first created life and the wheel of time that governs it . . . , so as to escape its lonely prison.)*
>
> *This seemed by far the longest portion of the experience although I have no way of knowing how long it actually was. The length of the earlier part of the experience isn't even*

comparable. I woke up at this point (or maybe my lonely, immortal self started dreaming again) Saturday morning in a hospital bed hooked up to an IV with my wife on my left side and my mother on my right. When I asked my wife what had happened this was her story.

Apparently she had asked if I was okay and if she could go to bed, and I said, "Okay." She then asked if she could turn the light off and I said "Okay" again. She awoke 10–15 minutes later to a gurgling sound coming from the other room. She found me convulsing on the floor. I had pissed myself at least once, and my eyes were wide open, but rolled back in my head. She tried to wake me, but I was nonresponsive to her repeated attempts. Desperate, she called the hospital and had them send an ambulance, who in turn called the fucking cops like most stupid hospitals do in the event of an OD. (How can this be justified when this only results in more deaths from OD when people avoid medical attention for fear of the police?) The ambulance came and the cops shortly thereafter.

—liftyourskinnyfists[18]

Modern spiritual thrillseekers who inadvertently damage themselves with the use of entheogens are usually trying to blast their psychic centers open. They have heard that the sacred plants—or, in some cases, their chemical extracts and analogs—will force open the doors of the mind and enable psychic powers. Traditional spirit workers, however, will tell you that such openings occur only with the aid of the plant spirit, and only if that spirit has already made its will known beforehand, and all the proper offerings are made. Usually an experienced practitioner who already has these alliances will discern whether the plant spirits will extend their aid to the novice and make the proper ceremonial introductions. What happens when this path is tried alone, with no existing spirit alliance, is usually one of two possible outcomes. Either the would-be shaman has a wild drug trip to little effect or the door to the seeker's mind is actually blown open so violently that the psychic "wires" are damaged. The door slams shut just as quickly, and the equivalent of scar tissue forms around the wound. After this, it will be many years, if ever, before that door heals enough to open again.

Additionally, while plant allies can be useful for increasing signal *sensitivity,* they often cause problems with signal *clarity.* Users may become caught up in exploring their fantasies, or they may "tunnel" into their own psyches and find themselves facing down their deepest fears. While these experiences may prove useful in and of themselves, it may be impossible for the Divine to reach through that self-absorption and provide any kind of useful message that doesn't get lost or hopelessly muddled. This can be countered to some extent by preparations like fasting, prayer, and study. Alas, only rarely do amateur shamanic practitioners take these important steps; most are just looking for a mystical shortcut. As a result, we can only recommend that this path be avoided by any but those who are willing to put in the required work and accept its inevitable risks.

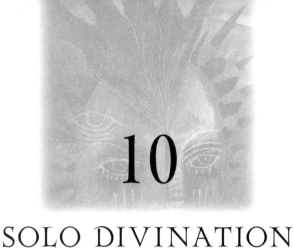

10

SOLO DIVINATION

The Process of Discernment, Part 2

The authors of this book admit to a certain bias for using divination as a method to verify one's personal gnosis, because we are both skilled diviners. In our defense, however, we are also both recipients of the kind of life-overwhelming gnosis that makes skeptical people back up and say, "Whoa! What do you mean, you're supposed to change your life in that way?" We got into divination more out of self-defense than anything else.

There are two ways to handle divination: be your own diviner, or find someone else to do it for you. (It's also quite possible to choose both, which we'll get to in a moment.) If you're already quite good at a divination method—tarot, runes, I Ching, or something else—by all means go ahead and do a reading on any spirit messages you receive. This isn't the time to try out new divination methods, though. Explore new methods with general life questions that aren't too important or questions about other people. For questions about UPG, you should use divination methods that you have already mastered. However, divining for yourself, especially on questions of major importance, requires more than skill. You also need objectivity. And while it's relatively easy to rise above emotional entanglements when you are reading for a stranger or casual acquaintance, it is considerably more difficult to do so when you are directly involved in the question.

The general key to doing your own divination is that the more emotion you have involved with the subject—such as very, very strongly wanting it to go one way or another—the less able you are to do a clean reading for yourself. If it involves loved ones, and especially if it involves your romantic partner, it is automatically in the far corner of "unable to be objective." We all like to believe that we can be objective about these things, but we usually aren't, and high-emotion areas are usually read more effectively by someone neutral, or—even better—someone who knows nothing about you and the people involved. (The one sort of reading that you can effectively do for a high-emotion subject is the question of "What do I really feel, think, or believe on this subject?" as a way of clarifying your own position.)

This is not to say that divination on these sorts of questions cannot be useful. A divination may point to aspects of the issue you have missed; it may also suggest ways of dealing with the problem that you have not considered. Even those who are skeptical about any underlying theological or magical explanation for divination sometimes find it an effective tool for shaking them out of their prejudices and preconceptions. The very process of interpreting a tarot spread or an I Ching layout forces us to see how the layout might apply to our question. In fitting our circumstances to the cards or yarrow stalks, we can find ourselves exploring the question in new ways and discovering new solutions to problems that seemed insurmountable. But even with those in mind, it is probably best to call on outside help in questions of personal gnosis.

Questions to ask may include:

Was this real spirit contact, or was it my own mind? As we noted in chapter 5, it can be very difficult to distinguish between a message and an ego projection. This can be especially true if you've put a good bit of time and effort into studying the Deity who is supposedly speaking to you. When you know most of the myths and events associated with your God, it's easy for your subconscious mind to take that material and use it to weave a very convincing image. Ego projections can be even more convincing than actual Deities; after all, they are exactly what you would expect your God to be like. A divination can help you determine whether you've achieved God contact. (And if you haven't, this isn't necessarily a sign that you won't or that your devotion has been in vain. If you're spending that much time thinking of your Gods, you are likely to be a good and devout servant to them whether or not you are called to walk on the Mystic Path.)

Who was it from? (Or: Was it from who I think it was?) If you're dealing with a lying spirit, you need to know that, and you need to take appropriate measures to send it away. If it will lie to you and pretend it is a God, it will almost certainly abuse your trust in other ways. If your spirit contact gets offended or defensive when you take these steps, that is an enormous signal that something is wrong. If it is telling the truth, it should have nothing to fear from procedures to verify its identity and its message.

Did I get the message right? If not, what parts are wrong, and what should that part of the message be instead? Deities can explain things to you, but they can't understand them for you. It's entirely possible that you have misinterpreted some or all of their message. Getting further confirmation and clarification is an important step in putting this gnosis into practical use. It can save you a great deal of embarrassment down the road, not to mention a whole lot of apologizing to your offended Deity.

What action am I supposed to take, now that I've heard this? Just because you've had a message from the Gods doesn't mean it's time to become a hermit, start a new religion, or take other spectacular steps. It could well be that the message was just a friendly introduction, and they want you to finish school and take care of various other mundane issues before going further on your path. On the other hand, they could be telling you they have waited long enough, and you need to get started on your spiritual work immediately. This is something that a divination can help sort out, as well as providing a tentative roadmap for your future involvement.

Is this just for me, or am I supposed to share it with someone else? If so, now or later? As we noted in chapter 2, there are various levels of gnosis. Just because Deities have spoken to you doesn't mean you have been tapped to be their representative to the world at large. It could well be they are asking you for a personal devotion and sharing it is not only not required but discouraged or even forbidden.

For really big questions (and asking whether you've been contacted by a spirit is a Really Big Question), there's nothing better than combining methods. In our book *Drawing Down the Spirits,* we suggest the following:

> When faced with really huge questions, such as "Should I leave my marriage and family and move to Faraway Place X to study Strange Art Y for much of the near future? Is this meant to be my path?" we suggest a Four-Fold Signal Clarity divination method that is used by many professional spirit workers, whose responsibilities are such that they cannot afford to be wrong too often in their divinations. This method utilizes both omens and traditional divination methods, and it goes like this:
>
> - First, do a divination yourself.
> - Second, have a friend who knows you and the situation do a divination.
> - Then have yet another divination done by an outsider who does not know you, your situation, or anyone involved.
> - Finally, directly after the third divination, tell the Gods that you are going outside into a busy and populated area, and that you want a clear and obvious omen immediately, within the next hour. Go out and look for one.

If all four steps give you basically the same message, then you've got something worth moving to Kamchatka over. However, if you start getting widely disparate messages, stop right there. Don't go on to the next step, or repeat things. It may mean that the future is heavily conflicted and things could go many ways. It could also mean that the Powers

That Be want you to figure it out for yourself, or that now is not the right time. Give it a period of days or weeks and then start over from the beginning. And remember also that sometimes signal clarity just doesn't come, because we are complicated beings with complex and ever-changing lives, and that's just the way of it.

The most important thing of all to remember as you go into this process is that it has to be okay for you to be wrong about it. You have to be sanguine about the possibility that divination will tell you something you don't want to hear—like, for instance, that the whole thing was your own unconscious. Even more confusing, it could say that there was some kind of spirit contact, but you got the message entirely wrong due to your own filters. That happens to everyone. Even professional spirit workers have bad days in which they misinterpret what appears in their heads. Both of us have done readings in the past about messages that we thought might be real, only to see (often to our relief) that they were only the product of our own fears and desires. It's all right to hope that it was real, but you have to be at peace with the idea that it might not be. If you go into the process with an open mind and as much objectivity as you can muster, you won't be so tempted to skew a reading in your favor that you miss important information.

But what if you've examined your situation and decided that you aren't objective, and you can't be, no matter how hard you try? At that point, it's fine to skip the do-it-yourself step and find someone who can be objective. That's not a matter of failure; it's a matter of common sense. Again, professional spirit workers consult each other all the time, for situations they know better than to read for themselves or for second opinions when an answer is fuzzy. It's more important to have done everything possible to get the information right than to pretend you're emotionally clear about it and risk real failure.

Many Pagan groups contain people who do readings professionally or who are spiritual practitioners who divine as part of their religious job. We suggest asking around in local Pagan groups to find someone or—even better—asking your friends if they have anyone to recommend, before you wander into Madame Juju's Tea Room without knowing anything about who might be behind the crystal ball. If you do end up going to a reader who is unknown to you, we suggest considering the points in the following section.

JUDGING A DIVINER FOR A PERSONAL READING

First, can you get a referral from someone you trust to have decent judgment? The best option is someone referred by a friend who is willing to talk about how he or she was helped. If you can't find a referral, pick out someone and then ask around to see if anyone has gotten a reading from that individual. Don't ask the reader for testimonials from former clients. It's not hard for any reader to come up with friends willing to swear that that practitioner is the "best psychic ever."

Because you are asking, "Is this message that I'm getting really from God X or Spirit Y, do I have it right, and what should I do about it?" you really should find out whether the diviner in question has experience in asking those questions. Some fortune-tellers are talented enough in their own way, but they haven't ever asked anything more supernatural than "Is my boyfriend cheating on me?" or "Will I go to jail for this?" If you really have a connection beginning with Gods or spirits, and if you really have a reader with a good "spirit phone," it's not unusual for the Deity or spirit in question to appear to the reader and start telling him or her what to say to you. This can be upsetting and disconcerting to a reader who has never had this happen before. If readers have experience with this subject, they are probably better equipped to hear any messages that come through for you—or, conversely, you can better trust their judgment if they say, "I'm sorry, but I can't seem to find any spirit involvement at all, around you or in this reading. I think that you may be misinterpreting something."

Take tradition into account, but don't box yourself in. By this we mean that if you think your message is from God A, then a practitioner who is knowledgeable about God A's pantheon and cosmology would be a good fit. However, it might not be God A after all—or you may not have such a practitioner around. Some readers may not know about that cosmology, but they're good at giving information and can handle any spirit that shows up. Don't give up if you can't find a Canaanite Reconstructionist priestess where you live, but it is good if the reader at the very least has a basic understanding of Neo-Paganism and its Gods.

Ask about fees. Warning flags include readers who give you a price and then ask for more money as soon as you enter, or who ask exorbitant prices, or who require you to buy a lot of ritual supplies from them. (If it is determined that a ritual is the right answer for you, and supplies are needed but you think that you can find the same quality of supplies cheaper, a reputable reader will allow you to do that. If the supplies must be blessed or charged by the practitioner, a reputable practitioner will not charge exorbitant prices to do it.)

However, be wary of relying on free readings from inexperienced people. The old saying about free advice being worth what you paid for it often applies. Your well-meaning friend who just got a set of runes last month is almost certainly unable to deal with the subtleties of interpretation or to treat serious spiritual issues with the gravity they require. Because this is an important reading, you are probably better off getting a professional to do it for you. The exception to this would be if you have an experienced friend or relative who reads regularly for you—but even then we suggest providing some kind of a gift or recompense for their time. When you get an important reading, it is important that there be an exchange of energy of some sort. There's a reason for the old custom of "crossing the reader's palm with silver." When you do so, you not only acknowledge the value of the divination, you also place the reading in a professional context: the diviner is now, by cosmic law and by social ethics, obligated to give you the best and most truthful service possible. A reading done for free can be a parlor game; a reading purchased from a diviner should always be treated as a sacred rite. If the reader doesn't understand that, you need to find another reader.

Be suspicious if readers or spiritual practitioners require you to join their group, make you swear some sort of loyalty or secrecy oath, or give you intrusive orders into areas of your life outside the scope of the ritual.

Be especially suspicious of threats, such as "If you don't take action X, the spirits will get you!" They should be able to voice their belief that a lack of action X would be a bad idea in their view, but they should also have the objectivity to let you know that you are an adult and can make that mistake if you choose to do so. Be cautious of any readers who try to force you into a course of action.

If the spiritual practitioner is a channeler of spirits, or uses spirit possession as his or her method of divination, try extra hard to find people who have seen that person work with his or her spirit guide. If you're not sure how to judge such things, we recommend our book *Drawing Down the Spirits* as a guide on how to judge possessory situations. Feel free to be skeptical about someone who approaches you out of nowhere and says, "God X told me that he has a message for you." While this has been known to happen, it is rare, and most instances thereof stem from the other person's psychological issues. Keep in mind that the Gods are not stupid, and they know perfectly well which sources you are more or less likely to consider true. In our experience, personal divine messages generally come unwittingly from people you already know well, not from wild-eyed strangers or self-important acquaintances. (In fact, when reputable spiritual practitioners get a message for someone they barely know and who is not actually a client, their first questions should be, "Is this any of my business? Should I even tell that person at all?" If the answer isn't a definite "Yes!" they should file it for future information and say nothing more. It may be that a better opportunity to pass it on may come in the future, or perhaps it should be passed on to another practitioner.)

Good Pagan spiritual practitioners should be able to explain clearly why they are asking you to do anything or why they are doing anything to you. It is true that many spiritual practitioners straight from traditional cultures, used to their own people and customs, may not be willing to explain much of anything. That's part of many indigenous cultures—the practitioner does things to you, and gives you orders, and you shut up and don't question. Anyone trained and educated in Western culture has no such excuse. Be suspicious if such practitioners refuse to keep you informed about what they are doing, including providing the translations of non-English chants they may want you to perform. They should be willing to explain before a reading or ceremony what is expected to happen and what is expected of you. Inability to do this suggests incompetence, and unwillingness to do it suggests unclean motives. (Kenaz adds: There is some secrecy in many African diaspora traditions. An Iyalocha [priest or priestess of an Orisha] is not going to give you the details of how a cowrie reading works, and a Babalao [priest trained to read using the Table of Ifa, a complex system of divination] is not going to go into lengthy explanations of the various *patakis* [stories] that may be connected with a particular reading. However, there's a difference between professional discretion—keep in mind that many of the details of how to perform these divinations are oathbound secrets—and a refusal to explain how the various taboos and requests they are seeing apply to you. If they say, "Oya says you need to give her X," they should not hesitate to tell you who Oya is, why she wants this, and why you need to do it. It's not unheard of for a cowrie or Ifa reading to reveal the querent needs to be initiated in the future. This does not mean "You need to max out your credit cards, empty your bank accounts, mortgage your house, and have me, the reader, do this ceremony next week.")

If you know how to psychically shield, you should do so before walking into the space of any readers you do not know. You don't know what has shown up in their magical space or what may still be hanging around, if only unclean negative energy from past clients. Experienced readers should be able to pull down information for someone regardless of their personal shielding; they're supposed to be reading your destiny, not your aura or your mind. You might also want to take a witness along, preferably a stable, grounded friend who knows you well and knows how you react. That person can provide a reality check afterward about whether the information sounded like your life or whether you were denying an accurate but painful point. (If you don't know how to shield, Raven recommends the book *Spiritual Protection: A Safety Manual for Energy Workers, Healers, and Psychics,* by Sophie Reicher, which has in-depth directions on many sorts of shielding and warding for Pagans. If you have no aversion to Christian iconography, Kenaz recommends purchasing a simple Saint Michael the Archangel holy card or medal and carrying it with you when going into situations where there may be spiritual danger. Saint Michael is tasked with driving away evil and will do that for anybody who bears his image.)

If you do any divination for yourself, or even if you have a friend who is willing to pull a rune out of a bag or something like that, it's no trouble to ask, "Was I given accurate information at this reading?" If the answer is ambivalent, ask, "What subject should I be suspicious of?" Just as it's fine to get a professional to give you a second opinion about your own readings, it's also fine to do your own reading as a second opinion on a professional. It's also fine to get readings from more than one professional to cross-check, and any professional who objects to the idea of you getting a second or even third opinion is, in our book, less trustworthy.

DIVINATION IN EXTREMIS

We also realize that not everyone has access to several diviners—or to any good diviners. A bad reading can be worse than no reading at all; if you get that bad reading from a phone psychic, it may not only be misleading but extremely expensive! To that end, here are some tips for things that might help if you're isolated from any sort of community or otherwise unable to find someone who can help you sort out the nature of your spirit contact and what steps you need to take next.

Try to learn as much as you can about the God who has purportedly contacted you. This will make it easier for you to spot any omens the Deity may send in your direction. It will also help you to determine whether the message you are given and the general bearing of your spirit contact is in keeping with ancient myths and rituals. You may also look to forums dedicated to that pantheon and get in touch with other worshippers. As with everything else on the Internet, caution is advised. If you look long enough, you will find sincere, knowledgeable, and dedicated followers of your God who are open to the idea of personal gnosis, but you will also find the usual share of kooks and cranks, along with believers who are hostile to the idea that their God would deign to talk to anyone—especially some newcomer who doesn't know as much as they do.

Facade.com offers a number of automated divinations—the I Ching, runes, tarot, and various other systems. Because these readings are computer generated, they are random; because their interpretations consist of rote descriptions of each card, rune, hexagram, and so forth, they are free of any kind of personal bias. Kenaz has found this website useful when trying to answer personal questions on the fly. It is no substitute for a real reading by a flesh and blood diviner, but it can definitely provide a neutral take on the questions at hand and give you food for thought. The key here is to treat the web-reading seriously. Light a candle beforehand or otherwise make your intent known. Repeat each question before you type it in, and ask your Gods and ancestors to send you a clear answer. Save each answer and treat it as if it came from a person rather than a computer. Don't reload the page if you don't like what you see, and don't ignore it because "it's just a webpage." The Universe will give you the information you need by whatever means are available if you ask, but it will expect you to listen.

Ultimately the best thing you can do with a question like this is to pray on it. If your Gods want to communicate with you, they will find a way of getting their message heard, verified, and acted upon. And because they are Gods and work on a divine timeline, they will be willing to wait until an opportune moment arises or until they can put you in touch with a reader who will provide an answer to your questions.

11

SILENCE AND FAITH

Even after trying all the suggestions in this book, not everyone is going to be able to clearly see or hear or sense Gods and spirits. That's another of the hard truths that we need to face before we go any further, because if we don't, some readers are going to end up throwing this book across the room in a fit of rage at the unresponsiveness of the Divine. Not everyone ever manages to communicate with Gods and spirits. However, we do know from experience that some people never get to the point of having any extrasensory experience, and very few get to the point of having regular conversations with Gods and spirits. Even in indigenous societies in which spirit contact is accepted by everyone, most people still do not have regular two-way contact with spirits.

This is made even worse by the fact that modern Neo-Paganism is very much an experiential religion with no doctrinal barrier on who is allowed to have divine connections. Unlike faiths in which the majority of people are expected never to be touched by the Holy Powers but to believe in them anyway, most Neo-Pagan sects enthusiastically tout that anyone can get to the point of having extrasensory experiences, doing effective magic, and connecting with Deities. We can all be mystics and mediums if we only give it a try, this view purports. Is it true, or is it designed to set a lot of people up for failure? Opinions differ, but practical experiences suggest that not everyone can or is meant to have mystical experiences.

The reasons for spiritual radio silence are many. Here are a few, although there may be even more that we don't know about.

1. **You could do it if you tried, but you're not trying hard enough.** Most people didn't grow up with families who encouraged them to be aware of or cultivate their subtler senses, and in fact most grew up in families who openly ridiculed such things. Children who had spirit encounters were told that they were imagining things, and later they learned the association of "imaginary friends" with mental illness. This meant that many people have repressed the subtle senses they have deeply enough that it may take decades to dig them back up again. Most people are also not encouraged to still their minds and listen, and our hurried lives often discourage this as well.

2. **You're afraid of what might happen if the Gods spoke to you.** Divine contact could mean that you're crazy, according to much of society. It could also mean that the Gods are real and could never again be easily ignored or put aside when their existence in your life becomes inconvenient. In addition, people who were raised with the idea that prayer is primarily a form of confessing your faults to God may not want to know what God, the Gods, or the spirits have to say, because they are afraid it will only be a litany of everything that is wrong with them. If you fear the voice of Spirit, even if only subconsciously, you will block it out.

3. **Your psyche (or body, or both) is damaged to the point that your subtle senses have been blocked by the damage.** Many factors could contribute to this, including neurochemical illness, post-traumatic stress disorder (PTSD), chronic physical pain, drug use, alcoholism, or general ill health. As diviners, we have seen plenty of people with wrecked lives who come in asking, "What's my spiritual path?" The answer that we receive from the spirits is "We're not even going to go there right now. You need to focus on the practical aspects of your life, and get off drugs, or take care of your health, or get out of your toxic life

situation, or whatever it is that's wrecking your life and could be changed. Fix that first, no matter how long it takes, and then we'll talk about spiritual paths."

4. **Your natural inborn neurological and energetic "wiring" is not able to sense things in this way.** This is a controversial reason; some spiritual thinkers believe that receiving spirit messages is possible for everyone, while others disagree. The idea that spirit communication is dependent largely on the luck of neurology is a difficult one for many people to swallow, and of course there's no scientific proof either way. It does seem that the more impressive (and difficult to manage) psychic gifts run in families and can be genetically inherited, a fact that is used by proponents of the idea of neurological "spirit wiring" to support their thesis. According to this view, being able to communicate with Spirit is an inborn gift held by only a few, and this is how it has always been. Just as not everyone can have perfect pitch or be an Olympic athlete or an Einstein-level physicist, not everyone can have the gift of the spirit phone. On the other hand, some modern spiritual teachers feel that everyone has the potential for this gift, and inability is not an inborn lack but a problem of lack of practice, as in reason 1. There's also the issue of improving what you have; many religious traditions offer practices of meditation and altered states that are designed to enhance and change the inborn "wiring." How effective these practices can be and how far one can go with neurology that resembles a psychic brick have been a matter of debate for centuries.

5. **It is your life's destiny this time around to concentrate on the physical world, at least for now.** There's no shame in living in the physical world and seeing its myriad beauties as sacred and worthy. People all have different life lessons to learn, and if yours is to appreciate this world rather than concentrate on Otherworlds, there's probably a very good reason for that. After all, someone has to do it! It is by no means a "lesser" destiny, and don't let anyone else tell you otherwise.

6. **It is your life's destiny this time around to make your own decisions, without help or advice or influence from Spirit.**
Again, everyone's life lessons are different. For some, the big lesson is trusting in the will of the Gods. For others, it is learning to trust themselves. This can be a temporary thing—*you need to figure this out yourself; it won't mean as much if you get a message from Beyond*—or it can be a life pattern. Ironically, we've found that while the people who have free rein on their life path complain about how much they crave some kind of direction, many of the spirit-ridden people on the other end of the spectrum whose lives are largely governed by divine will complain about how much they'd like to be able to do whatever they want with no direct spiritual consequences. The grass is always greener on the other side, which is a good indication that everyone involved is getting the experience that he or she needs to evolve and grow, if not the preferred experience.

7. **It is your life's destiny this time around to learn to keep faith in the face of divine silence and to model that faith to others who find themselves facing an unresponsive Universe.** This is perhaps the hardest reason of all, and the one that requires the most compassion from spiritual leaders if individuals are to fulfill their purpose. One of the most significant modern examples of faith in the face of divine silence is the Catholic nun Mother Teresa, who said bluntly that the single hardest part of her vocation was "God's silence." She apparently received some sort of visitation early in life that pushed her into helping the poor and dying in Calcutta, but after that she received nothing more for the rest of her days. Her constant round of self-doubt was evident in her writings and in her words to those who knew her, but so was her constant reorienting once again to her faith. In *First Things*, Carole Zaleski writes of how Mother Teresa converted "her feelings of abandonment by God into an act of abandonment to God."[1] Focusing on the idea of Christ's loneliness and sacrifice on the cross helped her to see her own silent isolation

and sacrifice as embodying Christ's experience in an everyday discipline.

Elizabeth Lev, Mother Teresa's biographer, writes of her:

Mother Teresa lived her doubts, not for an hour on Sunday, but every day as she tended the poor and dying in utter, relentless squalor. Her example reaches across from Christians to non-Christians. Time and time again, saints show us that when they suffer, the solution is to look outside oneself, not further within. . . . Particularly in our era that gives more weight to feelings than facts and to sensation rather than sense, Mother Teresa teaches the world to persevere through doubt, pain and loneliness.[2]

To say that some people may be fated, during this lifetime at least, to follow in Mother Teresa's path will not make us many friends, nor be satisfying to those who are shouting into the void to no avail. Mother Teresa herself clearly did not want that path, even though she made the absolute best of it, and most of us are not nearly as dedicated as she was.

Is it any wonder that many Pagans who are getting only radio silence firmly decide that Gods just aren't talking to human beings anymore? Is it any wonder that they salve their hurt with statements like "If you talk to the Gods, you're praying. If the Gods talk back, you're crazy." (To which a friend of ours once retorted, "No, if the Gods talk back, you're blessed.") It's not hard to see how people with this attitude could be locking on to the idea that there is no legitimate personal gnosis out of personal pain—after all, if the Gods are talking to those other people, why aren't they talking to me? It's less painful to decide that the Gods aren't really talking to anyone than to face divine silence.

The best response to this attitude is not defensiveness but compassion. Of all the reasons we as diviners have uncovered for a lack of communication with the world of Spirit, the one reason that we have never encountered is that the individual is a contemptible human being, unworthy of spiritual attention. That has never happened in our experience, and as far as we can tell, that's not the way the Gods work. Regular two-way communication with Gods and spirits is never, as far as we can tell, based on merit. Plenty of people have this experience who aren't the most evolved characters around, and plenty of very good people do not get it. The medieval mystic Julian of Norwich apologetically wrote that people must not think that her communications with saints made her a better person, that she knew many who were far better Christians than she, and she had no idea why the saints did not speak to them as well.

For the Pagan priest, priestess, or spiritual counselor who is facing individuals with one of the last four reasons, it's important to drive that point home. It's not that they are lesser beings; we cannot say for sure how the Gods choose whom they speak to, but we can say that it is never about being an unworthy person. Just knowing that it is not their fault, and not due to any lack of character or morals, may be a comfort to lonely seekers. Counselors can also emphasize the truth that, in many ways, it is more honorable to hold faith in the face of divine silence than to believe only because the Gods bother you so much that you can't do otherwise. (There's a telling scene in the movie *Constantine* in which the mortal main character—chosen for his psychic talents to be a demon slayer—argues with the angel Gabriel. He contends that he should go to heaven because he is a believer. Gabriel says, "No. You *know*. That's different.") It's not that people who talk to spirits don't have their own mountains of faith to contend with—including trust in the benevolence of the Divine—but the initial mountain of faith in its very existence is in many ways a far greater struggle, and one could consider it more worthy to conquer.

It's also important for people who *do* have spirit communications to internalize that point as well. The Yoga Sutras make disapproving references to supernatural powers gained by various yogis, and they point out that if one thinks that such powers make one a more enlightened person, one is very much missing the point. The attitude that it must be based on some kind of merit or worthiness is responsible not only for a great deal of insecurity on the part of those who aren't getting through, but also for a great deal of egotistical behavior on the part of those who are. Of course, it may only be a matter of time until the Gods decide that it's time for them to be publicly humbled, but as any spiritual counselor will have to say sooner or later . . . the ways of the Gods are mysterious, and we don't always understand their plans for others or why they are so different from their plans for us.

12

NEO-PAGANISM AND ITS ATTITUDES

The Neo-Pagan demographic (we are not referring to it as a "community" because it's actually a lot of small communities that share some faith tenets) responds in varying ways when a member of the group shares personal gnosis and hopes that it will be taken seriously in some way. In order to discuss the ways that this large and diverse crowd does things, we will first go over the current divisions in that demographic.

Two decades ago, if they'd been asked to talk about the different subgroups under the Neo-Pagan umbrella, many would have crinkled their brows and said, "Divisions? You mean like different kinds of Wiccan covens?" Some might have mentioned Asatru if they knew of its existence, or said something about women's spirituality, or the queer magical/gay activist Radical Faeries. However, generally it was Wicca, Wicca, and yet another version of Wicca. Decent histories of the early years of Neo-Paganism can be found in Margot Adler's *Drawing Down the Moon* and Ronald Hutton's *The Triumph of the Moon*.

Today, although Wicca is still the single largest division of Neo-Paganism (when explaining this to outsiders, we might sometimes use the analogy "Wicca is to Neo-Paganism as Catholicism is to Christianity"), other groups have grown and changed around it, forcing a revision of people's assumptions. New traditions (Pagan for "sects") are presenting rites at public gatherings that are far removed from traditional coven structures and symbols. In ancient and medieval times, it might take a religion centuries to do this kind of splitting and reforming; today, in the Information Age, when people can travel across the world in hours and share their ideas in seconds, it has taken Neo-Paganism mere decades to do what it took Christianity, for example, ten centuries to accomplish. We have literally as many sects as that major religion, with a far smaller population assembled in those factions. (In fact, we've been informed by liberal Christian theologians that some of them are closely watching the development of Neo-Paganism; according to them, its progress resembles the development of early Christianity, only hundreds of times faster and without the ability [or, at least so far, propensity] to slaughter conflicting groups. By watching us, they learn something about how their own faith grew, split, and argued its way through theological differences. We, of course, can probably learn something from studying the history of Christianity and its stance on gnosis within groups, if only how not to handle the situation in future.)

Modern Neo-Pagans are still rather bewildered about the number and type of subgroups in their faith demographic; some still use "Wiccan" and "Pagan" interchangeably and are taken aback when they encounter group after group that differentiates itself from that label. There have been fiery and tempestuous intergroup arguments about who ought to be under the "Pagan" umbrella title and who ought not to be, all of which are beyond the scope of this book, but provide a map of the growing pains of this highly eclectic faith.

However, we can still sum up the basic divisions as they stand now and their general attitude toward personal gnosis in groups. This list may be different in a matter of years and require reconceptualizing; that's how fast we are changing. We can divide Neo-Pagan groups into the following categories: British Traditional Wicca, Modern Wicca, Wicca-inspired traditions, Reconstructionist traditions, and Reconstructionist-derived traditions.

THE FIRST CIRCLES:
BRITISH TRADITIONAL WICCA

British Traditional Wicca groups, or BTWs, as they are called, are a much smaller percentage of the demographic (even of the Wiccan demographic) than they once were, but they still boast a good number of folk in the U.K. and America. This is the sect that started it all, coming out in the 1950s in England and stimulating the "Witchcraft Revival" in America. Classic BTW has an initiatory mystery tradition rather than a church-with-congregation structure—adults only, requiring a series of initiations, limited to small-numbered covens, and focusing as much on magical practice as on religious faith. Secrecy is emphasized to a greater or lesser extent, reflecting its nature as a mystery tradition. Their liturgy worships the Lord and Lady, a male and female God and Goddess pair also referred to as the Horned God and the Triple Goddess (due to her ability to appear in any of three forms—Maiden, Mother, or Crone). Occasionally they use the names of Deities drawn from historical records in place of the nameless Lord and Lady (Frey and Freya, Herne and Diana, etc.) but these are held to be aspects of the Lord and Lady. BTW practice could be categorized as "duotheistic," although it is probably more accurately called "pantheistic."

The way personal gnosis is dealt with in British Traditional Wicca is very much at the discretion of individual covens and practitioners. Contrary to what one might expect, experimentation occurs nearly everywhere in BTW, and such has been my experience in the Alexandrian tradition. It's true that permanent, conscious changes to established practices occur only rarely. (This normally leads to new denominational offshoots.) But that doesn't preclude invention. Most groups are quite willing to try something entirely new, whether to serve the religious needs of the coven's members, or just to see if it works. "Success is thy proof." If a coven ends up liking something enough, they might incorporate it into their regular practice; many covens have their own quirks and preferences that they've developed on their own, apart from what is traditionally handed down.

Aside from that, the way an initiate relates to the Gods and spirits is a personal matter. If the God or Goddess has a message for someone in circle (or out), no one, not even the presiding high priest or high priestess, would try to interpret it for her without being asked. There is relatively little anxiety about what one is supposed to make of her revelations or intuitions. Whether on an individual or collective level, we generally trust that the Gods will make their wishes known, one way or another.

Outside of spellwork, what I do at home is not usually anything you would call Alexandrian, so that's a bit of a separate subject. Although, you might say that personal gnosis was the whole reason I joined the Alexandrian tradition. Previously, I had been practicing with another BTW group that wasn't serving my needs at the time. After making the acquaintance of my current high priest and priestess, I had a dream in which the Horned God silently took me by the hand and led me to their house, pointing. It was pretty unambiguous as far as nocturnal visions go. It took me a couple of years to act on the God's advice, but I have no doubt now that it was the right decision. Every good omen I could have sought has appeared, and in any case, I'm pretty happy with the situation so far. Having learned from experiences of this nature, my general attitude is that the only way to verify one's gnosis is to act on it.

—Nicole Hernandez, U.S. Alexandrian initiate

THE GREAT WAVE: MODERN WICCA

From the roots of British Traditional Wicca exploded a huge number of groups that used the basic Wiccan structure, values, and symbolism, but embellished their practices in different ways from the original

Gardnerian version. The Alexandrian tradition may have been the first official offshoot, but it was similar enough that today it is generally relegated to the first category above, and Modern Wicca is made up of groups with more strongly varied catechism. These groups generally keep to the custom of organizing in small covensteads and "hiving off" when they become too large and unwieldy for their spaces and manageability.

This is a domestic religion, in the sense that it is usually practiced in people's homes (or, in many cases, outdoors in secluded areas) rather than in any central building made for the purpose. Due to a good deal of influx during the 1980s from environmentalist, antiwar, feminist, GLBT, sex-positive, and other politically radical individuals seeking a religion that could be made to support their goals and values, Modern Wicca has tended to become more progressive and liberal, and in some cases more radical, than the BTWs from whence it sprang. One of the side effects of this influx is a great reduction in the emphasis on secrecy; Wiccan arts and rituals exploded into major publication during the 1980s. Where once initiates had hand-copied rites and spells into their own Book of Shadows, now Pagan presses were churning out the mysteries for anyone to see—and to start a coven on the strength of a book or two.

Modern Wicca groups, like their forebears, are initiatory mystery traditions. They tend to place a strong emphasis on teaching and practicing magical arts, have an adults-only demographic, require initiations, and work with a male/female Deity duality. Modern Wicca groups tend to be strongly pantheistic, seeing all historical Goddesses and Gods as aspects of that divine duality, and sometimes using their names interchangeably. Some place an emphasis on a particular culture, incorporating that ancient pantheon's Deities and symbols into a Wiccan framework, such as Celtic Wicca, Seax-Wicca (Anglo-Saxon), and Faery Wicca.

The attitude of Modern Wicca groups toward personal gnosis varies depending on tradition and, most commonly, the personal preferences of the high priest or priestess who sets the standards within the individual coven or other group. Some are open to a great deal of gnosis as long as it is not personally offensive to group members and can be molded into the general framework of their practices; others prefer to stick to a set theology and not move from that path. Because these are usually small, intimate groups, it is not unusual for them to judge gnosis from a member by the member's reputation or by group prayer or divination.

> *The witchcraft community I practice with feels that personal gnosis is critical, but must be balanced with tradition. Others in the wider traditional witchcraft community can sometimes be far more wary of personal gnosis than myself and those in my small coven, and because of the overemphasis on personal gnosis in some prominent contemporary Pagan sects, I think that there is something of a minor backlash against personal gnosis in the Reconstructionist and traditionalist communities. I am not attaching value to that claim, only that I see it as true. It's tricky business. I recognize that personal gnosis, taken to its extreme, leads to all kinds of ridiculousness, and that tradition is critical in connecting us to our roots, to our ancestors, and to a form and structure that unites and grounds us. On the other hand, I find any religion that lacks poetic, prophetic, and divine communion/ inspiration to be just as obnoxious.*
>
> **—Ruby Sara, U.S. Neo-Pagan**

WANDERERS THROUGH A MILLION FIELDS: WICCA-INSPIRED AND ECLECTIC TRADITIONS

Today, although Wiccan symbolism permeates the Neo-Pagan community if only in its familiarity, the largest subgroup of Paganism consists of groups that could be called Wicca-inspired, even if they now bear little resemblance to their Wiccan progenitors. These groups still tend to have a pantheistic focus that sees many Gods and Goddesses as facets of two or even one, and they share with Wicca an immanent rather than a transcendent focus, a reverence for the Earth and for diversity, a belief in the body and sexuality as sacred forces, the teaching and practice of magical arts, and an emphasis on personal responsibility in morality. They may also use the symbolism of the four elements and the four directions, cast a "circle" or other related form to create sacred space and delineate ritual time, and utilize many of the other tools of Wiccan practice. Their Gods may reflect Wiccan divine duality, or be any number of ancient Deities in any number of combinations, or in some cases be pantheons entirely created (their worshippers would say "discovered") by modern practitioners.

Where they differ is radical changes in structure. Many folk who came into the Wiccan revival found its mildly hierarchical, initiatory, secrecy-laden, small-domestic-group structure to be unable to meet their needs, and they carried the spirit and the symbolism over to groups formed on different structures. Some added more hierarchy; some took it away entirely and created horizontal consensus groups in which roles were rotated. Groups differ in structure as vastly as consensus-based, spiritually oriented, political-action covens to large churches with congregations. In fact, probably the most drastic change was the transition from small initiatory mystery groups to large, open church/congregation models, with education for children, community service, Pagan chapels, liturgical cycles, tax-exempt church status, donation boxes, and all the other structural trappings of the mainstream faiths that many people had fled to Wicca long ago to avoid.

The aforementioned radical-political influx that affected Modern Wicca to an extent practically forged the outflow of the Wicca-inspired traditions, and one finds among the newer groups a pervasive community atmosphere of tolerance toward progressive politics and alternative lifestyles. So many nonheterosexual and transgressively gendered individuals defected to Neo-Paganism that there is now a higher percentage of them here than in any other religion, and it is not uncommon to have small Pagan religious groups that are entirely queer oriented. A few Pagan churches do weddings not only for GLBT folk but polyamorous ones as well. There are groups dedicated to men's mysteries and women's mysteries, to political work as a sacred task, to the worship of a single ancient Deity, and to Pagan versions of monasticism. Environmental reverence is almost a given in most communities, as is a general ethic of tolerance. The ability to "sacralize the ordinary"—whether that means creating sacred space in a concrete warehouse, seeing the body in all its physicality as sacred, or performing magic in the kitchen with a wooden spoon—has been a guiding force in many Wicca-inspired communities; it is all about sacralizing what one already is rather than trying to become some different ideal.

One of the more surprising theological trends that has arisen in the Wicca-inspired demographic is the significant number of folk who ardently take part in Pagan ritual and community, yet consider themselves to be atheists. For them, ritually calling on Gods is a way of communing with transpersonal archetypes, gaining self-knowledge, and being spiritually moved by sacred theater. Referred to as "archetypists," theirs is a new phenomenon, and one that creates an interesting fault-line among Neo-Pagans who consider themselves to be theistic, whether pantheistic or polytheistic. A greater percentage of religious atheists might be found only in Buddhism. It will be interesting to see how the tolerant but theistic Neo-Pagan majority reacts to the growing number of atheists.

Most of the Pagan groups who refer to themselves by the label of "eclectic Pagan" could be described as Wicca-inspired, just from the sheer amount of influence that Wicca has had on Neo-Paganism. However, a few would fall more accurately under the "Reconstructionist-derived" label, or be a combination of the two. While Wicca-inspired groups also vary widely in their attitude toward personal gnosis according to sect rules and leader preference, it cannot be denied that this general group contains the most gnosis-friendly traditions. Some sects were founded, in fact, on the strength of one person's gnosis; the resulting group may be completely intolerant of other gnoses (if the founder is dedicated to his or her own vision above all), or completely open to nearly all other personal visions based on principle, or anything in between.

I am an eclectic Pagan in a group with other eclectic Pagans dedicated to exploring and celebrating the mysteries of the local land here in Sussex, and I have never felt that my personal gnosis has to toe any "party line." In the course of our rituals and discussions, we have each been encouraged to share any personal revelations that we feel we have received. Whilst any objective intellectual or historical proof is always welcomed, intuitive conviction is also respected, and acted upon if the other members agree that it is relevant to the group rather than just to the individual involved. So I would say that "valid" is taken to mean "applicable and useful to our purpose."

—**Rose Alba, U.K. Pagan**

As an overall practice, the group I currently work with is respectful of UPG. Only in case of extreme hardship ("I understand Odin wants X, but we won't have the equipment to do such a thing!") or in the rarer case of conflicting UPG, we will discuss the merits of the ideas with the qualifier of it being personal gnosis taken as a given. For the most part, we regard all UPG as "intuitively true," but are more likely to give it weight if it is also "applicable and useful."

In the wider Pagan community, where I do a large bulk of my shamanic practice, UPG is a difficult thing to talk about at best. Too many Pagans concentrate solely on what they can learn from books, and when you expose them to something that may be more recent, or incongruent with the lore they have studied or memorized, you challenge the basis of not only their belief, but the way their religion works. The Pagans I've interacted with like their rituals, their interactions with Gods, to be something easily relegated to a proverbial box—if I'm dealing with Papa Ghede, I need cigars and rum in a cemetery. If I'm dealing with Frigga, I need a freshly made loaf of bread and a piece of the family hearthstone.

When you start adding in your personal experience, the first shock is that you're having direct, one-on-one communication with your Gods and guides. To some people, that's just as good as admitting that you're a wacknut who belongs in an institution. (I hear the quote "It's okay if you talk to the walls, as long as they never talk back" thrown around a lot in this situation.) They don't understand the experience of the Immanent Divine, and within the confines of such an egalitarian religion (where everyone who wants to be clergy is, and everyone who wants to learn the dark secrets supposedly may) it has proven to be incredibly difficult to point out that some of us hear the voices of the Gods better than others. It's not something that can be taught in an hour-long class at a Pagan gathering, for starters. Some of it is raw talent, some of it is technique, and some of it is just being open to whatever the experience will be, rather than trying to force it into the outcome you were hoping for. Many Pagans are hostile to UPG because it's something that is outside the understanding of the core tenets of their religion. Don't even get me started if the UPG in question changes how someone might feel about a certain guide or Deity.

—Del, U.S. Pagan

Each member is an individual with individual experiences. We are a group of like-minded people who have had similar experiences and share similar thoughts and beliefs regarding those experiences. How can they judge what is valid and what is not? Each individual's personal gnosis is valid. Differences do not invalidate any one person's gnosis. What does "valid" mean—objectively and provably true, intuitively true, or applicable and useful? Three people look at the same tree. Three perceptions are made. One calls it a tree. One calls it an elm. One calls it friend. Still looking at the same tree, all three feel the wind blow. One sees the leaves of the tree shake.

One hears the rustle of the leaves. One hears the tree say hello. None of the perceptions are any more or less valid than the others. Life is a personal journey. No one else can validate nor invalidate anyone else's spiritual needs or experiences or beliefs or truths.

—C. J. Maxey, U.S. Pagan

The use of the word "gnosis" is very rare in the Reclaiming tradition—I actually can't recall having ever heard it used. Perhaps you will find some parallels if I describe our work and how it looks to me. Each person in Reclaiming creates and pursues an individual path. The parallel with gnosis might be the process of discernment, which of course is ongoing. But I would describe this more as "practice" than as knowledge or gnosis or insight. If something I do seems to have a positive effect, I do it again—it's not really a spiritual insight, but a practical, behavioral process.

Naturally, people talk with one another, and what one person finds useful might be shared or even taught to others. Our teachers are sharing not a "curriculum," but practices that have worked for them. What we share tends to evolve over time. In the end, each person, from the most experienced teacher to the newest participant, decides what works for him or her. We say: "You are your own spiritual authority."

Although we all decide for ourselves, I would say that many Reclaiming people would agree with this statement: The Goddess is within me. Perhaps she is external as well, but the place I first seek her is within myself. For me, this means that any insights would come from within myself—which might contradict the usual definition of "gnosis."

What's "real" is a practical question, and in the end each person answers it for him- or herself. At a personal level, I guess my criterion for "real" is that afterward I feel more powerful, more grounded, more emotionally flexible; I feel that I have grown stronger and more capable of dealing with whatever life throws at me. If I develop a practice that helps me feel more grounded amidst turmoil (for instance, at a protest or at a job interview), I might share this with others. If others find it useful, it might eventually be something we teach as part of a class. Because this is entirely voluntary, it is up to the participants to decide whether the new practice is useful. If enough people start doing something, we'd say it "caught on." But it can also fade away. Our practice is ever-evolving.

—George Franklin, U.S. Reclaiming Pagan

ANCIENT ECHOES: RECONSTRUCTIONISTS

At the same time that the Wiccan Revival was exploding, some individuals and small groups were working on more specific aspects of Pagan religion. Reconstructionists attempt to "reconstruct" the religions of the ancient world and practice them as closely as possible in a modern context. This means that their groups center on a specific time and place in ancient times—Hellenic Greece, republican Rome, Pharaonic Egypt, pre-Roman Gaul, Eire and Britain, and early medieval Iron Age Scandinavia being the most common. (Those particular traditions tend to be referred to as Hellenics, Romans, Kemetics, Celtics, and Heathens, respectively, at least in this area.)

Adapting ancient faiths to modern contexts is challenging, as many practices and social beliefs of our ancestors do not translate well into modern society—sexism, forced slavery, blood vengeance, and human sacrifice being good examples of those. Reconstructionists walk a fine line when they must choose what to keep and what to discard. They also struggle with the issue of practicing beliefs that are the product of a specific society, one to which they do not belong and whose mindset they cannot fully re-create, with specific sets of Deities. As might be expected, a great deal of emphasis is placed on academic scholarship and research as the foundation of Reconstructionist liturgy, ritual, and belief. This often places adherents in the difficult position of taking most of their theological foundation from the written works of academics (and sometimes ancient writers who are the only primary sources) who are not only unbelievers, but find the idea of actually practicing the religion ludicrous, and whose attitudes about this permeate those sources . . . a situation with which no other faiths have to cope.

We often find among Reconstructionists a strong atmosphere of reverence for the past, ancestor worship (of literal or spiritual ancestors), and soft to hard polytheism—the belief that all the ancient Gods are separate entities who can personally interact with their worshippers, but tend to do so only when addressed as separate entities rather than as vague aspects of a pantheistic whole. This polytheism/pantheism split is the major theological difference between Reconstructionist groups (and their derivations) and Wicca-inspired groups, which tend to a more pantheistic theology, with the aforementioned percentage of archetypists.

Reconstructionist groups grew up simultaneously inside the growing Wicca-derived community, founded by people who were interested in historical re-creation and liked the idea of re-creating authentic-feeling Pagan religion as well, and outside, in separate groups not linked to that demographic. During the 1990s, a good deal of crossing back and forth between these internal and external groups occurred. Some left the greater Pagan demographic, and some entered it; others existed on the fringe. To this day, some Reconstructionist groups consider themselves firmly part of the larger umbrella of Neo-Paganism, and reflect that in their social values and political alliances, while others shun the name and are hostile to the association. A few find themselves somewhere in the middle. Even so, because a good percentage of converts to the latter groups come out of Neo-Pagan collectives, the influence still remains.

Because Reconstructionist groups did not come out of initiatory mystery traditions, their beliefs adapted quickly to public temple/congregational-style structures, to tribal/clan-style communities, or to domestic hearth-and-home family worship (not unlike solitary Judaic structures) that include whole families and households. As the externally developing groups missed the influx of politically progressive seekers from the 1980s, some of them have much more conservative values and gain most of their converts from conservative Christianity rather than a mix of faiths. Their small numbers and lack of concentration in much of America (or in Europe in countries where their specific ancient culture is not the ancestral one—for example, Hellenics in Germany or Asatru in Italy) is a difficult handicap to overcome in faiths that evolved within a homogenous community, but members are usually hopeful that the future will resolve this issue.

There are several different types of Reconstructionist sects, grouped loosely by cultural and cosmological specificity. While we cannot explore the varying opinions in every one, we tried to get a sample of opinions from most of them. Hellenismos, or ancient Greek reconstruction, seeks to re-create the religion of the pre-Roman-conquest Hellenic states and countryside. In modern Greece itself, Hellenic Reconstructionism tends to take on a more nationalistic tenor.

The Ekklesía Antínoos is very friendly toward and accepting of personal gnosis, as long as explanations are provided. If something that is suggested seems to stem from desires and motivations that are not being expressed by the people making the suggestions (e.g., a ritual that was suggested in the preschism period, of essentially picking an attractive individual, or paying a prostitute, to play the role of Antínoos, and then having a circle jerk on his feet), then it is questioned. If specifics of research, or of how one got particular ideas, or of spiritual experiences that suggested particular items of information are not given and outlined with each suggestion of new practice, then they are also questioned (and possibly dismissed) as unqualified. The main question of "validity" with all such matters is whether the practice is appealing, meaningful, and productive to engage in, and that question must be answered by individuals, because there is no enforced structure or necessity to conform as part of the group's standard operating procedures. (If a public ritual is performed, then it will run according to the preferences of the person who is organizing and performing it; thus far, that has been myself, without exception.) The cliché "when in Rome" certainly applies to this: follow the directions of the person or organization hosting and sponsoring the event, respect that person, and be a good guest just as they're (hopefully) being a good host.

—P. Sufenas Virius Lupus, Hellenic Pagan

Kemetism, or Kemeticism, is the reconstruction of ancient Egyptian religion, based on the word *kemet,* the name of that land in the original language. There seem to be two main branches of Kemeticism, which evolved entirely separately; one is a sister-faith to other Neo-Pagan Reconstructionist sects that grew out of a mostly European-descended Pagan demographic, and the other is an African American sect that grew up on its own as a way to free African Americans from the religion of the oppressors. The two are still mostly separate, and somewhat wary of each other, although forays are being made into diplomacy between groups. Because both use the term *Kemetic* as their own (although the latter sect is often termed *Afro-Kemetic* by outsiders), there is sometimes confusion between them. The quotes that follow include opinions from both sects.

The general openness to UPG is one thing I really appreciate about the Kemetic community in general. There's emphasis on this being a living faith, not a slavish reenactment of a different time and place. For a religion to be a living faith, it has to have relevance and meaning to its practitioners and the cultural context of the adherents, and it has to have a dynamic element—a living faith is one that can evolve and grow.

Which is not to say that the community accepts all UPG blindly. A faith also has to have stability and structure and a base set of consistent tenets and values in order to have coherency. Generally, if something does not contradict the lore, it's accepted as possible, as a valid experience even if not a universally true experience. It becomes more accepted if many people independently have similar experiences (PCPG). And so it's a pretty common belief that the Netjeru are fond of chocolate even though it wasn't available to ancient Egyptians. It's a common belief that Heru-Wer (Horus the Elder) is fond of rum as an offering. And so on.

Kemetic Orthodoxy, the House of Netjer, has a structure of its own, and is more rigidly defined as a faith than the general Kemetic community. As such, there are more generally accepted tenets of the faith. UPG is generally accepted or tolerated if it does not conflict with lore and generally accepted tenets of the faith.

Mind you, it takes a lot to conflict with lore, as our lore is not set in stone. One key concept in Kemetic Orthodoxy is polyvalent logic, in which multiple things that seem to contradict can be simultaneously true. For instance, there are many different creation stories. They all contain truth and are valid lore and valid myths, and no one really thinks that the Seen world was literally created by spittle and tears and semen—it's mythic truth, mythos, not logos. In addition, Kemetic lore is made up of a conglomerate of stories and local Gods who had different versions in different cities and eventually got syncretized together—so people can have very individual experiences of various Netjeru, which may have great personal truth and reveal something about the more universal nature of those Netjeru, without being an experience of everyone within the community.

There don't appear to be hard, set-in-stone methods across the community (I am assuming this is in regard to the community as a whole, rather than on a personal level) for judging what is real or appropriate. It seems to go thus: If the message contradicts the lore and the established community-wide experiences/tenets, it's viewed with a great deal of doubt if not outright rejected. As far as if the message is appropriate and relevant . . . that seems to depend on who it comes from and if it "sticks," so to speak. Sometimes someone will share an experience or message, and it'll be rapidly forgotten or not even noticed. Other times someone shares something, and people have correlating experiences and talk about it, and it gets absorbed into community lore.

—Meirya, U.S. Kemetic

Kemetic spirituality is the oldest known African religion. In spite of its commitment to sophistication, ceremony, protocols, and high spiritual development, the Kemetic practice depends a great deal upon signs and wonders through Nature as confirmation for messages from the Divine. These messages usually come in multiple forms, so there is little or no room for doubt. Modern-day Kemau, or Kemites, incorporate our ancestral spirituality into our daily lives—we "live the culture," as we say, and also rely heavily upon the use of oracles through cards, shells, pendulums, and the like. Our attentiveness to health consciousness through fasting, holistic diets, and clean living spaces heighten our vibratory rates so that we become one with our environments.

Ultimately, the goal is to become living oracles, so that we no longer rely on tools. (Ua em Ua—"I am One from/of the One.") When people in our spiritual community share words that are considered valid, sound, necessary, uplifting, profound, or prophetic, they are metaphorically weighed on the scales of Ma'at, as far as how they resound within the community's bosom. To be a Kemite is to be governed by Ma'at, the Goddess (Ntr-t), with a balanced intellect, heart, and intuition. She is also justice, order, reciprocity, balance, harmony. As Kemau, we govern ourselves according to the forty-two Laws of Maat, which guide our moral and spiritual compasses, and hone our intuitive natures. As such, a true Kemite will seldom drink the Kool-Aid. The checks and balances are designed to be too high for a mentally unstable, weak-willed, delusional, or morally bereft person to slip through.

Unfortunately, because of today's vast Internet landscape where folks reinvent and misrepresent themselves, it happens with greater frequency than in smaller, personal communities. We still warn each other, however, when someone is out there who thinks he or she is the newest McGuru. And because, overall, Kemetic spirituality calls for personal accountability, Kemites are more likely to question if a "new spiritual message" holds weight and is worth retaining or rejecting. Kemetic traditions highly encourage community, but not lemmings.

—Queen Mother Imakhu, U.S. Kemetic Priestess

Celtic Reconstructionism, which re-creates the religion of the ancient Celtic peoples, has a particularly difficult time with regard to lack of surviving documentation. This is due largely to the destruction of that work by centuries of Christian occupation. The stories that have been passed down are mostly garbled folktales. On the other hand, Celtic Reconstructionism does have a documented tradition from ancient times of judging gnosis, which we will explore in a later chapter.

Within Celtic Reconstructionism, different groups and people in different regions are developing their own methods and ideas, and when one is among them, one should respect their hospitality by following what is directed. If they ask for individual responses and input, one should give it, but not be disruptive to things already occurring or be belligerent and disrespectful when offering critique. At worst, one can always opt out of doing particular things, because to force someone to comply on condition of hospitality (or other such threats) would then be an offense in itself.

—Philip Bernhardt-House,
U.S. Celtic Reconstructionist Pagan

Within the larger Celtic Reconstructionism community, personal gnosis is often entirely disregarded in favor of scholarly sources, whether literary or archaeological. This is not always the case, but in some ways I do believe we err a bit too much on the side of caution. CR tends to prefer things that are historically verifiable, though there is often not much to go on within the source material that is authentically Pagan in origin.

I think it's important to point out that there is a difference between "validity" and "authenticity"—a practice can be valid because it works, but inauthentic in any historical or cultural sense. Chanting "awen" in an OBOD (Order of Bards, Ovates, and Druids) circle is a valid practice in that it works for the group doing it, but it's not culturally authentic for any pre-Christian Druids I'm aware of. It might conversely be culturally authentic, but not particularly valid as a modern practice. Human sacrifices are certainly culturally authentic in some places, complete with archaeological remains of said sacrifices, but they're not exactly a valid modern spiritual practice!

Celtic Reconstructionism is often so preoccupied with debates about "what is Celtic" that it's difficult for newcomers to feel welcome or even competent to engage in a beginning practice. While it is an important question, it's certainly not the only one, nor should it be the sole focus of the movement as a whole. CR traditions generally demand a comparing of personal gnosis against scholarship within Celtic studies and the historical record. Folklore and folk practice are considered important sources as well. Personal gnosis that falls too far from the patterns established in such sources is usually discarded or disregarded. In more extreme cases, any personal gnosis at all tends to be rejected. The struggle to balance cultural authenticity and modern spiritual needs is a large current within CR debate.

As an example of the necessity for personal gnosis, we know for a fact that the Irish and other Celtic cultures had sweat traditions. We know almost nothing about how those traditions operated and nothing at all about the words of any rituals that may have been performed in those sweat houses. Unless we explore ideas that we get through our own personal gnosis and do some actual experimentation with our own bodies, we will not be able to in any way reconstruct sweat practices for modern use. Research, meditation, and experimentation are all necessary if we are going to develop this into something that any practitioner with the necessary physical resources can use. To dismiss personal gnosis regarding this work simply because it can't be proved through historical sources at this point would be to dismiss any possibility of creating a workable tradition. That is, very simply, not a useful answer.

—Erynn Rowan Laurie,
U.S. Celtic Reconstructionist Pagan

Probably the largest sect of Reconstructionists is that of Norse/ Germanic Heathenry. Heathens—of which Asatru is the largest interior group—have the longest history as a group in several countries, including Iceland, where Heathenry was recognized as a legal religion in 1973. While all branches of Reconstructionism have struggled with the issue of personal gnosis and its place in religions based on incomplete historic documentation, Heathenry has been in the forefront of that battle, taking the brunt of the struggles between "lore" and UPG. (In fact, it was this demographic that coined the term *UPG*, with various original meanings including "unusual personal gnosis" and "unverifiable personal gnosis." People finally settled on "unverified personal gnosis.")

Some of the bitter conflict stems from the fact that this is simply the first group of Reconstructionists to become large enough, and to develop a cohesive enough doctrine, to run aground on the need for deeper theological inquiry. In addition, a greater number of converts to U.S.–based Heathenry come originally from conservative Christian as opposed to liberal humanist backgrounds, and bring some of their assumptions about holy scripture with them, and that might drive some of the conflict as well.[1] European-based Heathens in the original countries of this faith tend to be more tolerant and have their doctrine and practices less rigorously based on primary sources. While some of the most violent disagreements have come out of Heathenry—including accounts of death threats by more conservative members toward members with "unacceptable" gnoses[2]—this battle is an important benchmark in the theological growth and maturity of Neo-Paganism in general.

People vary in how they feel about UPG in Asatru/Germanic Heathenry. Most are open to the possibility, but to various degrees and with various degrees of skepticism. UPGs are judged by extant lore when available and relevant, by its fitting in to Heathen practice in some coherent way. Asatru is so nonauthoritarian that one group or individual usually has no way to enforce his or her beliefs beyond at most one small group.

—Jordsvin, U.S. Heathen

Asatru generally is opposed to such things. They traditionally require historical documentation for "validity" at the core levels.

—Scott Mohnkern, U.S. Heathen

The current state of Heathenry is (with few exceptions) extremely ambivalent and even overtly hostile to the idea of personal gnosis having any normative authority within the community at all. Those who readily discuss their personal experiences or, even more so, those who find points of PCPG, are openly mocked and vilified. The tools used to determine validity within large swaths of the Northern Tradition are lore and other related sources (none of which, incidentally, were ever intended to function as religious texts), community consensus, and status quo. Little validation is given to intuition, passion, or personal gnosis, particularly when it challenges the prevailing status quo. It is accepted only when it flows from that status quo and continues to support it . . . and one might question whether such instances actually qualify as "gnosis" at all.

—**Galina Krasskova, U.S. Heathen**

NEW LEAVES FROM ANCIENT ROOTS: RECONSTRUCTIONIST-DERIVED TRADITIONS

Just as Wicca spawned a great number of traditions that built on those roots, so the Reconstructionist traditions have spawned their own offshoots. While these offshoots may borrow the rituals, liturgies, cultural ceremonies, and pantheon of Gods of the "Recons," as they're casually known, they tend to use these researched works as a base and build from there, through intuition, prayer, divine mediation, and sometimes imagination. One of the main differences is that in "Recon-derived" traditions, it is considered acceptable to use divine inspiration as a primary source to fill in the missing holes in lore. Historical documentation is displaced as a primary source and becomes merely the means to an end—providing enough religious context to access the real primary source, which is the Gods themselves. It is also considered more acceptable to openly adapt the ancient religion to modern social values; Recon-derived groups almost themselves part of the Neo-Pagan demographic and tend to share similar ethics and values.

One of the biggest differentiations is the creation of "eclectic" Reconstructionist-derived traditions, where rather than concentrating on re-creating one particular religious era, a group may work with several of them and rotate "cultures" among their rituals. This eclecticism of practice reflects an eclecticism of theology: unlike many Recon groups that practice theological separatism (the idea that one should deal only with the Gods of one's chosen pantheon), Recon-derived groups consider it acceptable to deal with the Gods of many (or any) pantheons. A few even reach across the divide to Wicca-derived groups and consider Wiccan beliefs, Gods, culture, and symbols as a separate "pantheon," as legitimate as Greek, Roman, Celtic, Norse, or Hindu, to also be honored on a rotational basis.

In addition, there are sects who began as non-Reconstructionist Pagan groups who simply chose to focus on, or be inspired by, a specific cultural cosmology—however, they never declared themselves Reconstructionists nor placed those limitations on their doctrines. These cannot be referred to as Reconstructionist-derived per se, as they did not split off from Reconstructionist groups, but because they did derive their culture and customs largely (if not completely) from historic sources from a specific ancient culture, they tend to have the same attitudes about personal gnosis as Reconstructionist-derived groups. One example of such a group is Ár nDraíocht Féin, or ADF, a Druid-based sect and one of the oldest cosmologically specific groups in Neo-Paganism.

> *ADF welcomes UPG so long as it is presented as such, and not otherwise. Presenting it as fact or tradition is severely disdained. Personal gnosis, when and if it becomes accepted and shared by the group (becoming PCPG), can become tradition. We are not wholly Reconstructionist; we are self-consciously Neo-Pagan, so this is entirely possible and indeed likely for us.*
>
> **—Brandon, U.S. ADF Pagan**

In ADF, no one seems to judge another's personal gnosis unless it begins to intrude on the grove or the public. Our grove requires that a seer use a symbol set for public ritual, and that the seer's divinations correspond at least somewhat to the basic meanings for the symbols drawn. This is due to past bad experience with a seer using UPG for public ritual. For public ritual, "validity" means something at least objectively true. For private working, a person's UPG is not questioned, but recognized always as UPG.

—**Julian Greene, ADF Pagan**

I consider myself a Pagan, or Neo-Pagan, if you want to get technical. Personal gnosis in the Neo-Pagan community is generally treated with tolerance, so long as you aren't perceived to be "oppressing" other people with it—that is, you have to be careful to talk about it only as "just my opinion," because a lot of Neo-Pagans are threatened by statements made without such qualifiers. Folks in Reconstructionist traditions are much more severe about their acceptance of UPG, particularly if it's the sort that strikes them as being contradictory to "the lore," or primary sources. But among local Neo-Pagans, as near as I can tell, UPG is judged mostly by whether it fits the liberal, PC viewpoint of most of the demographic, and whether it makes people feel good about themselves. I find this attitude to be less than helpful at times, as it often leads to accusations of "intolerance" if you state an opinion that contradicts the prevailing attitude. But that's speaking in generalities. If I had to guess, I'd say that approaches to UPG vary just as much as individual approaches to Paganism, which is to say, quite a lot. Some people will accept anything that sounds good, and some have more rigorous standards. Some communities are far more reticent about UPG, while eclectic Wiccan types are often the most tolerant of it. It depends on who you talk to.

—**Elizabeth Vongvisith,**
U.S. Northern Tradition Pagan

Germanic Neo-Pagans differentiate themselves from the Germanic Mesopagans (e.g., Asatru) by having increased reliance on UPG. Like many shamanic paths, what is "valid" depends—at least in part—on the individual. Who am I to judge others' inherently subjective experiences? Does it matter if someone else considers my experience as "valid" to them when they are valid to me? If someone starts talking about "Thor the Moon Goddess," I can simply say "I have had no experiences associating Thor with the Moon, much less Thor as a female." I can point out how this is ahistorical, but I cannot say that the person didn't have the experiences that are claimed or that those experiences aren't useful to that person. However, I'm not going to go so far as to invalidate all the experiences of anyone whose practices significantly differ from mine. For example, I've been fairly critical of the core shamanism concept that most entities are benign, but I've also had personal misgivings about conceptions of Deities and spirits that in essence say that we must give in to their every demand as a way to placate them, because that's the way it's supposedly done genuinely. Either way, softer or harder than what I do, I'm looking at things from a more practical viewpoint, and less automatically critical. I will call things as I see them, but so long as people are practicing respectfully and in earnest I will not invalidate their experiences, though I will point out that what they are experiencing is not what I'm experiencing— maybe learning something about myself in the process. That said, in the interest of building a coherent tradition, there is a need for some sort of limits on UPG, but I believe that this is a theological discussion that needs to be had on a case-by-case basis, and that there are few "hard and fast" standards here at the moment.

—Hrafn, U.S. Heathen

Northern Tradition Paganism typically respects any shared personal gnosis. I've never yet seen anyone saying someone else is wrong. At worst, it's a case of shaking one's head and strongly suspecting that the person is listening more to his or her own desires than to the Gods. When that happens, the gnosis is more likely to be ignored than contested.

Someday we may have enough collected gnosis on lesser-known Deities to be able to decide that this bit is superior to that bit. In the meantime, we have so little of it that there are rarely contradictions, and even when there are, we seek only to resolve them when there is a need to do so. If someone says a Deity's favorite color is blue, and the other orange . . . well, they might well both be favorite colors. Humans are complex, multifaceted, and able to change their minds. I don't think our Gods are any simpler than we are. All written lore had a start as someone's personal gnosis, or someone's artistic license based on gnosis. I must assume the Gods are real, interested in us, and able to communicate with us. Otherwise, there's really no point to honoring them.

We pretty much take personal gnosis at face value. If someone makes the effort to give offerings, pray, commune, or journey to talk to one of the Gods, we generally accept it as a valid experience. If something sounds dubious, it may be that it's just that person's private way of relating to that Deity or that it's what that individual needed to hear. We record the information, and people are free to go talk to that Deity for themselves if they don't think it sounds quite right. Sometimes we can test the information in a devotional rite and see how it goes over with that Deity. Often, it's the only information we have, until someone else gets more information. The lore can't help us decide whether Skadhi likes her meat rare or well done, for instance. We can guess, but asking her is probably the best way to go.

—**Linda Demissy, Canadian Pagan**

I am largely a Northern Tradition Pagan, but I also have loyalties to other Gods and traditions. There isn't much room in Reconstructionism for dual-tradition or multitradition people, because Reconstructionism by its nature demands that one believe only in one worldview— the view of one single ancient people. To attempt to see the world through the eyes of multiple cultural cosmologies is considered antithetical, or impossible, or "tainting," and disrespectful to each cosmology. The problem, of course, is that when Deities from multiple cultures approach you, you can't just tell all but one group to go away. In my experience, the Deities themselves don't seem to mind, but of course this brings us back to the issues of personal gnosis that you're asking about.

I became a Northern Tradition Pagan with ties to both an NTP (Northern Tradition Pagan) kindred (group) and an eclectic Pagan group because I didn't feel that I could do any kind of Reconstructionism justice, working as I do with Deities from multiple cosmologies (though mostly Norse). The NTP group is open to personal gnosis and has multiple ways of judging its validity and whether it will be accepted, including divination and theological discussion. The eclectic Pagan group tends to judge entirely on "Is this something that's going to work for most of the people in this group, or is the majority not going to get anything out of it?" A new gnosis by a member is more likely to be scrapped if it falls flat when discussed in the group, if no one has any enthusiasm for it. If there is enthusiasm among a small number of members, they are encouraged to try it out in a small private ritual and report back.

—Seawalker, U.S. Northern Tradition Pagan

WHEN PERSONAL GNOSIS GOES WRONG
IN GROUPS

It seems that when we bring up the issue of personal gnosis going wrong in groups, the first situations that people think of are usually non-Pagan cults that ended terribly, such as Jonestown and the like. While such cults certainly do exist and do suck in gullible members, Neo-Paganism in general (as far as we know) has been remarkably free of both controlling cults and gullible, unquestioning people. In fact, Pagans often pride themselves on being skeptical and allergic to heavy-handed groups that attempt to prevent them from leaving or to tell them how to live their personal lives. The modern Pagan ethic of "if you don't like it, start your own" may contribute to the lack of numbers in most traditions, but it is definitely a deterrent for dictatorial groups. We haven't had any Jonestowns, and the authors feel it is unlikely that this will be a problem in the future. Nearly all the destructive behavior that comes out of the personal gnoses of Pagans affects only the individuals themselves, as we've discussed in the first half of this book.

Unfortunately, in mainstream Western culture, having direct experiences with Spirit is more often conflated with Son of Sam than with Julian of Norwich. A liberal Christian friend of Raven related that his branch of Christianity has basically decided that God no longer speaks directly to human beings. This decision was made out of self-defense; the largest part of their modern experience of people who claimed to have messages from God in Christianity tended to be hate-speech types who bombed clinics because "God told them to." For Raven's friend, the idea of a religious community in which divine communication in any reasonable way might be an expected event made him incredulous. After his first questions about how to prevent people from abusing the potential authority that being perceived as divinely inspired might bestow, he tentatively asked, "So . . . who do you think those other Christians are talking to? Is it God, or something else?" Mainstream religion, it seems, stopped asking these discerning questions some time ago . . . because it was just too confusing and dangerous.

Of course, this is a lot easier if the majority of people live under the assumption that there is really only one God, and only a handful of religions under that God, and the beliefs of those religions are not only the air that the followers breathe but the air breathed by everyone else around them. When you bring multiple religious and Deity choices into the picture, people start asking, "Why are we assuming that the Holy Powers don't speak to people anymore, just because the lunatics make the loudest and most disastrous splash?"

However, this doesn't mean that trouble doesn't arise from personal gnosis gone wrong. At the very least, a group ritual based on someone's personal gnosis can fall flat; it may turn out to have little meaning for those who didn't get the original message. (Of course, so can a ritual based on other sources.) In rare cases, a message bearer with a great deal of charisma can persuade others to make unwise decisions for themselves and for the group. The most common problem, however, is when an individual in a Pagan group wants his or her personal message validated by having it incorporated into the group's practice and beliefs, and that request causes discord and argument.

Sometimes, from the perspective of the group, the problem is someone clumsily insisting on making a change in group ritual that bothers some members. Often this happens without adequate discussion or explanation, and the inspired individual is too caught up in his or her own ideas to thoughtfully weigh how to make the inspiration palatable to the rest of the group. (For suggestions on how to do this, check out the Responsibilities of Message Bearers section in chapter 14.) The unpolished inspiration can seem childish, ridiculous, self-serving, or awkward in the context of the group's current practice, especially if it puts the inspired individual in a starring role.

A newbie in a kindred I was once in and who had a reputation of being more than a bit melodramatic told us after a blot (ritual) that Tyr told her to carry a big spear around to ward the blots from now on. She was plainly informed that while she had every right to her own spiritual work and any UPGs that came from it, they would not necessarily be taken at face value. She was somewhat upset that she didn't get to carry the spear but eventually dealt with it.

—Jordsvin, U.S. Heathen

The reason our grove instituted its rules about having a symbol set for divination is that we had one seer who would do this goofy thing in public ritual. At the time of the omen, he would close his eyes and put his hands on his head as if he were "receiving a message." His divinatory "pronouncements" usually smacked of his own personal interjections about whatever his current irritation was with the grove.

—Julian Greene, ADF Pagan

Other times the problem is that the group sees the message as offensive to its theology or, in some cases, to specific people's lived experience. The latter is really a bigger problem than the former; theology may bend or change or figure out a way to absorb new information, but a message that directly contradicts the real experiences of people (and here we're not talking about their own gnoses, but their practices) needs a second and third look. There may be information that isn't being seen or understood. Perhaps the message is true only in certain limited contexts whose boundaries have not been clearly perceived and expressed, or there are exceptions to the message, or it is being muddied with cultural assumptions (ancient or modern). In any case, it should be studied further to see if distortions or limitations can be cleared up.

An example I could point to comes from the community of contemporary neoshamanism, which draws most of its inspiration from Native American practices. Many authors in the field make generalized statements with the formula "Native peoples believe X." These statements are quite often the personal gnosis of the authors. I have seen people in the neoshamanic community eat those statements up uncritically, not bothering to subject them to reason or compare them impartially with a broad spectrum of different Native peoples. They come away with severely distorted views that do not represent any one of the numerous and diverse peoples that might be subsumed under the expansive label "Native peoples." Fortunately, I haven't seen such misunderstanding result in outright conflict, but it is not hard to see that it's headed in that direction.

Likewise, I've seen a shamanic teacher use her personal gnosis in a logical syllogism to draw a bizarre conclusion. When asked whether the shamans of Native peoples traditionally work with chakras, she replied, "Well, shamans know their bodies well, and chakras are real, so yes, they must work with chakras." Wow. I stood in awe of this person's complete lack of respect for accurately representing the traditions of Native peoples. She was willing to combine a shoddy, sweeping generalization (shamans know their bodies well), with her personal gnosis that chakras are real, to derive a conclusion that she then passed off as truth to her class. (As an aside, note that the conclusion is logically valid, yet its truth content is well open to question, since it was derived from questionable premises.)

—Brandon, U.S. ADF Pagan

There is, however, one other point that we are forced to mention, even if it is an uncomfortable one. While it can be hubris to assume that the Gods will smite a group on your behalf, it is not unheard of for the Gods to interfere in a rite in which the main players (or the majority of the congregation) were participating with less than clean attitudes and motivations. U.S. Heathen Galina Krasskova remarks, "I also have to be the bad guy and point out that what the Gods think is going horribly wrong and what we, in our limited humanity, think is going horribly wrong can be two distinctly different things." Sometimes what seems like a short-term period of discord can later become a necessary phase of questioning assumptions that heralds greater understanding. The Gods live longer and see further than we do, and just as they are not static, they understand that we cannot be static if we are going to evolve spiritually as people. Sometimes they are not above creating some discord if they know that the long-term result will come out well, and it's not unreasonable for a conflicted group to ask that question directly of an oracle or diviner.

> *One of the most disastrous rituals I ever participated in was a sacrifice to a Deity who was known for using chaos to teach people lessons. Doing it was the vision of at least two people who had a close relationship with that Deity, and they assured us all that the rite was desired by its central spirit. However, the entire rite was fraught with issues from the start. It was the main rite at a small yearly public event, and at the start two participants demanded both that their own personal gnosis be respected during the event (by allowing them to hold an unscheduled, disruptive, and inconvenient ritual in the middle of the event), and that the main ritual be changed, as they found it offensive. The priestess running the event gave in to their pressure and granted them the ritual time, but refused to change the main rite. They chose to watch anyway from a distance, making unpleasant comments, and the priestess felt too harried to tell them to go away.*
>
> *Everything went wrong with the ritual. Chaos reigned, but specifically the "targets" were people who had come in with a careless "I've done this before, I don't have to be mindful" attitude (and promptly dropped and fumbled important things) and ones who overstated their skills in order to get difficult and high-status parts in the rite (and promptly made abysmal errors that required more experienced people to step in and save things). All this, and it all got to happen in front of judgmental people who were likely to report negatively on the whole mess on their online journals the next day.*

The Gods knew what they were doing, all right. At a post-ritual discussion, all but one of the fumblers admitted their initial mistake and noted the lesson learned. The priestess learned a hard lesson about being the one to guard boundaries, and instituted rules banning gawkers and unscheduled impromptu rites. Divination confirmed this, and also confirmed that the Deity in question had definitely wanted the ritual done, for good or ill—the "good or ill" part had all been on us. If we hadn't done a ritual in which we called the Deity directly into the space through the spiritual anchors of two devotees, it all would have gone much smoother . . . and we wouldn't have learned anything. We could have gone right on being sloppy and unmindful and self-congratulatory. Thank you, O Gods, for the wonderful and terrible gift of your attention.

—Seawalker, U.S. Northern Tradition Pagan

13

HISTORICAL PRECEDENTS

Gnosis in Ancient Times

Today the monotheistic faiths draw a hard and fast line between the prophetic ages and the world of today. Judaism distinguishes between great
historical teachers such as Maimonides and Menachem Schneerson and
divinely inspired prophets such as Elijah and Joshua. Islam declares that
Muhammad is the Seal of the Prophets and that there will be no further direct communications from Allah after the Qur'an. Christianity
holds the New Testament in similar regard. While a few denominations
(notably the Church of Jesus Christ of Latter-day Saints) have put forth
other scriptures, they have been loudly condemned for their presump-
tion by the majority of Christians. As a result, many who come to polytheism from monotheism look back to a Golden Age from whence all
wisdom springs. They assume that their role in this time and place is to
apply the old myths and wisdom to contemporary problems.

If we are going to re-create the traditional worship of the Old Gods,
we may first wish to consider how those traditions formed. What we
see today as a mythic past was to our ancestors a very real here and now,
with many of the same worries and concerns afflicting those incarnated
in this era. The ancient myths were once new tales being shared for the

first time. While it is important to show proper reverence and respect to those legends and rituals, it is more important still to consider their source. Instead of relying solely on past discussions with the Gods, we might want to use myths and traditions as stepping-stones to our own conversations.

Many denominations today have professional clerics who act as spiritual leaders, teachers, and arbitrators of their doctrine. Few have offices dedicated to speaking directly to the Divine. This is a comparatively modern development; since before the dawn of history there have been those who carried messages between our world and the world of the Gods. Exploring the varying roles they played in different societies may help us to establish their role within our own. And we may want to start our exploration by rethinking the way we view the interaction between humanity and the Gods.

Today, most social scientists assume religion is shaped by culture: as societies grow and evolve, they change their Gods to better fit into and serve their new paradigm. But what if we came at the problem from a different angle? What if our cultures regularly attract the attention of new Gods who provide us with the tools and ideas necessary to enter the next stage of development? Instead of taking as a given that we mold our Gods based on our needs, suppose they mold us based on theirs? It seems like a radical, even an insane, idea. But only during the last two centuries has there even been any real doubt that the Gods intervened directly in our history. If we accept that our ancestors were as intelligent as we are—and there is no evidence that brain capacity has improved markedly since the dawn of *Homo sapiens*—it behooves us to approach their beliefs with an open mind.

HUNTER-GATHERERS

In the beginning we lived as hunters and gatherers. By relying on edible plants and edible animals, small pockets of humanity could survive in suitable environments. (Note that suitable does not necessarily mean idyllic; Inuit hunter-gatherers have survived for millennia in the harsh regions above the Arctic Circle.) While we may consider them "primitive," hunter-gatherers often show extraordinary skill in crafting tools, tracking game, and distinguishing between edible and inedible plants. They are also remarkably efficient at what they do; it is estimated that most hunter-gatherers spent between twenty and forty hours a week engaged in the search for food. The rest of the time they devoted to leisure activities like singing, dancing, conversing, and journeying to neighboring communities to visit friends and relatives.[1]

Unfortunately, few if any pure hunter-gatherer cultures are in existence today. Most are at least tangentially involved in the market economy, relying on trade or donations for supplies or medicines. Any efforts to understand or re-create the hunter-gatherer spiritual worldview will involve speculation (and, if we're lucky, avoid romanticizing and wishful thinking). Perhaps the best we can do is examine historical records and explore the beliefs of contemporary hunter-gatherer cultures to reconstruct their religious ideas.

Among the hunting societies of the Siberian forest, it is believed that animals and fish, like humans, have sentient spirits. To ensure a good hunt, the shaman is tasked with obtaining good luck from those spirits so that the hunters and fishers may keep the tribe fed. The hunt is seen as part of a great exchange. As humans eat the blood and flesh of animals so too do animal spirits eat humans, thereby bringing sickness and death. The shaman acts with the fish-giving and game-giving spirits as a negotiator, ensuring the greatest possible success in the field at the least possible cost to the tribe members. A shaman who cannot ensure a fruitful hunting season will be replaced by another next season; shamanic authority is based solely on shamanic success.[2]

For a long time it was thought a given that hunter-gatherers lived in small, simple, and self-contained societies. But twelve-thousand-year-old megaliths at Göbekli Tepe in southeastern Turkey give the lie to that assumption. Nine-foot-high (2.8 meter) stone pillars are arranged throughout the site in circles ranging from 25 to 100 feet (8 to 30 meters) in diameter. Many are carved with elaborate reliefs of lions, foxes, bulls, cranes, ducks, and other wildlife; bones of gazelles, vultures, and other animals scattered about the site suggest animal sacrifices were made there. Klaus Schmidt of the German Archaeological Institute estimates at least five hundred people were required to hew the 10 to 50 ton slabs of limestone from local quarries, haul them some 1,300 feet (400 meters) and then erect them.[3]

Between 64,000 and 75,000 years ago, the ancestors of today's Aborigines arrived in Australia. Today there are five hundred distinct Aboriginal peoples and two hundred Aboriginal languages. The specifics of their religious beliefs vary, but there is a universal recognition among these peoples of a "Dreaming" or "Dreamtime" when the ancestral powers shaped the world and embodied their power in humanity, in the land, and in the flora and fauna. The Dreaming exists both in the past and the present; the wisdom of the ancestors is passed down to their descendents and embodied in various totems and taboos.[4]

This small sampling suggests the innumerable variations that exist among various hunter-gatherer cultures—or, more precisely, among the different spirits of place and time that they have encountered. But there are commonalities as well: they have mythologies concerning the prey animals that feed their tribes and the landscape in which they travel. The binary divides between sacred and profane and between human and nonhuman are not sharply defined. While within the social unit some people typically have a more close and personal relationship with the spirits, their authority is limited, and most people within the group recognize and work with the spirit realm on a regular basis. U.S. Pagan Aleksa gives an example from a mixed hunter-gatherer/agricultural society of how changes made by one individual can resonate beyond that person's original circle.

> *I take my inspiration for handling things well from Native practice, which is part of my own lineage. A classic example is the Jingle Dance, which was first performed in the early 1800s. The Jingle Dance is done by girls in a dress covered with little silver cones that jingle together like bells as they dance. The dance came to an Ojibwa elder who was very*

ill. He was close to death and dreaming when four women, representing the four cardinal directions, came to him in a vision. He was instructed in the steps of the dance, and that its purpose was to ask for healing, and he was told to teach the dance to his granddaughters.

He was also told how to make the dress, and that making the Medicine Dress would make him whole and bring healing to those who made them. When he awoke, he told his granddaughters, and they helped him make the dress. When the dress was complete and the dance performed, the elder was healed. Certain beats of the drum, known as "honor beats," initiate the raising of a hand (the old way) or a feather prayer fan (the new way) to ask for and give thanks for the healing. This ceremony spread to other members of his band and the Ojibwa nation.

The dance was welcomed not only among the Ojibwa, but also among the Lakota and Dakota people, and since its origin it has also spread to tribes in Taos, Hopi, Navajo, Micmac, and even Wampanoag lands. Today the Jingle Dance is a staple among Native people and very popular at powwow.

AGRICULTURE AND DOMESTICATION

As hunter-gatherer societies master the arts of agriculture and domestication, their ability to support a larger population increases. Instead of wandering about in search of food, the tribe can settle down on a fertile patch of land and set up permanent settlements. While once it was feasible to possess only what you could carry, now acquisition of heavier and larger goods becomes possible. Instead of tents and lean-tos, permanent dwellings are constructed in wood, brick, and stone. While once we negotiated with the spirits of the land and the plants and animals that sustained us, we can now bring forth a living from the soil through our own efforts. But for all the benefits it brings us, agriculture exacts a great toll on our lives and on our way of living. It changes irrevocably the ways in which we deal with ourselves, with our human and nonhuman compatriots, and with our Gods. As philosopher and author John Zerzan says:

> "To level off, to standardize the human landscape, to efface its irregularities and banish its surprises," these words of E. M. Cioran apply perfectly to the logic of agriculture, the end of life as mainly sensuous activity, the embodiment and generator of separated life. Artificiality and work have steadily increased since its inception and are known as culture: in domesticating animals and plants man necessarily domesticated himself....
>
> Food production, it is eternally and gratefully acknowledged, "permitted the cultural potentiality of the human species to develop." But what is this tendency toward the symbolic, toward the elaboration and imposition of arbitrary forms? It is a growing capacity for objectification, by which what is living becomes reified, thing-like. Symbols are more than the basic units of culture; they are screening devices to distance us from our experiences. They classify and reduce, "to do away with," in Leakey and Lewin's remarkable phrase, "the otherwise almost intolerable burden of relating one experience to another."
>
> Thus culture is governed by the imperative of reforming and subordinating nature. The artificial environment which is agriculture accomplished this pivotal mediation, with the symbolism of objects manipulated in the construction of relations of dominance. For it is not only external nature that is subjugated: the face-to-face quality of pre-agricultural life in itself severely limited domination, while culture extends and legitimizes it.[5]

Agriculture is a far more labor-intensive lifestyle than hunting and gathering. Egyptian farmers could thank Asar (Osiris) for teaching them the cultivation of grain and his wife, Aset (Isis), for the annual Nile floods that deposited fertile soil on their fields. The rich dirt required relatively little in the way of plowing and hoeing to prepare it for crops. Yet even for them the labor was backbreaking. In his instructions to his son (a literary work also known as "The Satire of the Trades"), Middle Kingdom scribe Dua-Kethy described the Egyptian farmer's lot:

> The vintner carries his shoulder-yoke. Each of his shoulders is burdened with age. A swelling is on his neck, and it festers. He spends the morning in watering leeks and the evening with corianders, after he has spent the midday in the palm grove. So it happens that he sinks down (at last) and dies through his deliveries, more than one of any other profession.[6]

For hunter-gatherers bad weather means going farther afield in search of food and possibly losing a few of their weakest members should hunting and foraging prove exceptionally poor. For those tied to their soil, the harvest may be the difference between life and death. Between 1315 and 1317, Europe experienced the Great Famine, three years of cold, wet weather and failed harvests; this was followed soon thereafter by a series of livestock epidemics that only added to the general population's misery. As much as 10 percent of the population died during these lean years, while the starving survivors were forced to resort to extreme measures. According to monk and eyewitness John Trocklowe of Saint Albans Abbey, "men and women furtively ate their children and even strangers in many places."[7]

Agriculture and sedentary lifestyles allow us to acquire more possessions. But they also enable class inequalities that are not supportable in a hunter-gatherer culture. One person who controls a small plot of land is a subsistence farmer; one person who controls large plots of land is a noble. Sedentary societies offer new opportunities for advancement. It becomes possible to set up forges and engage in more intricate and demanding crafts, while merchants, scribes, innkeepers, and other new professions spring up to meet the demands of an expanding culture. But the most onerous and backbreaking work is reserved for a growing peasant class—or for slaves. And much as hunter-gatherers made little distinction between human and nonhuman, the rulers in an agricultural community see little difference between laborers and beasts of burden.

While the shamans negotiated with their spirits, the priests of city-states worshipped their patron Deities. The reverence granted to the Gods was like the respect granted to kings and queens, only writ large. As political power became vested in fewer hands, so too did religious power. Instead of the shaman who engaged with the local land spirits, we got the priests and priestesses who made sure that the ruling party retained divine favor, and thereby kept control of the kingdom. Officially sanctioned oracles and prophets provided their input to the kingdom and those wealthy enough to afford their fees; mystery cults offered both wisdom and social status for a price.

But this does not mean that contact with the Gods was reserved for the wealthy and powerful. In Greece, people living near streams and forests honored the nymphs living there. The *vaettir* (land spirits) received offerings throughout northern Europe, while certain areas were avoided as the homes of the *Alfar, Duergar, Jotnar,* or other nonhumans. Within the city-states the various social strata worshipped the Gods in ways befitting their station. We tend today to think of a Greek religion, a Celtic faith, a Norse pantheon, but the practices within these areas, and the spirits honored, were as varied as the roles played by different people within their complex societies. Our tendency to homogenize them and see them as part of a monolithic whole comes largely from the influence of later cultures.

The spirituality of agricultural societies seemed to be conservative, but still somewhat open to the gnosis of small groups, most of whom would branch off into mystery cults of specific Deities. Most of these mystery cults were regarded with tolerance, and eventually many became well known and integrated into state religions. Some, like the mysteries at Eleusis, became downright famous. When a mystery cult was suppressed, the reasons—even the stated reasons—had little to do with religious intolerance and everything to do with politics. The Dionysian maenad cult, for instance, was persecuted mainly because of the roving drunken orgies (and occasional murder) of its practitioners, which disrupted the flow of ordinary life.[8] The famous execution of the Athenian philosopher Socrates on a charge of "impiety" was largely trumped up to get rid of a popular political gadfly; aside from defacing temple property or disrupting public ritual, the "impiety" charge was kept around as a convenient all-purpose pretext for dispatching politically inconvenient people.[9]

Egyptian pharaoh Akhenaton provides an example of radical personal gnosis affecting an entire country. He overthrew centuries of polytheistic worship, tried to eradicate its priests and temples, and forced the country to worship only the Sun, of whom he was the sole priest and living embodiment. He even forbade and refuted history in order to bolster his absolute claims.[10] However, after his death the worship of the Old Gods returned, and his works were destroyed in vengeance. Even this was more of a political statement than a religious one; while the new concept of centrally organized or state religions was useful as a political weapon, if a cult behaved itself and did not challenge political views in its earlier days, it seemed to be understood that time would decide on whether it would be integrated or die off on its own from unpopularity. The existence of mystery cults was not seen as any kind of a religious threat, only a political one in rare cases.

PASTORALISM AND HERDING

Camels helped Arabian nomads cross the harsh deserts of the Middle East and northern Africa, and their rich trade caravans spread silk, spices, language, and religion throughout much of the world. Horses changed the face of agriculture, transport, and especially warfare, and mounted cavalry played an important role in campaigns from the earliest days of history to the advent of the Petroleum Age. Yaks provided transport over rugged Himalayan passes, and even today herders throughout the cold, inaccessible Tibetan plateau rely on their meat and milk for sustenance, their wool and skins for warmth, and their dung for fuel. Many lands that offer only marginal farming opportunities can be home to large herds of grazing animals, and to those who domesticate them.

Pastoral social groups tend to be smaller than those found in an agricultural state. The patriarchal family unit is the monad upon which the extended family is built. These come together in clans, tribes, and other larger groupings that may squabble among themselves but that will generally unite when faced with an outside threat. Women typically have less power in a pastoral society than in an agricultural one; they may be treated like the flocks, as objects of prestige to be acquired and protected from outsiders rather than as independent beings with free agency.

Settling into permanent villages is difficult when life revolves around following the herd animals to various grazing grounds. Part or all of the population lives a nomadic or seminomadic existence, traveling with the flocks and watching over them as the seasons change. They must protect their livestock from predators. They must also defend them against raiders from other clans. Feuds over grazing areas and rustling are not uncommon, and despite the idyllic picture painted in pastoral poetry and art, violence is an ever-present threat in the lives of most herders. As a result, pastoral societies tend to be particularly warlike and expansionist.

Many pastoralists have used their skill at arms not only to protect their herds but also to garner tribute from their neighbors. While their land may not be suitable for extensive farming, they can always acquire tools, vegetables, and other valuable items. These may be taken in raids or obtained in exchange for protection against other herding clans. For centuries, the Xiongnu rode out of the steppes of northern Central Asia to raid Chinese settlements; in 370 a branch of the Xiongnu crossed the Volga River and entered Europe, where they would become legendary as the Huns. Eight hundred years later, a Mongolian herder named Temujin would unite the feuding tribes and make himself known to the world as Genghis Khan. Coming to Kiev in 1246, six years after the Mongols sacked it, Papal envoy and Franciscan friar Giovanni de Plano Carpini wrote:

> They attacked Russia, where they made great havoc, destroying cities and fortresses and slaughtering men; and they laid siege to Kiev,

the capital of Russia; after they had besieged the city for a long time, they took it and put the inhabitants to death. When we were journeying through that land we came across countless skulls and bones of dead men lying about on the ground. Kiev had been a very large and thickly populated town, but now it has been reduced almost to nothing, for there are at the present time scarce two hundred houses there and the inhabitants are kept in complete slavery.[11]

In a pastoral society, the more land you control, the larger the herd you can raise and the greater your wealth. Those who would steal your lambs or take your cattle to their fields must be driven away. Those who would take away your grazing rights must be stopped. Those who are not strong enough to defend their own rights will lose them. Your herds are your property and your responsibility, and you have absolute control over their lives and their deaths. And at least some of the Gods who have inspired pastoral societies have taken a similar view toward their followers.

Many of the patriarchs of Judaism were shepherds, most notably Abraham, Moses, and David. The Jewish G-d demanded that his people worship only him and forbade them to wander into pastures controlled by other Gods. Later Christians identified Jesus as the "Good Shepherd," and bishops in many denominations still carry a shepherd's crook as a sign of their rulership over their flock. And in the Arabian Desert a herdsman named Muhammad received a vision and a message that he was to carry to the world. Many Deities have demanded tribute; these Gods stand out for their stern insistence that they and they alone be worshipped.

The Gods of these religions care greatly for the sheep they have earmarked: while the God of the Jews is content to look over the affairs of his tribe, the others work aggressively to expand their holdings and build up wealth in worshippers. This is not to say they are evil, although many would blithely dismiss them as such. While there has been a great deal of evil done in the names of Christ and Allah, we should not forget that many good deeds have been done as well. But if we are to understand their motivations, we may wish to look to the fields, deserts, and mangers where they first reached out to humanity.

These monotheist religions incorporated many different societies and cultures. Their missionaries spread their message by word and by sword, through compassion and through conquest. The Huns and Mongols, who showed little interest in the religions of their foes and who were more interested in plunder than proselytizing, were able to create large empires but had much less success in keeping them for more than a few generations. The followers of the One God, by contrast, showed a remarkable staying power. The Christianization of Europe and the Islamification of much of Asia and Africa took place over centuries, but once those lands were claimed, they stayed under their pastoral yoke. Churches and mosques stand like watchtowers in their streets to this day. Not until over one thousand years after the conversion of Constantine and Muhammad's meeting with Jiv'reel would they find themselves faced with a real threat—a social change that shook the very underpinnings of their faith.

Once established, monotheistic religions generally dealt with the personal gnosis of their congregants by first attempting to suppress it. If the congregants meekly stood down, it was reasoned that the gnosis couldn't have been that important. If they raised a ruckus and gained a following, the choices were generally either to suppress them more violently or to wait until they were safely dead and then incorporate their vision. Which of these choices happened depended on how politically troublesome they were during their lifetime. Many saints and honored teachers were actively denounced (or at least suspiciously tolerated) while they lived, but once they passed on, the faith could integrate their vision, perhaps reinterpreting it to fit better with existing doctrine. The classic example of this is Joan of Arc, whose unprecedented rise and disastrous political fall was followed, centuries after her death, by canonization. In her rise to influence and kingmaking, Joan herself took advantage of an old myth that a virgin would emerge from an oak wood and save France. She spoke with voices while standing under the trees in a wood formerly sacred to Pagans, a gnosis that set the church's teeth on edge, but once she was safely in the past, she could be embraced as a true carrier of Christian wisdom. She herself was hardly the only mystic burned by the church even during her era—prophets such as Marguerite Porete, Prous Boneta, Guglielma of Milan, and Jeanne-Marie de Maille preached both their divine visions and their political opinions. The first three were burned; de Maille was protected by the Franciscans who valued her and thus escaped; like Joan she was canonized well after her political protestations were forgotten.[12]

THE SCIENTIFIC REVOLUTION

We say, pronounce, sentence, and declare that you, the said Galileo, by reason of the matters adduced in trial, and by you confessed as above, have rendered yourself in the judgment of this Holy Office vehemently suspected of heresy, namely, of having believed and held the doctrine—which is false and contrary to the sacred and divine Scriptures—that the Sun is the center of the world and does not move from east to west and that the Earth moves and is not the center of the world; and that an opinion may be held and defended as probably after it has been declared and defined to be contrary to the Holy Scripture; and that consequently you have incurred all the censures and penalties imposed and promulgated in the sacred canons and other constitutions, general and particular, against such delinquents. From which we are content that you be absolved, provided that, first, with a sincere heart and unfeigned faith, you abjure, curse, and detest before use the aforesaid errors and heresies and every other error and heresy contrary to the Catholic and Apostolic Roman Church in the form to be prescribed by us for you.

And in order that this your grave and pernicious error and transgression may not remain altogether unpunished and that you may be more cautious in the future and an example

*to others that they may abstain from similar delinquencies,
we ordain that the book of the "Dialogues of Galileo Galilei"
be prohibited by public edict.*

—**Papal Condemnation of Galileo Galilei,
June 22, 1633**[13]

While many today consider it one of the Catholic Church's greatest blunders, in retrospect the panel that condemned Galileo was responding to a very real threat. It was not so much his claims that the Sun revolved around the Earth. In 1533, Pope Clement VII listened to and approved a presentation of the heliocentric theories of Polish cleric and astronomer Mikołaj Kopernik (who is more famous today under the Latin form of his name, Copernicus). Rather, it was the idea that the Universe could best be understood not by philosophical or theological speculation but by mathematical formulas and models. As Galileo put it, "with regard to those few [mathematical sciences] which the human intellect does understand, I believe that its knowledge equals the Divine in objective certainty, for here it succeeds in understanding necessity, beyond which there can be no greater sureness."[14]

Galileo was also at least partly the architect of his own misfortune. His old friend Maffeo Barberini (Pope Urban VIII) offered some commentary in 1623 in letters defending Galileo against his detractors. Galileo reproduced the Pope's arguments in his 1632 *Dialogue Concerning the Two Chief Systems of the World*—but put them in the mouth of a thick-headed geocentric proponent unsubtly named "Simplicio." After Galileo lost the support of his most powerful patron, his enemies in the Vatican were finally able to bring him to trial on heresy charges.

However, the church was fighting a losing battle. From 1617 to 1621, Lutheran astronomer and mathematician Johannes Kepler published his three-volume *Epitome of Copernican Astronomy*. While the Vatican placed it on the *Index Librorum Prohibitorum* (List of Forbidden Books), their edicts held no weight in Protestant countries. In 1687, English scholar Isaac Newton published the first edition of his

Philosophiæ Naturalis Principia Mathematica (Mathematical Principles of Natural Philosophy), wherein his theory of gravity explained both the fall of objects on Earth and the orbits of heavenly bodies. The stage was set for a new worldview; instead of relying on scriptural and canonical laws, we would now seek out the universal laws through reason, experimentation, and direct observation.

This is not to say that the giants of the Scientific Revolution were atheists. Copernicus was a devout Catholic, albeit one who fell under suspicion during the Counter-Reformation; his works were placed on the *Index* in 1611 and not removed until 1835. Despite his difficulties in getting along with church authorities, Galileo too was Christian. And though Newton's interests in alchemy, prophecy, and various occult subjects are widely known, he also believed "There is one God the Father everliving, omnipresent, omniscient, almighty, the maker of heaven & earth, & one Mediator between God & Man the Man Christ Jesus."[15] But their vision of the world and of Deity's place in it was one in which the Good Shepherd and the Loving Father were replaced by the Great Architect who created the Universe and the natural laws that govern it.

In prescientific societies, miracles were seen as a real and important sign of divine presence. Within a Deist or scientific worldview, a miracle makes no sense. God created this world according to his divine plan. Why would he violate his own rules? Accounts of the miraculous are written off as charlatanry, delusion, or superstition. Alternately, they are seen as descriptions of natural events, colorful tales that have now been superseded by rational explanations. Adherence to orthodoxy and holy scripture is less important than logic and reason. Galileo believed in the importance of biblical accounts, but felt that they had to be interpreted in light of available evidence rather than the other way around. And Newton's anti-Trinitarianism and his questions about the Divinity of Jesus would have certainly disqualified him from any academic positions in England and might even have sent him to prison.

Newton showed the force that held the planets in their orbits was the same force that sent falling apples to the ground. Scientifically inclined scholars of religion sought the *ur*-faith, the Truth behind all religions. They looked to Egypt and India for evidence of the primal myths underlying every faith. Some did this to show that European Christianity was the apex of human spiritual and moral development; others wanted to prove that all faiths were equally true, or equally false. Holy books and myths were treated not as sacred objects but as evidence to be used in reasoned arguments and academic studies.

Deism allowed the educated and enlightened to hold onto both their faith and their reason. But its distant Creator God who watched over the world with mathematical equations and thermodynamic principles rather than with saints and angels was not especially appealing to the emotions. If he could be seen only in his creation and no longer deigned to intervene, many wondered if he was necessary at all. Religion became not a means of spiritual enlightenment but a social tool by which proper ethical and moral behavior could be encouraged—and, increasingly, as a dangerous superstition that causes far more problems than it cures. And after Darwin's 1859 publication of *On the Origin of Species,* it became increasingly clear that humanity was not "created in the image of God," but was rather a hairless tool-using primate whose closest relatives were not angels but chimpanzees.

There were (and are) religious movements that hoped to bridge the gap between these ways of thinking. In his *Equinox* publications, Aleister Crowley promised "the method of science, the aim of religion." Spiritualism began as an effort to verify the existence of the spirit world and thereby make worship a matter of science rather than mere belief. Many in the New Age movement have used (if not necessarily understood) concepts from quantum physics and string theory. Many others have channeled alien astronauts or messengers from various galactic brotherhoods. Science is not necessarily hostile to religion or spirituality, but it is an implacable enemy of faith. It demands proof for beliefs and privileges thinking over feeling.

However, the Age of Reason culminated not in utopia but in the brutal First and Second World Wars. The industrial technology that gave us mass-produced automobiles in Michigan also gave us assembly-line murder in Nazi concentration camps. Those who hoped for a classless Marxist paradise were disappointed when faced with the reality of Stalinism and Maoism. While increased social mobility meant higher standards of living, it also meant increased feelings of rootlessness and alienation. In a lengthy 1947 poem of the same name, W. H. Auden declared our era "the Age of Anxiety." Philosophers who had long ago renounced faith now found themselves forced to question the limits of rationality and reason.

MODERNISM AND POSTMODERNISM

A style of clothing emerges from a film. A magazine promotes clubs which promote various fashions. The gadget expresses the aberrant: when the mass of commodities slides towards aberration, the aberrant itself becomes a special commodity. In keyrings given with prestigious purchases and later sold and exchanged in their own sphere, we see the mystical abandonment to the transcendent merchandise. The one who collects these keychains, which were made solely to be collected, accumulates the indulgences of the merchandise, a glorious sign of his presence among the faithful: he shows proof of his intimacy with the merchandise. Like those transported into ecstasy or healing by the old religious fetishes, the fetish of the merchandise reaches moments of fervent exaltation.

**—Philosopher and critic Guy Debord,
in *The Society of the Spectacle*[16]**

Religion sought Truth in revelation, scripture, and direct contact with the Divine. Science sought Truth in experience and experimentation. Postmodernism claims both these paths are misguided. There is no universal Truth, no great Meaning of the Universe just waiting to be decoded by mathematician or mystic. Everything is relative and subject to interpretation; those who say otherwise are generally trying to sell you something. It follows science in rejecting argument by authority, then questions scientific authority. It distills human relations down to economic transactions in the best Marxist tradition, but rejects the idea that one can break free of capitalistic and hegemonic oppression. Instead of mathematical proofs or elegant dissertations, it favors satire and irony as ways of pointing to cracks in society's various power structures.

Instead of looking at "primitive" societies with the eye of an anthropologist, a missionary, or a tourist, postmodernist and postcolonialist scholars attempt to peel back the veneer of "othering" and exoticism. They seek to give voice to those who have suffered under a colonial yoke and to understand them on their own terms rather than judging them by Western moral and cultural standards. In theory, this allows for deeper encounters with traditions such as Haitian Vodou or other religions of the disempowered. In practice, these faiths are often reduced to a proletarian reaction to capitalism, or explored by indigenous postcolonialists schooled in Western institutions and the convoluted language of academia, upper-class locals whose actual connection to their traditions may be tenuous at best. Despite these shortcomings, postcolonialism has contributed a great deal to forcing outsiders to explore their privileged position vis-à-vis their gurus and teachers. It may be more important for the questions it raises than the often facile or impenetrable answers it provides.

Postmodern religions like the Church of the SubGenius interrogate the very idea of faith. The SubGenius movement is an elaborate satire poking fun at those who are credulous enough to buy into various apocalyptic and fundamentalist cults. Not even the most devoted members believe in the second coming of "Bob" Dobbs, nor expect flying saucers to come take them off to Dobbstown on X-Day. By sending in membership dues or buying SubGenius merchandise, members signify that they are in on the joke, unlike those who have not yet given their lives over to "Bob." They make themselves a people set apart while simultaneously mocking the idea that a religion can set you apart. Discordians draw inspiration from surrealism and absurdism, their "holy book," *Principia Discordia,* is subtitled *How I Found Goddess and What I Did to Her When I Found Her, Wherein Is Explained Absolutely Everything Worth Knowing about Absolutely Anything.* Their theology is not to be taken seriously—but then, nothing else is either. Discordianism inspires many contemporary Neo-Pagan and occult movements, most notably chaos magick. Following is an exchange from the *Principia Discordia,* illustrating Discordian ideals.

> GREATER POOP [GP]: Are you really serious or what?
>
> MAL-2: Sometimes I take humor seriously. Sometimes I take seriousness humorously. Either way it is irrelevant.
>
> GP: Maybe you are just crazy.
>
> M2: Indeed! But do not reject these teaching as false because I am crazy. The reason that I am crazy is because they are true.
>
> GP: Is Eris true?
>
> M2: Everything is true.
>
> GP: Even false things?
>
> M2: Even false things are true.
>
> GP: How can that be?
>
> M2: I don't know man, I didn't do it.[17]

At their best, these movements bring a refreshing sense of fun and frolic to contemporary religion. They remind participants not to take themselves too seriously and to steer clear of dogma. They allow worshippers to use cut-up, samples, and mixes to create their own unique spirituality. Much as a hip-hop artist might lay a snippet from a soul tune, a segment from a commercial, and a riff from a progressive rock anthem atop a rhythm track to create a new song, many modern Neo-Pagans freely incorporate Gods and ideas from various pantheons and cultures. At worst, frolic can degenerate into frivolity, and the Gods can be reduced to decorative items used to give the proceedings a suitably "spiritual" air. A movement that honors snarky irony and feels authority is inherently bad is likely to have problems with any kind of spirituality based on reverence and worship.

In the end, there are a variety of historical views toward people's personal visions, but ideally we would hope that Neo-Paganism would err on the side of the ancients whose Gods we actively revere . . . without, ideally, their all-too-human use of religion as a political tool with which to beat each other. Plenty of evidence indicates that our ancestors cheerfully adopted the Gods of newcomers alongside their own, making room for them in temples and shrines and even pantheons. Most of these interfaith amalgamations seem to have occurred completely peacefully, with time and general popularity deciding their fate, not theological wars. We can learn from the patience of the ancients, especially in the wake of all their history, and agree that there is room for all—if not in the same circle, then next door in the spiritual marketplace.

RESPONSIBILITIES

Sorting Out the Tangled Mass

Integrating personal gnosis into group beliefs is a complex process, one that could affect a good many people. Each person has a small (or not so small) burden to bear when it comes to making that process as healthy as possible for everyone involved. In this section, we'll touch on the challenges of each party—the seeker, the group itself, the message bearer, the group leader, and the diviner—discuss obligations, and suggest how each can facilitate the process of integrating inspiration.

NEWBIES, SEEKERS, AND CONVERTS

Neo-Paganism is largely a religion of converts. A small number of members were raised in it and decided to stay, but the vast majority were raised in other faiths (or none) and converted at some point in their adult lives. This means that there is a continuous trickle of folks who look into various Neo-Pagan groups to see if they're right for them. Some will stay; some might move on to other Neo-Pagan traditions; others might leave entirely and become Buddhists or Hindus (or even go back to the faith of their upbringing). This is common, and expected.

Spiritual quests take many paths, each of which rings true in some small way, until seekers find the one with the truest ring for them. It's also true that human beings change over time, and the path that was right for us this year may not fit as well a couple of decades later. People aren't static, and neither is their spirituality.

In some mainstream religious denominations, great efforts are made to persuade potential converts to stay and to prevent them from leaving and seeking out a different group. Part of this may be due to a doctrinal dictum that stresses gathering a large quantity of members at all costs or that warns of terrible consequences for any human beings who aren't part of the group and honestly wants to "save" them. Usually, however, it is due to the entirely human emotional reaction of wanting group validation of one's beliefs from as many people as possible. In these groups, schisms are seen as entirely negative and unwanted, and it is considered acceptable to attempt to restrict exposure to other religious ideas. (Most Neo-Pagans, being of a more tolerant bent, would tend to consider these groups "repressive.")

Because many of these denominations strongly value a generational continuation of their structure—meaning the children of the members grow up to stay in the group and pass on their beliefs to their children rather than seek out other truths—it is considered especially effective to restrict the spiritual explorations of children and adolescents. One hears "But what about the children!" often when theologically "threatening" practices are brought up, as in, "The children might hear about this and be led astray! We must prevent them from ever finding out about it, because of course they'll value the shiny new dogma over the familiar, because they're too young to know any better."

In Neo-Paganism, the subject of children's religious rights has been a controversial one. Because we're generally suspicious of groups claiming theirs is the Only Way and the practice that all human beings on Earth should follow, and because we've historically embraced the idea that all people should choose their own path, we've usually (although not always) been liberal about allowing children to learn about a multiplicity of religious choices. Some groups—generally the initiatory mystery traditions, which will not initiate people too young to make their own decisions—have erred on the side of teaching children about many different religions and refusing to privilege their own over any other. Others raise their children in their own tradition, but do not prevent them from exploring other options in adolescence and do not punish them for doing so.

Second-generation Neo-Pagans, however, are still only a small percentage of our number, so we rarely hear objections on the "but what about the children!" topic. Ironically, though, we do hear that same language with the word *newbies* inserted to replace *children.* "But what about the newbies! They'll hear (alternative theology X), and they'll be confused, and they might stray!" And so forth. One assumes that this is largely coming from people who were raised in the above "repressive" sort of groups, and who have not yet abandoned the concept of quantity-at-all-costs, or who take every defection as a personal invalidation of their beliefs.

The difference, of course, is that newbies are not children. They are, one assumes, mentally competent adults. (If they aren't mentally competent adults, there will be some sort of legal caretaker to deal with, and one should proceed as if they are someone else's child. If the state considers them mentally competent and you don't, letting them into your group is probably going to cause more problems than it's worth.) To treat newcomers to your denomination as if they were children, as if they were not capable of weighing opposing views, asking questions of multiple people, and making the decision that is best for them, is a profound insult. To even speak of newcomers, as a group, in this way is a profound insult.

It's a rare Pagan who will admit "Yes, when I first came to Neo-Paganism, I was so stupid and incompetent that I was incapable of reading multiple books, asking questions about anything unclear, and judging opposing viewpoints. I'm so indebted to the group that I joined for raising me to the level of being capable of making decisions when faced with a movie marquee or a restaurant menu. I'm so glad that they've prevented me from sullying my delicate mind with alternative concepts that will no doubt turn me into a confused, quivering wreck were I even to contemplate them." Yet by even suggesting that certain concepts should not be available to newcomers, you are implying that this is the norm among them.

Most newbies—and personally we'd rather use the term *seekers,* as it's less diminishing—have a strong concept of what they don't want, even if they're not sure what they do want. They know, for example, that wherever they came from is not what they want, or they'd still be there. They came looking for something that resounded in them, and they may leave looking for something that resounds more closely. For seekers to look elsewhere is not a failure on the part of the group they are currently involved with. For seekers to leave is also not a failure—in fact, it may be a success, if you count "successful" as "knowing what you are supposed to do, and being willing to risk in order to get it." It may not be easy to see it as a success when you're a member of the "abandoned" or "rejected" group, but good spiritual leaders will be objective about the reality of spiritual seeking and will help their group members understand this as well.

You'll notice that we deliberately used the words *abandoned* and *rejected,* with all their strongly emotional connotations. It's not unusual, and not entirely abnormal, for members of a religious group to take someone moving on just that personally, with the same anger that they would have about a jilted lover. It's also not unusual for them to react to a member looking into alternate paths (especially ones who have values or practices in opposition to those of the current group) the same way that a jealous spouse would react to his or her partner drooling over an attractive person in a club. This is because we're all human, and we all have irrational weaknesses, and love of one's faith can be just as strong in us as love of one's partner and family. We're not perfect, and the emotions carry over.

However, it has long been acknowledged that one's spiritual or religious practices are the best forum for improving oneself and struggling to overcome such irrational and destructive emotions. Good religious leaders are able to gently challenge those emotions, in their members and (ideally publicly where they can lead as an example) in themselves, and prevent them from being acted upon. Indeed, if this does not take place, the result is almost always a toxic rise of fear, anger, and repression within the group. For proof of this, we need only scrutinize the history of thousands of years of mainstream groups making those mistakes on a grand and murderous level. In a sense, they have done us a huge favor by giving us these examples, and they paid for that experience in blood and pain. We, as members of a new religion, should be grateful that they did it for us and that we have the opportunity to learn from their mistakes . . . and learn we should.

This brings us to the issue of schisms. When it's not just a lone seeker but a whole subsection of the group that leaves, fires of insecurity can burn even higher. The usual jilted-lover feelings are often accompanied by a (perhaps justified) fear that the schism will leave the group too structurally unstable to continue. Neo-Paganism has historically upheld a more phlegmatic view of schisms than other faiths because its earliest groups were initiatory mystery covens that deliberately limited their numbers for reasons of spiritual intimacy; when membership numbers became insupportable, people were expected to "hive off" and form their own "sister" groups. The "hiving" policy was often used as a way to head off at the pass potential doctrinal arguments that might split a group—"Well, if you feel that strongly about it, maybe it's time to form your own group." This practice—directly in opposition to mainstream "quantity-at-all-costs" values—was touted as the best way to peacefully propagate (mostly Wiccan) groups.

Today, Neo-Paganism is an umbrella faith with nearly as many denominations as Christianity, and they differ as drastically in their structure and doctrine as Unitarians, Mennonites, and Russian Orthodox Christians. Some retain the old value of "splitting a group willingly and with good will is better than breaking it up angrily after attempting to keep people." On the other hand, some argue that the ease of hiving off means that people leave too soon rather than stay and work out their problems; one Pagan likened it to the high divorce rate in modern Western countries and the attendant unwillingness to stay and work out conflicts, a result of the comparative ease of acquiring a modern divorce. Because the last few decades of Neo-Pagan history have seen the rise of legal Pagan churches and congregations that exceed fifty people, the justification of keeping groups small and intimate seems outdated except in the remaining initiatory mystery traditions. And, of course, people don't convert without bringing in baggage from their prior faiths.

Differentiation is also a point to consider. When there are only a few obviously different traditions, it's easy to tell one from the other. When there are a myriad of small groups with only a few subtle variations (which, while they might seem superficial to an outsider, were theoretically crucial enough to cause a schism), it might take seekers awhile to differentiate them. This is often one of the areas where the cry of "Keep that information from the newbies!" is most frequent, as groups become offended that a newcomer might mistake them for that other group.

This all means that the question of whether to split and form a new group is no longer so simple and will vary in smoothness from tradition to tradition. What does all this have to do with personal gnosis? It's the single biggest reason for schisms in Neo-Pagan groups today. Ten or twenty years ago, when there were fewer variations in Pagan theology, the foremost reason tended to be personal differences among group members. There's still plenty of that today—certainly enough to run a close second—but in the anecdotal evidence we've gathered, personal gnosis (and the divided reactions to it among group members) has surpassed simple infighting over personality clashes as the bedrock group-splitter. (It can cause a good deal of infighting, though.)

For the seeker, there are a few simple truths. First, any group that suggests, even subtly, that you ought not to read or look into other spiritual viewpoints (especially opposing ones, and most especially viewpoints that are based on the personal gnosis of someone outside their group) is in essence telling you that you are not a competent adult capable of making spiritual decisions for yourself. Second, they are also telling you that they do not have faith that their own practices will speak clearly to those who are meant to embrace them. In other words, they don't trust you, and they don't trust their Gods and spirits. Third, while groups are not obligated to never mention other groups or theologies in unflattering ways, a wise seeker will be suspicious of groups in which bitching about specific outsiders, or comparing themselves positively to such people, seems to be the most popular topic of conversation. The old adage about people who continually put down others out of low self-esteem applies to groups as well as individuals.

A seeker contacting a particular group is like a stranger entering someone's home, and as such, all the rules of hospitality apply. In many Pagan religions, hospitality is a sacred obligation on both parts. The host has an obligation not to make the guest uncomfortable, and the guest has an obligation not to be rude to the host. When it comes to religious group activity, we could lay out the mutual obligations like this:

1. The group has an obligation to be clear about its beliefs and values. Ideally these should be written down where a seeker can read them. If joining the group is going to require specific changes in a person's behavior outside the group, this needs to be made clear. For example, if a group believes that associating with, marrying, giving money to, or reading about certain individuals or other groups will bring bad energy to (or make a bad example of) the group, that needs to be laid out up front where a newcomer can find it easily. If new members will be expected to become vegetarians, they have to know that rather immediately. It is indicative of a lack of maturity in the group to have clusters of unwritten rules that "everyone" knows about but no one can be held accountable for. Seekers should be wary of groups uncomfortable with openly "owning" their rules or putting them in writing. (Certain practices may be secret and open only to initiated members, but basic theological beliefs, values, and rules of living can't fairly be in this category.)

2. The group has an obligation to be clear about how personal gnosis is handled in the group. How is it judged? By what people? By

what standards? What's an example of how it was dealt with in a way that the group finds acceptable? While a group does have the right to ban all personal gnosis from entering group practice, be suspicious of groups that don't have a clear process for judging it or have a history of handling it badly (meaning in ways that create backbiting and disharmony).

3. The group has an obligation to be clear about who is in the group and who it speaks for. This requires being honest and up-front about which values and beliefs are shared by other groups, both inside and outside the group's tradition. Right now in Neo-Paganism, almost no traditions recognize a central religious authority that is allowed to define beliefs and practices for all groups within that tradition and to cast them out if they dissent. Therefore, when a group claims that its beliefs and practices are shared comprehensively among all other groups in the tradition, be suspicious. The wise seeker will cross-check that with other groups in that tradition, especially ones that are geographically far away or have no connection with the group in front of them. (Some groups will claim that everyone in their tradition does things their way, largely in the hopes of making it true by announcing that it is so. If there is inter-group conflict over these beliefs, you'll want to know about it.)

4. The group has an obligation to make sure that the person who explains the group values and beliefs to newcomers is actually authorized to do so by all members of the group.

5. The group has an obligation to make it clear how belief during ritual events is handled. For example, if newcomers are not sure that they believe in the group's theology, can they take part in participatory rituals, or should they refrain out of respect? Can they "act as if" without actually believing, or is that sacrilegious? Does belief make a difference at all, or is the only issue polite and appropriate behavior?

6. The group has an obligation to be clear about the customs and behavior expected during events, and to designate someone to

brief newcomers. This is especially important if the group has a fairly closed structure and has created its own specific internal culture or requires a good deal of formal ritual protocol. If a newcomer badly violates a custom, the first person to call is the designated "protocol handler." If the protocol person didn't explain that rule properly, the newcomer is blameless. A reasonably decent newcomer will feel embarrassed about the violation, but he or she also might be sensitive to the lack of warning; calling the newcomer out for the error adds insult to hospitality injury.

7. The group has an obligation to refrain from deciding what is spiritually best for any given newcomer.

The seeker, on the other hand, has the following responsibilities.

1. The seeker has an obligation to remember that every group has the right to set its own rules. If you don't approve of the rules, no one's stopping you from leaving. (See that part about schisms we mentioned earlier.) You may feel that the rules are stupid, destructive, or sacrilegious, but it is a breach of trust to say that while enjoying that group's hospitality. If you really have questions about the group's practices, speak to the leader or to designated spokespeople in private—not in a roomful of people—and keep your tone respectful and not contemptuous or accusatory. Ask in a way that's designed to foster good communication, not defensiveness.

2. The seeker has an obligation to wait on asking the group to incorporate any of his or her personal gnosis until the individual has been in the group long enough to make a commitment and earn a place as a member. It's neither fair nor terribly effective to walk in and start telling people how they ought to do things differently.

3. The seeker has an obligation to bring up personal qualities, practices, deeply held beliefs, or existing spiritual commitments that might conflict with the group's practices and theology. There's no point in waiting until one is invested to find out if the group

is homophobic, or to let them know that you want to belong to another religious group at the same time or that you really believe that the Flying Spaghetti Monster is your true patron. It's best to get a rejection out of the way first thing, to the relief of both parties. This may seem to violate the previous responsibility, but there's a clear difference between saying, "I believe this, even though it's just my own thing" and "I think this is the way that groups in tradition X ought to believe." If the group has trouble seeing that difference and treats a careful statement about personal beliefs as a general reproach, that's good evidence of a lack of objectivity and reason. Similarly, the seeker has a spiritual obligation not to lie about his or her actual beliefs in order to please the new group.

4. The seeker has an obligation to respect the customs and protocols of the group at every event that the seeker chooses to attend. There's no excuse for acting rudely or challenging the group on its customs and procedures. If the seeker cannot follow one particular custom for personal, ethical, or spiritual reasons, he or she should privately seek out the leader or an elder in the group to discuss the concern beforehand, and see whether participation in the event is acceptable without taking part in that custom. An example of this is an abuse survivor who has trouble being touched by strangers facing a ritual that requires embraces as a greeting, or a ritual in which participants are requested to make a promise that conflicts with an existing vow. A mature and responsive group leader will try to make a newcomer comfortable if possible, but if the rule cannot be bent, the newcomer has an obligation to step aside and not attend. If the newcomer's personal practices are such that they cannot attend an event without violating group customs, for the Gods' sakes don't inflict yourself on them.

While a seeker who moves on from a group isn't obligated to explain why, it is a courtesy. If the reason is just "It wasn't for me; no harm done," it might relieve worried members who are afraid that they offended. If there was an actual problem, it can be useful to members if a recently departed newcomer courteously points out ways he or she was made to feel unsafe or unwelcome, so long as it is done with an attitude of "It might not occur to you folks that someone might be made to feel bad about this, so I'm just giving you useful information for the future," and not "You bad, horrible people hurt my feelings" or "You're doing it all wrong!"

If a seeker acts like a competent adult, he or she has the right to expect to be treated like one. If a group expects a newcomer to act like a competent adult, he or she should come through. One hopes that if such codes of conduct were socially encouraged in our demographic, they might end the problem of infantilizing "newbies" and make welcoming a newcomer a less suspicious activity.

RESPONSIBILITIES OF MESSAGE BEARERS

I find people who engage in long, drawn-out battles on their UPG (or even their PCPG) boring and pedantic. It really all boils down to whose "invisible friends" are bigger, louder, more important, and more right than someone else's "invisible friends." What is spiritually significant and relevant for me may have no bearing on your life, and in order to motivate me to do the work my Gods want me to do, they may tell me things meant to rile me up and inspire me; these things do not necessarily apply to everyone else who follows the same Deity or tradition. Call me a special snowflake, but I like to think the majority of what the Gods tell me is meant for me alone, or for the person they instruct me to tell it to and no one else. Even if the Gods really wish you could "correct the record," and set you out on that journey, they understand that it's an incredibly difficult task that you have little chance of succeeding at. Remember that many times, for them, the journey is as important as the destination.

—Del, U.S. Pagan

Sometimes, as we've said, the message from the Holy Powers is for the person who received it and for that person alone. On some occasions that's pretty clear, but other times people want to share the message—perhaps because they want to know if this sort of thing has happened to other people or because it's so life-changing that they just can't keep it inside themselves. Sometimes the message even comes with a dictum: *Share this. Put it out where others can see.* The message bearer might write about it or talk about it in workshops or discussion groups. In this case, the message bearer has the responsibility of acknowledging in the writing or the discussion that this is a personal message, his or her own gnosis. He or she need not apologize for it, and one clear acknowledgment should be enough.

The problem comes in when the message bearer brings personal gnosis to his or her religious group and asks to have it integrated into group practice and values. Sometimes the message may even be something concerning the group practice itself, which always has the potential to be controversial. While we've already established that a group needs to have a clear process by which to judge people's personal gnosis, the message bearer is not devoid of responsibility for the process.

If the Gods and spirits have given you a message and indicated that you must take that message to other people, you have been given a sacred trust, and you must not abuse the trust that they have in you. Certain obligations will be landing on your head, and if you shirk them, you will be dishonoring their gift of knowledge. If you're a spirit worker—if you're the one with the "spirit phone" who gets messages on a regular basis—you have an extra obligation to be scrupulous about these obligations, because you're going to be in this situation a lot, and you'd better learn to get it right.

1. **First, cross-check your information.** Get divination on the matter. We suggest getting readings on the subject from two different people—one who understands your spiritual situation and is sympathetic, and one who is distant and does not know or care about your situation. If they differ, something's wrong.

Discard the reading that is the one closest to what you want to hear, and try another one with a similar person. If you still get different results, replace the other diviner and try again with someone similar. If there's no cohesion after all this, put the matter aside and pray, asking the Gods and spirits to send clarity. Don't try anything with the information for at least three months.

2. **In order to best carry out the trust that the Gods and spirits have placed in you, you have an obligation to pass the message along in the way that will get it heard most effectively.** If you simply throw it out and your target audience doesn't get the message or gets it wrong and becomes angry with you, you've failed in the Gods' mission and dishonored the message that they trusted you with. Getting something heard most effectively may require using language that is familiar to and respectful of the target group, or speaking from a persona that is nonthreatening to them and emphasizes what you have in common. It may mean giving out part of the message and creating a foundation that might eventually support the rest of it. It might mean intimately studying the attitudes and biases of your target audience or seeking help from sympathetic members for ways to craft the "packaging" of the message. While the Gods don't want you to compromise the meaning, effectively carrying out their trust may mean coming as close to that line as is humanly possible in your attempts to make it hearable to its target audience.

3. **Ask not only whether you got the message clearly, but whether you are the best person to pass it along.** We all like to think that we're special, but it may be that you're meant to pass it to someone to whom your target audience will be more likely to listen. That may require some swallowing of pride, but the Gods are less concerned with your pride and more concerned with getting things done properly.

4. **Be clear on who is in your target audience.** If it's "people in general" or "random unknown people out there who are in the

same situation as me," your obligation is correspondingly less. You should indicate in your spoken or written message that the material is intended for that audience, and that it is your own personal gnosis, and that's all you need to do. If your target audience is a specific demographic, it's on you to make the message as effectively heard as possible, which might mean get expert help from sympathetic people in that demographic who can aid you in your slant. When you are a divine messenger, you need to remember that the medium is as important as the message, because if the audience rejects the medium, the message dies and you've failed. You also need to remember that you and your public behavior are part of the medium.

If your target audience is a specific group with a leader, then the best thing that you can do is go to the leader and ask how to get the message across to the group in a nonthreatening way. Remember that to be the spiritual leader of a group is also a sacred trust; leaders are gatekeepers who protect their people, and that's their appropriate job. Be wary of personal gnosis that casts you as the implacable enemy of the leader (or the whole group) with no compromise but that individual's surrender, or the one who is charged with "teaching them a lesson," or the victimized and misunderstood voice in the wilderness. Those are extremely likely to come out of your own baggage. If you are fairly sure that the leader is going to reject your message, it may help to talk to members who know the leader well and can give advice on how to present it convincingly. But be careful how you go about this. Unless you intend to supplant and banish the leader (which is a dangerous game), don't begin shilling your idea without first talking to the person in charge. It's unlikely that you'll get the leader's cooperation after that, and things will probably go downhill at that point.

5. **Make sure that you know who *is not* in your target audience.** If you're writing for people in one denomination, the disapproval of people in other denominations can be ignored, so

long as you are being courteous about other groups and their differences from your own. You're not trying to please everyone; you're trying to get a message through effectively to a specific bunch of people. Achieving that, whatever it takes, is your job . . . and in this instance, if you don't decide whose biases to take into account and whose to ignore, you aren't doing your job.

6. **If all else fails and you can't find a way to pass on the message effectively, it's time to throw yourself down in front of the altar and say, "Holy Powers, I want to do your message justice and get it heard and accepted by the greatest possible number, but I don't know how to do that! Please give me some guidance on how I can make this happen."** If they gave you the Word to pass on, they're obligated to help you do it . . . but sometimes you have to ask for help rather than stumbling in with guns of enthusiasm blazing and making a mess.

Throughout history, mystics have tended to be divided into two groups: the ones honored by the current social structure, and the ones who are outcasts. Sometimes the dividing line is political—those who say what the current group in power doesn't want to hear will be blacklisted. Sometimes it's about social standards—one recalls Saint Francis and how his poverty lifestyle horrified his rich Italian family. Sometimes it's because the Gods and spirits pick someone who has good "psychic hearing" but isn't the most stable of people (and there are many anecdotal reports indicating that having a really strong psychic receiver throughout one's childhood isn't exactly conducive to perfect sanity). Sometimes it's because the Gods and spirits lay taboos or demand behaviors from mystics that clash with their culture and make them seem somewhat less than respectable. In fact, it seems like the most famous mystics didn't start out as anyone "respectable," and the few who did quickly turned away from what had given them that socially stable reputation in the first place. The call of the Divine can be all-encompassing, and in the face of it, human rules can seem extremely trivial.

Still, it is up to mystics who feel driven to get a message through to a discrete group to find the best possible balance of who they must be to be true to their calling and who they must be to actually communicate most effectively. That can be the barest knife's edge, but one assumes that the Gods and spirits would not choose people who couldn't eventually figure out how to do that . . . maybe after a few years of hard knocks. Still, some mystics were reviled curmudgeons to the end of their days, and it was not until well after their death that their works were revered. Perhaps to the Gods and spirits, with their long view of time and the Universe, that's good enough, but it can be fairly demoralizing to the message bearer in question.

Does living on the edge of society make you more likely to hear the Gods? Does hearing the Gods place you on the edge of society? We don't know for sure, although speculations have been rife for hundreds of years. But they are still valid questions to ask, especially for the message bearer who is trying to balance looking trustworthy to the people and being true to the Gods, and shirk neither . . . because in this case, to shirk the one is to betray the other. It will never be an easy road to walk.

> *If no consensus can be reached, it may be the case that someone, or a group of someones, cannot participate in a ritual or activity because their Gods tell them so. Yes, I've had to quit organizations that my guides disagreed with, and I never explained, "Well, my Gods don't like you, so I'm going to play in a different sandbox." I just quietly resigned and went elsewhere. It's more courteous that way. I've bowed out of rituals halfway through if my UPG tells me to, and I share the reason only if someone really asks.*
>
> **—Del, U.S. Pagan**

RESPONSIBILITIES OF GROUP LEADERS AND GATEKEEPERS

By what authority is it decided? That would be me. I am the Gythia, and one of my duties is to uphold the lore and traditions. But I don't judge people too harshly, and I welcome an open exchange of ideas and flow of information. I want to hear what they are experiencing, and if I need further help, I will call in someone I trust within my kindred to discuss it further. I try not to personally judge, but I make my determination based on what I know about the person. Is this person stable? I often ask myself what else the individual has done, read, written or said that might validate the message, but mostly I judge on what I know about the person. I try to read everything with a grain of salt, so that I am not swayed one way or another.

—Mist, Canadian Heathen

In the early days of Neo-Paganism, many groups strove to be as non-judgmental as possible, usually as a reaction to the religions of their upbringing. Some group leaders were careful to point out that while they might have administrative duties—making sure that the incense was purchased, candles of the proper colors were on hand, and the ritual speakers had all their lines—they weren't there to tell anyone what to believe. Eventually, as some groups created more unwavering doctrine and dogma, it was slowly accepted in many of them that if belief in a certain theology is integral to the practice of the group, the leader (or the Council of Elders, or whoever else is chosen for the task) has the right and obligation to take on the task of sacred gatekeeper, refusing admittance to those who don't share that belief.

Part of the reluctance of leaders to take on the gatekeeping task has been the reluctance of Neo-Pagan group members to let them. Many Neo-Pagans left religions in which they had bad experiences with gate-keepers, and they are wary of allowing anyone else to decide anything about their spiritual experience, ever again. Some individuals (and even some groups) commit strongly enough to this ideal that they staunchly believe not only that all people may choose their own personal spiri-tual path, but that there should be no boundaries around what anyone might choose to do spiritually at any moment during group practice.

People being who they are, however, this sort of thing rarely works for a mixed group. Spirituality may be deeply personal and individual, but religion is a group practice, and any group practice requires compromise, if only to figure out what the heck this random bunch of people is going to be doing together tonight.

So now, to one extent or another, we have group leaders (or elders, or whatever title is used) whose job is to decide on and guard the boundaries of what-the-group-does-do from what-the-group-doesn't-do. Part of that job will inevitably require them to evaluate the personal gnosis of anyone who wants to make changes based on inspiration of some sort. This is a heavy and uncomfortable responsibility. Most don't relish the job of having to tell the bright-eyed member brimming with devotion and enthusiasm that after long and thoughtful scrutiny, this innovation does not fit with the concepts that the leader has been charged to protect. It's hard to say those things in the face of someone else's spiritual dreams, knowing that the decision may well be interpreted as a denigration of that person's devotion, psychic ability, intelligence, or even sanity. It's even harder to remain open and compassionate in the wake of the bitterness and resentment that often follows. The temptation to rebuff, to enclose oneself in the righteousness of one's position as rules-guardian, is often strong.

This is why the leader of a religious group needs to remain compassionate and flexible about how the boundaries are enforced, and must be able to come up with imaginative ways to make situations work. If it isn't appropriate to do an activity that Quetzalcoatl has asked for in the main Greek-oriented solstice ritual, might it be possible to hold a separate small ritual on another day? Could a workshop or discussion be held about Quetzalcoatl instead? It's also possible to tell the message bearer that things have to move more slowly; perhaps the group members need some information over time to get used to the idea of Quetzalcoatl, and patient "prebriefing" over a number of months will bring a better result than forcing something onto a reluctant group.

If the personal gnosis is not something that the leader believes the group can endorse at all, a lot of credit can be built by actively helping the message bearer find a group that accepts the gnosis, or at least assisting the person in getting in touch with like-minded people. Just the fact that the gatekeeper is willing to help with that, or designates someone to help with that, goes a long way toward counteracting the potential impression of all the personal denigrations listed in the last paragraph. There's also a good deal of high moral ground in having done everything one can to be respectful of a member's gnosis while still refraining from compromising the group's boundaries.

In the event that the message bearer states that God X demands this, and there will be consequences to pay if it doesn't happen, the leader needs to be willing to verbally accept those consequences, even if the leader secretly believes that they are imaginary. (If nothing else, there will be social consequences regarding the leader's relationship with the message bearer and any other members who bear witness to the exchange.) This is the reason it's often good for a leader to have a couple of trusted diviners who can be called on—to answer what might happen if the leader refuses to do what a message bearer asks. Will Quetzalcoatl really smite the leader, or is this particular message bearer overreacting and misinterpreting?

It also lends credibility if the group has a process for judging personal gnosis that isn't just the leader's whim. While the leader may have given the matter several days of deep thought and prayer and a couple of tarot readings, it can still look like a whim to the people who don't see that part. A public process that is moderated by the leader, or at least a public advisory committee, can lend more transparency and thus more trust to the process. (We'll discuss a few examples in future sections.) More credibility is also extended to the leader whose own personal gnosis is publicly submitted to this process when there is any question in the group.

It's fair for a leader who is facing down an intractable message bearer to point out his or her responsibilities as per the last section (perhaps by giving the individual a copy to read or reread) and then to calmly ask how the message bearer intends to find a way to make the message convincing and acceptable to members of the group who honestly believe X or Y. It may help for the leader to remind the message bearer that those people are also under the leader's purview and also deserve to be part of his or her sacred trust to protect and be fair to all. Simply squaring off in oppositional positions of "Champion of the Gods" and "Champion of the People" will be counterproductive; it behooves the leader to undermine the assumption that those archetypal roles are inevitable, in any way possible.

So, given that, what standards should group members—new and long-term—hold for the people who carry the sacred trust of being spiritual gatekeepers? We asked a number of Pagans this question over a period of time. How would a group leader have to behave in order to gain your trust as someone authorized to judge any personal gnosis you bring to the group? The following list is a reflection of those responses. (Some groups don't have single leaders, but rotate the leadership function according to consensus. For these groups, the challenge is even greater. It doesn't mean that they can ignore the standards below. Instead, it means that every single person in the group with influence must be held to these standards, without exception. No one ever said that taking responsibility would be easy.)

1. They are generally honorable people with a good track record of keeping their commitments and treating their members well.

2. They are known for being honest and not deceptive. They know what they know, and what they don't know, and are clear about that.

3. They accept criticism gracefully and maturely, apologize and make amends for their mistakes, and firmly hold to their decisions when they don't think the criticism is valid.

4. They are clear and open about their spiritual beliefs, including the values that they extrapolate from those beliefs, and how those values might be put into practice. ("One of our sacred poems says X, and to me that means that I should always do Y, and in a situation that called for Y, I'd react this way.") They are willing to talk about both their passion for their faith and

the times when they've been assaulted by doubts. (Be suspicious of group leaders who say that they've never had doubts, if only about their ability to live up to their own faith's tenets.)

5. They are clear on where their authority begins and ends, how those boundaries were set, and whether all the members of their group agree on those boundaries. They are clear on the group's core values and beliefs, and whether all members of the group actually believe them, and to what extent those core values and beliefs are held in other groups of the same tradition. They do not claim moral or spiritual authority over people outside of their group who did not consent to it.

6. They have handled the personal gnosis of members skillfully in the past. "Skillfully" means in ways that have not created clouds of drama and have satisfied all members to the greatest extent that they could be satisfied while not compromising the structure of the group. They have implemented (or inherited and used) a workable system for judging personal gnosis that has proven to be reasonably reliable.

7. They speak courteously about the personal gnosis of others, both inside and outside of their group. They do this even when—perhaps especially when—it differs strongly from their own. They encourage similar courtesy among their members and quash backbiting. They may firmly disagree with someone else's position, but they do not descend into personal attacks or unfounded accusations designed to throw suspicion on the character of people with opposing gnosis, and they openly discourage such reactions among their members. They differentiate between unwanted behavior and unwanted gnosis in former members—rather than "Joe was an evil pantheist who thought that Pan and Frey were the same God," it should be "Joe disrupted a ritual and upset people by calling Pan by the name of Frey even when we'd asked him not to bring that up in group rites."

8. They react to accusations of bad behavior by group members by thoroughly investigating the problem before stating an opinion

on it, and they ask group members to similarly reserve judgment until the investigations are finished and a report made. (This should be especially true with regard to bad behavior that stems from someone's personal gnosis.) They discourage intragroup hysteria and drama, and provide a constant voice of reason. They investigate multiple sources of the accusations and cross-check all sides equally. They do not consider harm to be done unless someone is willing to come forth and claim that he or she has been harmed; accusations that "I heard on the Internet that someone was hurt, but I don't know who that is" should not be counted as useful information in an investigation.

9. They react to accusations of bad behavior by people outside the group by first thoroughly investigating whether the actions of the accused will actually affect the group in any meaningful way, besides providing gossip fodder. If the answer is no, they remind the group of this and refocus them back on their own practice. If the answer is yes, they thoroughly investigate the problem before stating an opinion on it and ask group members to reserve judgment until they are finished. They remember at all times that most people enjoy a state of exciting drama over a state of boring peace and that people will consciously or unconsciously attempt to proliferate the drama. They remind people over and over that if something is alleged, it should be proven before it is believed. A good group leader is a speaker for the truth, and rumors are the enemy of truth.

10. If someone has at one point claimed to be harmed by someone's actions, but is unwilling to discuss this or stand forth, the group leader should offer his or her protection for speaking the truth. If this does not suffice, the claimant must be told that the experience will be discounted if he or she is not willing to stand behind it. This is a hard point, and many group leaders give way before someone's wish to be safely anonymous and still have the "attacker" punished, especially when it's near impossible to tell whether the "accuser" is simply too frightened or is unwilling to defend a partially or

completely untrue accusation. However, the leader owes it to group members to provide trustworthy evidence as to whether to believe something that may affect them, and this sometimes means making unpopular decisions between privacy and group stability.

11. They react to fears of possible outside negative influences by calmly and objectively investigating the likelihood of the influence affecting their group (beyond merely frightening people). If the possibility proves to be negligible, they calm down the fearful in the group.

12. If, for whatever reason, they are unable to investigate any of these problems calmly and objectively due to personal issues, they appoint someone whose judgment they trust. They seek out someone who can be calm and rational about the problem (perhaps because that person is not involved with the group) to investigate for them. This assumes that they have such trusted individuals to call on, which they should.

13. They have good problem-solving skills, and they are quicker to attempt to resolve conflict than to start it. They are good at conflict resolution, and they encourage courtesy and appreciation for each other in all their members.

14. They are appreciative of the strong points of their members and accepting of their personal idiosyncrasies. For example, one Pagan woman speaking on the subject commented that she was more able to trust the opinion of a group leader who accepted her as a person. Another commented on the importance of giving credit where credit was due: "Joe, if I wanted advice on X, you'd be the first person I'd come to. However, this is Y, and I need to listen to someone who's as experienced in Y as you are at X. Where the problem infringes on X, that's where I'm going to take your opinion more seriously."

Being the leader of a religious group is one of the most difficult jobs ever given to a human being. It's often assumed (even if it's not part of your group's official doctrine) that you will be some sort of intermediary between the Divine and the people, especially if you're a priest or priestess and not just an administrator. When a message bearer shows up, it can create insecurities: "I'm the priest; why didn't they give me the message?" In some cases, it may be useful to ask whether the message was sent by this medium for a reason, a reason that has nothing to do with the group you protect and everything to do with learning lessons about your own triggers and issues. While that may not be the case, it's certainly worth musing about, if only when you're home alone. It might even be true if the message is entirely false; it might be the Universe testing your ability to gracefully handle such things. So long as we deal with real Gods and spirits, and they continue to be interested in assisting our evolution, such ambivalent lessons will keep occurring throughout our lifetimes.

RESPONSIBILITIES OF COMMUNITY DIVINERS

By now you've probably read several references in this book to divination and how it is one of the most useful tools a group can have when it comes to judging gnosis. Divination for religious questions was endemic to the ancient world, and even during the medieval period (when it was generally considered the work of the Devil) bibliomancy was sometimes used to settle questions among monastics and theologians. As several of the scholars who responded to our surveys have pointed out, the ancients had their own divinatory systems set up to judge questions, and inevitably those questions would sometimes involve the personal gnosis of some ancient dissident. Unlike mainstream Abrahamic religions, Neo-Paganism's long-standing (though not ubiquitous) discipline of using magical practice as part of spiritual ritual has given us not only a familiarity with divination, but a wealth of diviners of all sorts in our communities.

One Reconstructionist author admitted in an essay that because the ancients had such processes of spiritual discernment, an authentic process should ideally be utilized as the way to slowly integrate personal gnosis even into Reconstructionism, the most historically resistant of the Neo-Pagan denominations. After all, if it was an authentic practice to divine, judge, and integrate such things, then it should be allowed. He then sadly acknowledged that acceptance of the practice was held back by more than just the problem of reconstructing authentic divination. It was the depressingly modern issue that within contemporary Pagan groups, we just don't trust each other. Even those Pagans who acknowledge divination as useful and trustworthy—and not all do by any means—may not be able to bring themselves to trust any specific diviners.

Part of this is the spotty reputation of divination in this country. Illegal in many places as "panhandling" and relegated to the margins of society, foretelling the future has overtly been the province of frauds and con artists. We continually see images of people trying to separate other people from their cold hard cash through "love spells," blessing candles, or just keeping someone on a 900-number call for as long as possible with promises of a sunny future. Given that there is no certification for diviners and that even proof of effectiveness is by definition hard to come by, how is the average Neo-Pagan to figure out which of the spooky-looking people at the psychic fair is trustworthy and which is delusional, inexperienced, or just plain fake? When it's a matter of using one or more of those spooky-looking people to help decide a crucial question of theology in your religious group, average Neo-Pagan leaders might throw up their hands in despair.

While we tend to think of the ancients as gullible, superstitious peasants, they did not necessarily take the word of anyone who threw some sticks and claimed to be a seer. Along with their time-tested and community-accepted methods of judging personal gnosis, they also had time-tested and community-accepted methods of judging diviners. Some of those methods were fairly harsh, in that the seers who had incorrect information too many times—especially when it impacted the community negatively—could be shunned or even killed. Tales abound concerning shamans or soothsayers who couldn't predict the weather or the herds and were slain by angry villagers; one could consider it something of a dangerous job for that alone.

Murder aside, if we look to modern indigenous societies that use divination and have a respected place for their seers, we find two important threads: lineage and results. The most respected diviners have both—they were taught their trade by someone respected, and they get reliable and useful results more often than not—but those with no lineage can also be respected if word of their accuracy spreads. And, truly, this is the way that trusted diviners are "shared" in the contemporary Western world and in Neo-Paganism—people see good results over a period of time and refer their friends to their favorite fortune-teller.

To be a religious community diviner is a heavy responsibility, as bad in its own way as the job of community leader. You won't be called upon as often, but when you are, everyone is breathing down your neck, including the leaders or elders. Even the best diviners can't guarantee that their signal clarity will be good on any given day, as we're all human and psychic abilities are often limited by illness, exhaustion, hunger, stress, or emotional involvement with the subject. No matter what you say in circumstances such as those we've described, someone will be angry with you. In spite of this, you are obligated to tell the truth as you see it, even if it's unpopular. People who received unwanted answers will revile your abilities, and questioners may grumble when you say that you can't do it today because you just broke up with your partner and aren't clear-headed enough.

Diviners in general complain about the issues of ungrateful, pushy, and clueless clients and the hot-button topics of love and work, but diviners for a religious community face questions of religious passion, and that sort of thing has inspired millions of killings over the past centuries. You're dealing with emotional dynamite, and you have to get it right. Add to that the fact that any diviners reading for a religious community are probably strongly spiritual in their own right, with their own relationship to the Gods and spirits and their own obligations to them, and it's clear that this is not a job for the faint of heart.

What people want most in a diviner, of course, is a reliable track record, which in practical terms usually stems from a combination of inborn knack and long-term experience. Coming in a close second is some assurance of character and professionalism—honesty, integrity, sanity, humility, and good boundaries. If leaders whose job is to judge personal gnosis should be held to standards of behavior in order for us to trust them with our spiritual inspirations, the diviners who may be used as the very tool by which they make their decisions had better be held to standards as well. This doesn't have to be a bad thing; diviners who agree to follow a certain set of professional standards not only enhance their own reputation, but that of diviners in general.

Frankly, if we are ever to get to the point of trusting each other, we need to give each other good reasons for that trust. If a collection of community diviners were to agree to strive for certain standards, and hold each other to them, we might be able to start building that trust, brick by brick. At the very least, it couldn't hurt, and it would give the confused questioner something by which to judge those spooky people with their cards and stones and painted sticks.

STANDARDS FOR PROFESSIONAL COMMUNITY DIVINERS

The following characteristics should be sought in a proficient community diviner.

1. A community diviner should be well trained. Ideally, she should know more than one system of divination, because no one system works for every client. If she practices only one system, she should be able to adjust it to different circumstances, people, and cosmologies. She should be experienced at each system, enough to be able to do it in times of stress and trouble.

2. A community diviner should be objective, including being objective about his lack of objectivity. He should be able to tell when his own feelings or opinions are getting in the way of giving a particular client the cleanest reading possible, and be able to humbly refer the client to someone without his baggage.

3. A community diviner should have no ego or pride about the

divination job. Ideally, she should see herself as a vessel for the spirits or the Gods or fate or whatever, but no more than that. She should understand that having her gifts does not necessarily make her a more superior or less flawed human being than the flawed humans who come seeking her advice, laying their flawed lives out on the table for her to see. She provides a public service and nothing more.

4. A community diviner should be constantly working toward better signal clarity, using whatever techniques he can find—meditation, grounding, stress release, diet, herbs, drumming, or whatever works. Signal clarity is crucial, for without it we are idiots talking to ourselves. He should be better than most people at putting aside at will any emotions and stressors that interfere with his signal clarity. At the same time, he should be experienced enough to know when those stressors have overwhelmed his signal with static and be humble enough to step aside. See standard 2.

5. A community diviner should be actively and constantly working toward being more self-aware and mindful, and shedding her psychological baggage. Every bag we carry is a possible monkey wrench in signal clarity. Self-awareness maintenance should be a full-time avocation for a diviner. She should be more aware of her problems than most people and have better control over them.

6. A community diviner should be painfully aware of the state of his mental health and do whatever is necessary to make sure that any aberrations in brain chemistry do not get in the way of signal clarity. As a corollary, he should seriously consider concerned comments on his mental health and the quality of his readings by people he trusts, and not thrust them aside without due thought, discussion, and maybe getting a couple of readings on the subject. He should welcome such scrutiny from those he trusts and respects, because it's an important outside perspective.

7. A community diviner should have some sort of regular spiritual

path or discipline, and ideally some connection with Gods or spirits who help her interface with Otherworlds. If her signal clarity is good enough to get clean, clear information over the wire, it's good enough to get a spirit or God contact on the phone to cross-check in ways that human beings can't.

8. A community diviner should take disbelief in his abilities in stride and remember that no one is obligated to believe him. If he's right, it will all come out eventually; he should see the skepticism of other people as part of a healthy lack of gullibility and not take it personally. See standard 3.

9. A community diviner should stand ready to help those who ask, but should not push her gifts aggressively on others whether they want them or not. Sometimes it means more to a person to figure something out the hard way than to hear it come out of some random seer's mouth. If she is in doubt about when to keep silent, she should get a reading from someone else on the subject.

10. A community diviner should make alliances with other diviners, and not just to have other people to refer folks to. He should make a practice of cross-checking dubious information with other diviners he respects, preferably more than one at a time. The Gods don't mind if you want a second, third, and even fourth opinion—they'd rather you got the message right.

11. A community diviner should be grateful for the presence of other skilled diviners, seeing them as peers and colleagues rather than rivals. There's more than enough work to go around.

12. A community diviner should hold other community diviners to these standards and aid them in achieving same. If divination is to be considered a dependable source of otherworldly information—perhaps the most dependable source—then diviners must be openly committed to reducing error by any margin they can. There will always be error, but honesty, self-awareness, humility, and hard work can significantly improve things.

We should make it clear that when we speak of holding our community diviners to this standard, what we mean is simply to agree that this standard is optimal, and then quietly abstain from using diviners who don't meet it. There's no need to go on a witch hunt for bad diviners; just vote with your feet and the good ones will get solid reputations. Also, if you've had good luck with a particular person as a clear, objective, and useful community diviner, put their name out into the general community, especially directed toward people not of their tradition.

15

COMMUNITY DIVINATION

The Process of Discernment, Part 3

Divination is every spirit worker's friend. All public diviners need someone not directly involved in their practice or group who can ask for a spot check on signal clarity—theirs or someone else's. Even without all the spiritual mumbo-jumbo, when a group is having a disagreement about anything, it's usually a good idea to have an uninvolved party with no investment in the outcome waiting in the wings to help mediate disputes.

If this is just impossible, another good approach is to have everyone in the group conduct divination on the subject and report on the results—usually without interpretation. Let the group decide what the runes, cards, or tea leaves have to say. Look for any trends, repeated symbols, or clear-cut sets.

—Del, U.S. Pagan

In times past and in varying cultures, divination for a community question was sometimes handled as a private matter and sometimes as a public one. Modern Pagan diviners tend to lean heavily toward the first option, for a variety of reasons. There's huge pressure on a public diviner; doing it in private in front of a group of nervous people is bad enough, but doing it in front of a crowd (and especially a grumbling crowd that is divided on an issue) can be terrifying. The diviner may fear that half the crowd might accuse him or her of incompetence or of slanting the message, in a "Kill the umpire!" sort of way, and this fear might not be unfounded. If something goes wrong, many people will be disappointed. If the message is confusing and cannot be interpreted—something that happens to even the most skilled diviner—he or she may look inept and the reputation may suffer. If there are multiple diviners, a public argument about the results can undermine the people's trust in many directions. If messages come up that are personally humiliating to the individuals involved, it may seem like a terrible insult to bring that up as part of a public ritual.

Given all these potential drawbacks, why should any group even consider doing public divination on an important group matter? Because when it is done right, it creates a great bond uniting the people and can build rather than demolish trust. First, bringing the divination into the open can assuage at least some fears that the leadership is making secret deals behind closed doors or leaving out crucial information. Second, if the public divinatory process is accepted through frequent practice as a viable method of communication with the Powers That Be, it can actually cut down on postdivinatory arguments. If it gets accepted as part of the group culture, there will be a greater investment by everyone when it comes to trusting the process. Making it public turns it into a group activity; even those who are only witnesses can come to feel that it is their ritual, their sacred process, and their message.

As we've mentioned before, not all Pagans believe in the accuracy and legitimacy of divination as a method for achieving knowledge. Others may claim to believe, but doubts may crop up when the answer isn't one they want. As an example, a small private gathering of advanced Pagan spiritual practitioners started getting together every year to exchange skills and ideas. After a few years, word about their restricted gathering got out, and people began to petition to get in. The regular attendees wanted to keep the gathering limited to advanced practitioners, but who was to judge who was advanced enough or what the spirits might prefer? Divination was decided on, and the names of petitioners were sealed in envelopes by third parties and marked with geometric shapes. Three different diviners in three different places read on whether "Square" or "Circle" or "Wavy Line" should attend the gathering, then compared notes and opened the envelopes. Those with at least two "yes" votes could attend, although those without three "yes" votes were required to be silent during teaching until further notice. Some of the rejected petitioners accepted the verdict without question, but one or two suddenly became loudly skeptical about the veracity of divination as a way to make policy decisions.

Similarly, not everyone is going to like the idea of turning to the Gods for the answer, for a variety of reasons. They may not believe that it works at all. They may not believe that it works well enough or often enough to use it for doctrinal policy decisions. They may not like being unable to see the logical reasoning behind the decision—who knows why the Gods decide things? They may feel that bringing mystical forces into the equation removes the power of the humans involved. They may just be worried that the Gods will choose against them for some reason. Even people who believe in Gods may not believe in their infallibility or their benevolence. It's not easy to trust that they actually can see further and know better.

However, as we stated earlier in this book, divination is one of the mainstays for judging gnosis in ancient times, and public divination has a voluminous number of historical precedents behind it. Given that, it may behoove group leaders to gently introduce the concept to their people and see if they can eventually get behind it.

If there is a hierarchical structure and the group leader gets the final say on all decisions, then presumably this will also apply to decisions about acting upon personal gnosis, by the authority invested in the leader. (This could very well lead to ructions and resignations, but then so could any difference of opinion within such a structure!) If the group uses a consensus model of decision making, then the majority opinion will carry the day. A good procedure would be for the group to take some time as individuals asking for personal divine guidance on the matter, incubating dreams, contacting their higher selves, or making their own contact with the Deity concerned, and then to reconvene to see if the majority felt there was a clear sense of guidance on the issue. Authority would then hopefully remain with the Divine, as revealed to the greater part of the group, and any individual disagreements could be put down to the margin of human error. Hopefully.

It's bound to be difficult because personal conviction can be so absolute for the individual concerned, but the group should perhaps discuss and agree in principle that there is a margin of human error as regards the understanding of divine communication, and that this is well documented historically! No matter how great one's personal conviction, if the course of action is to involve others as well, it is always wise to ask for a "second opinion"!

—**Rose Alba, U.K. Pagan**

HISTORICAL DIVINATION

Like many syncretistic cults in late antiquity (e.g., Serapis, Asklepios-Imouthes, Nodons in Britain), dreams and dream incubation seem to have been a part of the cultus of Antinous (as indicated by the Obelisk). This would imply that the individual epiphanies of the Deity were very important and even essential on some matters for his worshippers. Dreams are remarkably unique and individualized, as we know from psychological studies as much as from surviving dream manuals and interpretations from antiquity. So allowing for this by saying that Antinous appears in dreams seems to give a great deal of leeway to the types of experiences that people may have ended up undergoing.

We also know that an oracle of Antinous existed. Oracular work is a topic unto itself, and there is some suggestion in certain sources that Hadrian wrote all the answers to the oracles (thus indicating some sense of spiritual fraud being possibly involved). But the ability to get answers from the Deity on individual matters of concern is an important aspect of a cult, and indicates that just as there were people who went and got answers themselves in dreams, there were specialists available as well who could get answers for others when called upon to do so.

In addition, there were mysteries of Antinous. Hadrian and Antinous were Eleusinian initiates, at the very least, and they were additionally known to have had associations with Egyptian mystics of various sorts. Hadrian was interested in religion and magic in general, and seems to have indulged in exploring it whenever possible, as well as being keenly interested in philosophy (and a variety of other topics). While we cannot be certain what the mysteries consisted of, there are some tantalizing fragments in various texts from Egypt that make some suggestions in this regard. Mystery initiations seem to have been a profoundly individual experience as well, even though they may have taken a structured and standardized form—ultimately, they set the individual up for a particular direct experience of the Deity and could therefore generate any number of possibilities in a person's perceptions and understandings.

—P. Sufenas Virius Lupus, Hellenic Pagan

In the year 1000 in Iceland, Thorgeirr the Lawgiver "went under the cloak" to determine the religious fate of all Iceland. The practice of "going under the cloak" was a shamanistic tool throughout the cultures of the northern half of Europe; it meant that diviners literally wrapped themselves fetal position in a cloak with a skin of water and did not come out until the Holy Powers had given them an answer—usually a maximum of three days. In some cases, they were bound into the cloak or blanket with only one hand free to receive more water or hand out a cup of urine. The combination of mummification, sensory deprivation, and fasting created an altered state in which seers were much more open to the words of the Gods, and their willingness to go through the painful process helped to show their commitment to truth and the Gods, as opposed to mere self-importance. Thorgeirr already had a reputation among the Pagans as a holy man who was touched by the Gods and among the Christians as an honest and sincere man of forethought and inspiration. People on both sides would trust his word.

This was a good thing, because many lives were hanging in the balance of his report. The question was this: Should all Pagans in Iceland convert to Christianity and give up their Old Gods, or should they organize and fight the attempts by the Christian immigrants and converted Icelanders—who were fast becoming a majority—to outlaw their religion and convert them by the sword? With what must have been heart-stoppingly painful awareness of the magnitude of his task, Thorgeirr went under the cloak for a day and a night and prayed to his Gods for the best answer.

When he emerged, he reported that the answer was wretchedly clear. The Christians, the Gods had explained to him, were too numerous and could call on help from allies overseas. Their closest trade neighbor, Norway, had a hostile Christian king who was holding many Icelanders hostage and would murder them if Iceland did not convert. If Iceland divided over the issue of religion and violence ensued—which was inevitable—the Pagans would be wiped out. The Gods could see no way for them to win such a war, and there would be a mass slaughter, with perhaps a third of Iceland depopulated. Afterward, there might be no one left to remember the old ways and pass them on to future generations. It was better to bow the head, convert, and secretly pass on the old ways—better for all concerned.

Ironically, public divination helped to unseat the faith that used it regularly and install one that would outlaw it. (While many modern readers may imagine the emotional reactions of Thorgeirr and his audience, we might also wonder about the emotions of the Gods who had to save the lives of their worshippers by effectively ordering that flock to abandon them, and run the risk of forgetting them altogether.) Thorgeirr's word was accepted, and Iceland became legally Christian. Thorgeirr himself, knowing that he had to lead the way his message pointed, ceremonially threw the statues of his Gods over a waterfall.[1]

In contrast, the traditional public divination system of Rome was presided over by the guild of augurs. Priests of this guild would sit on a hill opposite their temple and watch (or, in some cases, be blindfolded and have described to them) the release of a flock of sacred birds from the temple roof. The direction of the birds' flight, their behavior, and their noises would answer the question that had been asked of them, a type of divination known as *ornithomancy*. During the reign of Caesar, the previously militantly apolitical augurs gave in and accepted his money in order to claim that the augury was right for him to become dictator of Rome.[2] They may have been in fear for their lives if they refused, which was not an uncommon concern for public diviners in the ancient world.

Of the hundreds of divination methods catalogued by enthusiasts in the field—most of which end in the suffix *-mancy*—most were used by laypeople to ask domestic questions. A few, however, are clearly the sort of dramatic, showy event that works best as a public ritual adjunct. An example of this is *belomancy,* once popular in Arabia, Greece, Chaldea, and Tibet. It requires a line of archers with specially marked arrows all firing at once; the furthest arrow is the answer, and omens are also read from the flights of the arrows themselves.[3]

We also know that *haruspicy* (reading the entrails of a freshly slaughtered animal) was done in public; this practice still takes place in Africa to find answers to community questions. Haruspicy probably began around five thousand years ago in China, where reports of *scapulomancy* (interpreting the burned shoulder blades of food animals) arise, and it was found in over a hundred countries thousands of years later. According to the biblical book of Ezekiel, the Babylonian king of the time often used it as his public court oracle, and the second book of

Kings refers to comparable use by King Ahaz of Judah. Haruspicy was certainly the second mainstay of the Roman state oracles (after ornithomancy), who employed a specialist known as a *haruspex* to interpret the organs of sacrificial animals. Yet another popular divination method among the state-sponsored augurs was *molybdomancy,* or interpreting the shapes of drops of molten lead poured into water and allowed to congeal.

Both Babylonian priests and Druids divined answers from the smoke of burnt offerings, a practice called *capnomancy.* Those offerings were occasionally human. The Druids also burned twigs and leaves from sacred oak trees and their mistletoe parasites. Babylonian priests also practiced public *theriomancy,* or divining from the behavior of provoked animals. Water was splashed onto the heads of the sacred bulls, and one of seventeen specific reactions was watched for. Today in Polynesia, families gather to watch the progress of a beetle placed on the grave of a murder victim; its tracks will supposedly reveal the name of the murderer.

During the Shang Dynasty period of Chinese history 3,500 years ago, a divination system named *Kuei-pu* was developed and used extensively for public divination. This involved preparing tortoise shells so that they would break along carefully chiseled lines, and then placing them on a fire so that they would shatter (referred to in modern times as *plastromancy*). The pieces were examined and prognostications made from their pattern of breakage. Kuei-pu was the primary oracle at the Chinese royal court for thousands of years until the I Ching gained enough in popularity to threaten its prominence. It was later adopted by the Japanese and became an official function of the emperor's court oracles from 650 to the Meiji Restoration in 1868.

Queen Elizabeth I of England saw a comet streaking across the sky in 1583 and—being well versed in astrology—panicked about whether it meant disaster for her reign. She called her councilors and resorted to *cleromancy*—divination by casting dice or other small objects—which assured her that she would continue to reign for many years.[4]

We can't look at the history of public divination without addressing the term *prophecy,* a word that makes most modern people twitch and imagine sign-carrying lunatics standing on street corners and ranting at passersby, or perhaps prompts recollection of the astrological column in the newspaper. Plato called prophecy "the noblest of the arts." Socrates differentiated it from ordinary madness by calling it "a madness which is the special gift of heaven, and the source of the chiefest blessings among men." He pointed out that the oracles had conferred great benefits on Greek society when in an altered state, but had been of little use when they were in possession of their senses.

Much has been said about the famous Oracle of Delphi, but somewhat less about the oldest oracle of all—that of Dodona. Already old by the time of Homer, it is believed to have been established by the Pelasgian aboriginal people well before the Indo-European invasions of 2000–1200 BCE. It actually is thought to be a collection of oracles all in one place, of which the most famous was a sacred grove of oak trees. The grove was dedicated to the God Zeus after the Hellenes took over, but it may have originally been the province of the local Deity. It was said that the priests of the grove could listen to the rustling of the leaves and hear prophetic words. One large tree in particular was the "voiceful oak." This oracular practice may originate from tree worship or from the shamanic practice of speaking to tree spirits; however, it is also interwoven with the sacred voice of a Deity. It is impossible, now, to know how many of the prophetic spirit voices came from Zeus, how many came from an older God, and how many came from the spirit of Oak or that particular tree.[5]

We do, however, have tablet-inscribed lists created by the scribe-priests of Dodona that note some of the questions that ordinary people asked the oracle. (They did not list the answers; those were apparently personal and private.) While we think of oracles as being concerned with the future, other questions were far more common—what had already happened, what would be the best course of action, and so on. Questions abound regarding the paternity of children and which Deity a given individual should worship. One peasant asked whether he lost his blankets and pillows himself or they had been stolen. Some customers, of course, did not like their answers. One group of Boetian envoys disliked theirs enough to attack the oracular priestess and throw her into a cauldron of boiling water. The most famous oracular pronouncements, of course, were the ones that were so ambiguous that they could be interpreted several ways, likely to fit any future; these have come down to us still bathed in mystery, and are used to prove that such things are nonsense and not to be trusted.[6]

What we fail to understand—or dismiss out of hand—is that kings and statesmen regularly consulted oracles for decisions that would affect thousands of people . . . and, from their accounts, the oracles had a very good track record, so long as they remained apolitical. The Greeks and Romans were not unaware that public divination could be abused as part of political machinery, and they warned about the difference between "pure" oracles who had no interest in political gain and "impure" ones who should be cast out of influence. The Oracle of Delphi is recorded to have given correct and useful information to the vast majority of people who inquired of her; it's just that none of those answers were written down. Out of hundreds of thousands, we retain stories only of the handful of ambiguous and difficult ones . . . which were so unusual as to be memorable. Accuracy was the unremarkable rule for them, not the exception.

Some of the scraps of advice that come down to us from Delphi, which was first an oracle of Gaea and then later, after being conquered, of Apollo, is just and sensible. Foreigners who asked how best to worship were told "after the custom of your own country," and those who asked which God was best to worship were told "whichever one seems best to you."

Julius Caesar's reign was wrapped around with prophecies, as was his death; so many prophetic omens were told to him about the dangers of the Ides of March (including a dream by his own wife) that it is amazing he left the house at all. In fact, he is said to have cheerfully told a friend that morning that the Ides of March were here, and they didn't seem all that bad. The friend pointed out that the day was not over. Caesar responded that he had always been a gambler, and two hours later he was stabbed to death. (A week earlier, the Roman state-employed haruspex, Titus Vestricius Spurinna, saw an omen of disaster for the emperor in the liver of the weekly temple sacrifice and went straight to Caesar with the news. It was ignored, as Caesar was certain that he was so blessed by the Gods that he need never fear for his safety.)[7]

His successor Augustus, however, had so many prophecies of royal success thrown on him from his birth that his father supposedly considered having the child killed in order to spare democratic Rome a future tyrant.[8] All these prophecies (including several by astrologers) of his overwhelming political fortune allowed the young Octavian to grow up completely confident in his own destiny, and never once pause to worry about it. Some would call this simply self-fulfilling and his success a product of propaganda-inspired confidence. It's hard, when dealing with prophecy and divination, to sort out such chicken-and-egg issues.

Of course, to be fair, we don't know how much of history has been altered after the fact to make better stories and add to the glory of various rulers. (Plato himself complained that oracles and prophecy were a help to rulers only as long as the diviners stood fast and did not dilute their messages, even in the face of threats; he opined that it was when they began to tell powerful men what they wanted to hear that public divination became useless and false.) Still, these were not stupid men, nor nearly as superstitious as we might like to think. They were practical rulers and statesmen, and they consulted public oracles because it had been proven over time to make their decisions more effective. We can consider that superstitious and foolish, as society tends to do today, or we can perhaps make a careful test of trying it out, especially with the difficult issue of trying to decide what our Gods want from us. There's a reason why the word *divination* starts with the word *divine*—it is, first and foremost, a message facilitated by the Gods and spirits.

It has been pointed out, by the way, that the oldest extant public divination is the coin toss, which is essentially asking the Gods of fate to decide who should go first in any given activity, even if the people doing it don't see it that way. That's something to think about every time you see a ball game with the umpire doing the toss—it's our last bastion of public divination.

MODERN ADAPTATIONS IN THE FACE OF SKEPTICISM

It is true that not every situation is appropriate for divination in public, but nearly every one of the potential drawbacks of public divination can be counteracted by having protocols set up in advance. A few modern Pagan groups have found the following protocols for public divination to be very useful; feel free to try them out and adapt them for your own group's use.

First, don't decide on this policy until you have made sure that the group is comfortable with divination as a whole and can take it seriously. If the majority of members don't feel that it can be made reliable enough to base doctrinal policy decisions on, you may have to look for a different solution. People won't accept what they don't believe, and if at least half of your members don't trust the process, it will not settle their differences no matter how good the diviner is.

Ideally, each group should have at least two diviners. (More can be even better.) While they can be friends, their relationship should not be so close that group members would have a hard time believing that they would feel free to disagree with each other in public. They should also trust each other professionally and be willing to vouch for the divinatory skills of the other. All public diviners should have decent reputations as private diviners, both in and out of the group. They should be able to produce a variety of people who can vouch for their skills when applying for the position of an official group diviner.

It's important to make public divination acceptable to the group and integrate it into the group subculture before a huge issue arises that causes unrest and division. Start as soon as possible by having regularly scheduled public divinations—perhaps before, after, or during the rituals of yearly holidays that are associated with spirit connection or historic divination. The subjects should be general and not overly controversial—"What will the next year hold for the folk of this group? What will be our biggest concern as a group? What will trouble the majority of the people in their personal lives? What Gods would like to be honored at some point over the next year?" Encourage the group members to be present for and emotionally invested in the process, and make sure that the leaders or influential people in the group openly declare their belief in the process. It's not a bad idea for some of these preparatory public divination methods to be fairly showy as well as appropriate to the theme of the ritual event. This encourages people to watch, think, care, and above all get used to the idea. If the group has done the preparatory work well enough, people will be more likely to be enthusiastic about putting more incendiary questions to the process when the time comes.

Witnesses can do more than just witness. They can pray, for a set period beforehand, for the signal to be clear and for the Gods to bless the group with knowledge. Setting up a quiet ritualized way that this can be done—such as having people approach an altar or sacred space one at a time—helps with creating sacred space around the public ritual. Getting the witnesses involved heightens their sense of investment in the process. The diviner or the community leader should remember to thank them afterward for their prayers and energy.

The divination method used should be one that all the diviners are familiar with. They should also be well skilled in explaining their interpretation quickly and concisely to a group of people without needing to spend hours instructing them about the method. Witnesses don't necessarily want to know everything about that method; they just want to know enough about how the diviner made the interpretation to feel that it was done skillfully. For less crucial questions, a single divination could take place with a single diviner. For more controversial or politically important questions, a better method is to use two diviners. The first one asks the question and interprets the results. The second one asks whether the message has been heard clearly and if there is anything else the people need to know. Sometimes it's useful for the first question to be asked with a complicated system that can give in-depth answers (examples being sortilege methods such as tarot or runes) and the follow-up carried out with a clear yes or no omen divination.

The divination does not have to be a short one-day activity. Omen-style divinations can be set up to take days or months to come about; an example might be ritually planting seeds of a plant specifically beloved by the Deity of whom you are asking the question and observing how they come up over time. The wonderful thing about this method (and other long-term omen methods) is that an entire community can participate in them and thus be more invested. There probably should be a diviner overseeing and interpreting the project, but the more obvious the omen is, the better the community will accept it.

If the divination goes wrong somehow, the diviner should take this as a clear omen that the Gods want something else entirely. You can ask instead, "What do you want in this situation, O Gods?" If this also goes wrong, drop the whole thing for at least three months. Sometimes, during that time, something will happen to resolve the issue. If the diviner cannot interpret the omens or divination, that person needs to say that he or she is not the right diviner for this specific job. If the diviner is worried about his or her reputation, the community leader could say something supportive about how it is better to have honest diviners who know their own limitations than dishonest ones who fake their way through it. The divination should be postponed to another date. Giving the abdicating diviner the chance to choose a replacement is a courtesy.

All diviners run into this problem sometimes, and while it's especially humiliating when it happens in public, the community leader should not ask a diviner to step down on the basis of an occasional bad signal clarity incident. This is especially true if the rest of the diviner's performance was fine. If nothing else, firing your community diviners on the basis of such incidents will make future community diviners much less interested in being honest when it's their turn. Leaders should reward honesty, not appear to penalize it.

Once you have an answer to the problem, write everything down—the question, the method used, the officiants, the results in detail. The information may help those who have a similar question, or who have questions about how the policy came about, or who want to know more about the process itself. Document everything for posterity; you never know who might need it. It's even important to write down situations where it went wrong and how that was handled.

16

GROUPS AND GNOSIS

I believe in a moderate approach. Certainly I think that both cultural and scholarly sources should be used as important standards for authenticity, but I also think that if we are to have genuine mysticism and a living practice, at some point those sources will have to be transcended, and some innovations—usually based on somebody's personal gnosis—need to be introduced into the tradition so that Celtic Reconstructionism becomes practical in our lives and for our emotional and spiritual needs.

From my earliest involvement in what was to become Celtic Reconstructionism, I have been an advocate of "aisling (dream/vision) and archaeology"—a balance between gnosis and history. Today, I would add to that to make a triad with "argumentation," meaning not that we should be having rows over our practices, but that both our innovations and our history should be open to civil discussion and thorough debate about what is meaningful and useful for us within a Celtic context. Without all three of these elements, I do not believe we can develop a full and meaningful living practice.

—Erynn Rowan Laurie,
U.S. Celtic Reconstructionist Pagan

Controversies frequently arise when gnosis shifts from being a personal encounter with the Gods to becoming a divine engagement with a community of believers. One person's prophet is another's insane cult leader; one group's holy scriptures may be another group's collection of incoherent rants. Religious groups have been rent asunder over the question of whether a message is divinely inspired, and disagreement and disbelief often lead to accusations of unsavory and even criminal behavior.

Determining whether these claims have any merit can be a difficult task. History shows that prophets and seers have long met with resistance, but it also suggests that many people have played at being divine messengers for their own selfish purposes. But while we may not find any quick and easy answers in the past, perhaps we can at least discover some insights into how we might handle these problems when they arise in the present.

DOCTRINAL DISAGREEMENTS: THE "RIGHT WAY" OF SERVING THE GODS

Anytime someone starts with "the Goddess told me" or some such, it raises big red flags. When it's "the Goddess told me to tell you," I immediately dismiss it. When it's conveyed as UPG and recognized as a message for the hearer alone, even if it's shared as something that might be of interest or of use to all, that's fine with me.

—Julian Greene, ADF Pagan

Within modern Paganism, we frequently find that theological discourse begins from one of two extreme positions. The most common is the idea that there is no "right" or "wrong" when serving the Gods. The only sin is intolerance; the only blasphemy is to accuse another of blaspheming. If someone wants to serve hamburgers to a Hindu Deity or dedicate their mixed martial arts training studio to a peace-loving God like Kwan Yin, it is not our place to criticize. So long as nobody gets hurt, anything goes. (This, of course, leads to the thorny question of what constitutes "gets hurt"—but frequently that issue is ducked altogether or answered with platitudes about how everyone has life lessons to learn, and we shouldn't interfere with someone else's path.)

Often this approach is rooted in a belief that the Gods are merely symbols or tools by which we may better understand ourselves. Abstractions cannot be offended or take umbrage at blasphemers, and if rituals are merely psychodrama, their value lies solely in what they can do for the participants, not what they offer to the Divine. When the question is not "How can we serve the Gods?" but "How can the Gods serve us?" there is little need for doctrinal purity or ritual protocol. Neo-Pagans, who are often converts from other religions, may associate any kind of religious protocol with the rigid doctrines they grew up with, doctrines that assign unbelievers to eternal torment and damnation. *If we are going to reject our religion of upbringing and create a new one,* they say, *we might as well start by jettisoning all the problematic issues we may have with our former faith. After all, there have certainly been too many atrocities committed by people who were convinced they were doing God's will.* And to outsiders (and many insiders), the motivations for spiritual conflict can seem trivial and even silly.

But while this approach may be useful for avoidance of interdemographic conflicts (at least some of the time), it can be unsatisfying for those seeking a greater rigor in their spiritual life. The contrasting reasoning to the above voice is: *If my present spiritual path is no better than any other and no more likely to bring me closer to the Divine, then why waste time traveling on it?* Some folks with this preference have sought and found structure in existing living faiths. They become initiates in African traditional religions and master every detail of their tradition's practices; they memorize pages of Sanskrit and do pujas that would impress a Mumbai Brahmin; they become Thelemites who can tell you what Aleister Crowley had for supper the evening he wrote a poem that sheds light on an obscure line in one of his Class B publications. Others collect volumes of scholarly texts on history, archaeology, and related disciplines in an effort to re-create the religion of their ancestors with the most painstaking accuracy possible.

This kind of dedication is laudable and can definitely help seekers to better understand their Gods and their faith, but it can also become an end in itself rather than a means toward developing a deeper spiritual relationship with the Divine. Those who take a more casual approach to their faith are scorned as "fluffy bunnies" or "culture vultures" who are merely playacting. Devotion is measured not by how much an adherent loves the Gods or how important a role they play in the worshipper's life, but by how much obscure knowledge devotees accrue concerning the traditional ways Gods were served and how slavishly their followers re-create ancient rituals.

The possibility of a middle path is all too often minimized or ignored altogether. What if we accept that the Gods are real and that they can be offended by our actions—but what if we also accept that the rules for human engagement with the Divine are not universal Truths but individual and community guidelines? We stumble when we say that any convenient way of approaching the Divine is as good as any other, but we also stumble when we attempt to create too many detailed and petty regulations to fence in our connection to the Gods.

CIRCLES OF WORSHIP

Gnosis brought to a group should be judged according to the community standards it belongs to. A Heathen shouldn't be judged according to Wiccan standards, a Wiccan by Catholic standards, nor a Buddhist by Muslim standards. Nevertheless I think that there are several criteria that should be applicable regardless of tradition. First, is the gnosis consistent with community beliefs? Second, is the gnosis consistent with beliefs and practices expressed in applicable lore? Third, is the gnosis consistent with harmonious community and personal growth? Incidentally, I do not necessarily interpret number one to mean that a gnosis can't be groundbreaking, nor do I mean that an entire community must agree to the gnosis. What I mean is that, for example, if a gnosis teaches that Odin got the runes after fasting for forty days and forty nights in the desert, it's probably wrong. Now if that same person felt like nine days of hanging felt like forty days of fasting in the desert, then maybe it's consistent with community standards. If a person believed that Zeus worshipped Hecate, this may be valid, as the lore shows that Zeus showed her deference for various reasons and referred to her as existing as a Deity long before he did. It may also be potentially groundbreaking.

—**Aleksa, U.S. Pagan**

Many different practices are lumped together under the rubric of "worship." If we are going to understand the way spiritual practices help us relate to and understand the Divine, we may do well to examine those various layers and the ways they influence each other. "There are many different pathways to God" is a common truism, but few realize that every individual simultaneously walks on several of these pathways at any given time.

The core of this spiritual onion is the relationship between Deity and the individual. Since the Protestant Reformation and its focus on a personal relationship with Christ, this layer has received the lion's share of attention. Interactions at this level are personal and intimate. They may resemble the relationship between a king and his subject, between a mother and her child, between a lover and the beloved, between old friends exchanging helpful suggestions and entertaining anecdotes—the possibilities are endless.

From there we have the relationship between Deity and the family. Today we rail against efforts to "indoctrinate" children, but for most of history indoctrination was seen as a good and necessary thing. Parents were expected to pass down their religious teachings to their offspring; spirituality provided children with role models to follow and bestowed a moral and ethical foundation that would help them become strong and productive adults. Much as children might learn the family trade, so too would they learn the family prayers and become acquainted with the family spirits.

Still other layers of worship were placed atop these—for example, the family participated in the spiritual life of their village. Depending on the village's ethnic or cultural makeup, those rites might establish them as part of the greater community or set them apart; sometimes it would do both. In the classical world, different communities might serve the same God using different rites and representations. This did not give rise to war and to calls of blasphemy, but to pilgrimages. A merchant who wanted to repay a debt to Zeus might visit his temples in several different cities. There he might be regaled with different stories of the Sky Father's origin; he might hear of Zeus the wolf father, the chthonic Zeus who lived underground, or the ram-horned Zeus honored by Ammon in the Egyptian deserts. All these different tales of Zeus were proof of his glory and majesty; instead of focusing on their contradictions, devotees saw them as part of a greater whole, a mystery that could not be summed up in a single book or a single legend.

A vision or a visitation might result in changes to the practices within an area, or they might result in visionaries setting up temples elsewhere and putting their gnosis to practical use. This was not seen as irreverence, but as the highest form of devotion. Be it a small roadside shrine or a massive marble temple about which a city formed, gnosis led to the creation of another sacred place and gave us another myth by which we might come closer to the Gods. Worship was inclusive rather than exclusive; as the worlds of devotees changed and grew, so too did the worlds of their Gods. As time went on, new stories were added to the canon, and once-important and widely known tales faded in importance and were lost. (Indeed, many would argue that changes in the world of humanity were spurred by changes in the world of the Divine. While many today believe the sacred world is a pale reflection of mundane reality, many historical intellectuals believed our reality was but a shadow cast by the Divine Light—see Plato's thoughts on Forms for one particularly influential version of this theory.)

Religious controversies did not begin with the rise of monotheism. The Romans, for example, were horrified by the Carthaginian practice of infant sacrifice. (They also feared Carthage as a competitor, proving that the use of religious grudges for political ends also has a long history.) There were certainly doctrinal disputes and disagreements that might disrupt a community—the Bacchanals, for instance, frequently attracted negative attention for their frenzied rites—but by and large the ancient world enjoyed a great deal of spiritual flexibility. Groups were allowed to believe and worship as they saw fit, so long as their members functioned as peaceful and productive citizens. Within most groups there was little concern for what other spiritual practices their members followed, so long as they showed proper reverence and respect during services.

This is not to say that the liturgies and rituals of the Gods were completely flexible or that arbitrary changes were acceptable to the clergy or the congregations. Cities maintained their religious rites as diligently as their walls and defenses, and families protected their patron spirits as fiercely as their treasure. Traditions were not altered without very good reason; it typically required some combination of gnosis, charisma, and armed force to make changes in the way a city honored its Gods. Those who were unsuccessful in their campaigns could be jailed or killed for blasphemy. While this sort of violent response is less common today, the lesson remains valid: the larger the group you attempt to reach with your unverified personal gnosis, the greater the resistance you are likely to encounter.

PROPHETS AND ABUSERS: SPOTTING THE DIFFERENCES

In my small coven, we practice a form of received prophecy, and each of us has been the recipient of personal gnosis at one point or another. However, if the spirits were to instruct us to do anything that seemed dangerous or unwise, we would discuss the revelation as a group and come to a consensus on the matter before we proceeded. We believe that community discussion of received information will prevent ridiculousness or dangerous situations almost 90 percent of the time. In fact, we discuss all personal revelations in our group, whether or not it seems initially dangerous, unwise, brilliant, perfect, True, or whatever. This is why intimate, real-time, concrete, trusting, long-term, and authentic relationships are so critical to Paganism right now, in my opinion, and why we should truly have more of them. The Internet lends itself way too much to self-referencing fantasy. It's easy to be a messianic prophet on the web—it's not so easy to do so when you are in a deep relationship with a small community that keeps you grounded and can provide reality checks.

—Ruby Sara, U.S. Neo-Pagan

Western culture has developed a great distrust for "cult leaders." Those leaders who are perceived as overly controlling or intolerant are compared to historical bad guys like Jim Jones, Torquemada, or a certain failed Austrian painter with a Charlie Chaplin mustache. Hackles are especially quick to rise when these leaders claim to be speaking for the Divine. These suspicions are not unreasonable, as con artists regularly present themselves as holy men to take financial or sexual advantage of sincere but naïve believers. If we are going to discuss how to deal with gnosis, we must also address the issue of those who would abuse it.

Before doing this, we need to determine what is and is not "abuse." To that end, we need to distinguish between an arduous spiritual path and a dysfunctional one. Vows of celibacy and poverty may seem self-destructive and sex-negative to people seeking a more easygoing religious path, but monastics in a number of religious traditions continue to find value in these difficult exercises. Asceticism and ordeal may trigger people who have suffered from nonconsensual privation or violence, but they are not necessarily, in and of themselves, signs of an abusive religious group. (Indeed, most ascetics, monks, and ordeal workers would be quick to tell you that these paths are only for a select few and should not be attempted by those who are not ready for their rigors.) Orgies and sexual rituals can definitely be tools of degradation and coercion, but they can also be powerful magical operations in the hands of serious and consenting adults.

It is important to remember that freedom of choice includes the right of other people to make choices you might disagree with. You might not choose to become part of a monastic community, to be flogged or hung on hooks as a living sacrifice, or to act as a sacred prostitute for your Goddess, but others might make those choices of their own free will and find them to be meaningful and rewarding experiences. You need not approve of these rites and rituals, and for that matter you may believe sincerely that no Gods worth worshipping would ever demand these things of their servants, but it is important to refrain from demonizing those who perform them without some evidence of wrongdoing.

Consent is an important issue here. If members depart from a group, are they subjected to harassment, slander, poison-pen letters, and other sorts of unacceptable coercion? Are ill members allowed access to health care? Are they isolated from their families and friends and threatened with spiritual or physical injury should they violate the confidences of the group? Do the leaders use their gnosis to bludgeon critics inside the group? Are dissenting opinions and inconvenient questions silenced by prophetic proclamations that must not be challenged but only obeyed? Are reluctant members bullied into sexual liaisons? Are ordeals used not as spiritual experiences but as punishment? All these are warning signs that should not be ignored, nor justified in the name of some "higher cause."

However, we also need to approach reports of these abuses with some caution. "Witch wars" and theological disputes have historically led to allegations of devil worship, human sacrifice, and all sorts of luridly titillating practices intended to show that the opposing party isn't just doctrinally questionable but outright evil. When we are dealing with gnosis and personal interactions with the Gods, it is important to distinguish between doctrinal differences and actual criminal activity. We may disagree in good faith about how a Deity should be served, but there should be universal agreement that abuse and exploitation are unacceptable no matter the religious justifications the abuser puts forth. To sort out idle gossip from serious issues, it may help to apply the old journalistic "Five Ws."

Who? Who committed these alleged crimes? Who are the victims of these nefarious schemes? Who are the witnesses? Some of the people involved may wish to remain anonymous for one reason or another, but there should be at least a couple of verifiable names of both victims and witnesses to be found somewhere in the tale. If no actual human being can be found who will come forward and describe the wrongs that were directly done to him or her, be suspicious.

What? What are the specific offenses? Instead of nebulous comments about "brainwashing," look for detailed descriptions of actual incidents wherein the alleged perpetrators abused their power. When you hear someone is a "pervert," find out what the claimant means by that term. Are the critics talking about consensual or nonconsensual activity? What specific behaviors do they find offensive? If there are claims of involvement by law enforcement, that's easy to check—call the police in that state or town and find out if there was any sort of investigation or if that is a rumor as well.

When and Where? When and where did these events take place? Abuses don't happen in a vacuum. If someone remembered them well enough to share with a third party, that person most likely would recall the approximate date and location as well.

Why? Why would the offender do such a terrible thing? Christopher Lee and Vincent Price made careers out of playing villains who were evil for the sake of being evil, but most people are convinced they are doing the right thing and feel their motivations are perfectly reasonable and sane. And while we're asking the question, what are the motivations of the person or persons bringing this information forward?

An inability or unwillingness to provide specifics is a huge red flag. It suggests your source is mindlessly parroting gossip at best or engaging in an active campaign of smears and whispered innuendo at worst. If you can get a few clear data points, you're in a much better position to corroborate or refute claims. If it turns out the alleged perpetrator was in a different country on the day the "atrocity" took place, or that the "victims" were actually willing participants who found the experience enlightening or even enjoyable, that's one thing. If a little bit of digging reveals a large number of disparate people telling very similar horror stories *about their actual experience while in the group,* that is quite another.

However, all this brings us back to the question of what should be done if you believe that a group is honestly abusive. All too often unpleasant gossip—true or false—is simply passed along. This allows the rumormongers to feel good and virtuous; after all they are actually "doing something to protect the community." Unfortunately, what generally happens is that the story gets repeated to a disapproving audience. People cluck their tongues and shake their heads, but nobody ever takes steps to rescue the victims or to ensure the misbehavior stops. At worst, this can actually work for the abuser. Sociopaths are quick to present themselves as victims of witch wars and smear campaigns. As these tales are passed down, they frequently grow more embellished with each telling, making the original rumormongers look unreliable. Skilled abusers will use the most extreme accounts of their misdeeds as "proof" that all the allegations are ridiculous, and those who have grown tired of endless witch wars often wind up tossing out the baby along with the bathwater. In their quest to avoid ugly gossip, they ignore real issues as well.

If you have *actual evidence that someone is violating the law,* you need to contact the appropriate authorities. Statutory rape, assault, and theft by deception aren't topics for clucking condemnation; they're crimes that need to be handled by the police. Stories about the priest who "initiates" underage people by taking them to bed or the priestess who bilked an elderly couple out of their life savings need to be shared with people wearing badges. If you don't have enough information to take the case to law enforcement, you probably don't have the grounds to spread an idle rumor. If you do, then you need to put the case in the hands of people who can actually do something about the problem.

We understand that you may find dealing with police frightening. Mambo Zetwal Kleye (Kathy Latzoni) points out that abusers frequently try to convince their victims that the authorities will not take them seriously. Getting past this fear can be challenging, but in doing so you may well save a lot of other prospective victims from the suffering you have endured. If you cannot contact the police yourself, you may wish to speak to a social worker, an advocacy group, or someone else who may be able to see that your concerns are addressed.

More common is behavior that falls into the vast gray area of "legal but unethical." You may find a group's leadership to be emotionally abusive to vulnerable members, or you may have issues with the financial and social control they hold over their faithful and fear for those newcomers who fall in with them. Unfortunately, there is very little you can do to protect consenting adults from themselves. What steps you can take are limited, and they may prove ineffective when faced with charismatic abusers or well-meaning but naïve followers.

Should you wish to make your concerns public, we suggest first getting some divination on the subject. It may be that you are not the person to do it or that things are working themselves out quietly to a positive end, and a huge fuss would be the opposite of useful. If the Powers That Be give the go-ahead, go public in a calm and dispassionate way, presenting facts and accounts that support your contentions. But it is quite possible that those who most need to hear your warnings will shut them out or attack you for your "lies." It is also possible (and even likely) that the culprits will respond with innuendo about your motives, if not outright personal attacks. The best approach to this is to stay above the fray. If you can keep your cool while the objects of your concern fall into a frothing rage, they will go a long way toward proving your point.

If you are concerned with spiritual abusers, you can always call on spiritual assistance. The Gods often answer the requests of those who wish to defend the innocent. You can also appeal to their vanity; sins committed in their name reflect badly on them. This is not to say that all prayers will be answered or that prayer is a substitute for taking appropriate actions, but the Gods can pull strings that you can't, and those who would use the Gods for their own selfish reasons may well find themselves on the receiving end of a painful learning experience. Ultimately, however, you must realize that freedom of association works both ways. The rights that allow you to follow a religious path that many consider silly or even evil also allow others to follow leaders whom you find distasteful. You can make your disapproval clear, and you can take steps to distinguish yourself from these groups, but you may also find that the best way of dealing with questionable organizations and leaders is providing seekers with a safe, fulfilling, and nonabusive alternative.

On the other hand, if you are a leader or a member of a group that is the target of unfair lies and rumors—especially if those lies and rumors are happening due to a doctrinal dispute—the first thing you need to do is take a deep breath and remember that everything passes. This is especially true if the scuffle is taking place on the Internet. Do you remember all the "scandals" going around on the Internet ten years ago? Probably not, and most people probably won't remember Internet rumors about you ten years from now. If you are certain that you and your group are doing nothing ethically wrong, then just keep doing it quietly, as if the lies and rumors are not happening. If someone asks you directly, you can explain, but otherwise you look better if you take the high moral ground and don't get involved in the scuffle. Beginning your introductions with "Hi, I'm Joe Pagan, and all the rumors about me are lies" won't inspire confidence in people you meet.

It's also important to remember that graciousness counts. Targeting specific people by name and saying unkind things about them, even if they're saying unkind things about you, doesn't look good either. In almost all cases, your policy should be Do Not Engage. Let others do the engaging—for example, if someone who believes that your practices are evil tries to buttonhole you at a public Pagan event, don't rise to the bait. Avoid eye contact and graciously excuse yourself. If that person continues to harass you, inform the event staff and have them deal with the problem, not you. If someone contacts you about your participation in an event and makes threats or gives insult, don't respond. Instead, copy the correspondence and send it straight to the event staff. If actual threats of harm come, copy them and send them to the police. (If you really want to respond to a message, send a very polite reply thanking the sender for his or her concern and relate that the message has been sent to the proper authorities for perusal.) Most important, make a rule that public bashing of one's bashers is not appropriate for your group. People who aren't involved don't want to hear it, and you don't want to drag yourself or your group publicly down to that level. Remain above the fray and look unruffled until it all blows over—or, as the saying goes, "guard your honor and outlive the bastards."

Most important, start a plan to educate people about your practices and why those practices are sacred and fulfilling to you and the members of your group. Don't aim your education at your detractors—that's a lost cause. Instead, talk to the other billions of people in the world who haven't even heard about your faith yet. Write books, teach classes, and do it all as if you're not being libeled. Remember that Neo-Paganism has gone through a lot of changes in the past fifty years—as does every religion—and that the true test of spiritual belief and praxis isn't what the current people are saying about it, but how it is received ten, or twenty, or fifty years from now. Today, for example, nearly all Wiccan groups are fine with GLBT members, and same-sex Pagan groups are just part of the varied scenery. It's hard to remember that forty years ago, arguments raged regarding whether gay people should even be allowed in heterosexual-polarity-based covens. Time can make reasonably comfortable table-mates, if not bedfellows, of all sorts of Pagan beliefs. Give Time his head and let him do his work.

Neo-Paganism has a wonderful policy, in most cases, of seeing dissenters as a way of "hiving off" and extending our faiths, and we need to keep remembering that this a good thing. (If nothing else, someone else's group is a place for your dissenters to go and not bother you. The late Ed Buczynski, founder of the Minoan Brotherhood, was quoted as saying that when he had dissenters as students, his response was to get them through the Wiccan degree training as quickly and efficiently as possible in order to free them to start their own group.) After all, we are Nature-conscious people, and we know that diversity is survival while monoculture is decline. We just need to remember that when we gaze on people who may have taken our current doctrine in directions that we didn't expect.

17

JUDGING THE MESSAGE IN GROUPS

The Process of Discernment, Part 4

UPG is a great help to our kindred and has inspired others to venture into places that they were scared or hesitant of before. Everyone has become more open and more free to discuss things, which has brought us all closer as a group. I think, overall, the decision to share our experiences was wholly beneficial.

—Mist, Canadian Heathen

Personal gnosis in groups does not always have to be a can of worms—far from it. Many Pagan groups have had positive experiences with incorporating it, once members found a comfortable way to do it that fit with their standards. Divine inspiration can make the difference between a stilted, pedantic ritual and one that calls in a real sense of the numinous. Even the most conservatively structured and heavily delimited groups occasionally find an activity that becomes a small folk custom among their members. Karen Emanuelson, a U.S. Heathen, says, "We've adopted a few cute customs through UPG, such as Odin liking blackberry wine, and that when someone plays the 'Marine Hymn,' one must shout 'Hail Odin!' and drink, because the Old Man is the founder of the Marine Corps."

> *At an earlier point in the Celtic Reconstructionism community, a number of people working separately were given the sense that moss agate has resonance with the Irish Goddess Airmid, who is an herbal healer. It seems to work well in my personal experience and for those who have shared that insight. Nothing in the historical material suggests such a thing was part of Gaelic tradition—there is very little to suggest much work with stones at all—yet many people are getting good results with this particular bit of information. We don't label it as part of the traditional lore, but it does get discussed as part of a Celtic Reconstructionism modern development, and I do think it's been helpful for some folks pursuing healing work within that context.*
>
> **—Erynn Rowan Laurie,**
> **U.S. Celtic Reconstructionist Pagan**

One of the key points seems to be giving the whole thing time. Pushing some piece of personal gnosis too quickly into a group causes more difficulty than taking a slower route. Some people have reported good results with simply putting it out as food for thought, then perhaps discussing over a period of months or years how it works for their personal practice, and then—once it is at least not a brand-new concept—suggesting how it might be incorporated into a small (and perhaps experimental) rite for the group. Being open to divining on the subject, and being patient with other people's negative reactions, also helped.

Other things that may help include accurately and sensitively gauging the willingness of the people in the group to be told what to do, which often is connected with their continuing reaction to the religious group of their upbringing. Being careful not to couch uncertain new beliefs or practices in language that might trigger those memories may ease the initial approach. Groups actively wrestling with the problem also stress how important it is to let all sides be heard, even when only a minority objects. Making sure that all members are listened to and their opinions are given worth, even if they do not prevail in the end, goes a long way toward smoothing disagreements. Enthusiastic people need to remember that many folk just want their opinions to be heard and taken seriously.

It's also possible to find good compromises—"OK, you have a problem with this practice because you're worried about X happening; is there a way that we can structure this to prevent X? Can we add into our ritual prayers or invocations a poetic and spiritually effective way of asking the Universe to prevent X?" Sometimes all people need is a single piece of reassurance, or alternately, a way to gracefully step back from that ritual or practice without being seen as petty, flouncing, or less committed to the community. In addition, it may be deemed important to separate gnosis from political power struggles in the group whenever possible. This can be done by not allowing people to use a person's gnosis as a way to insult that person's general competence. Encouraging disagreeing parties to verbalize each others' good and honorable qualities, even when they continue to disagree about a particular issue, can make people feel less like they are being attacked for their beliefs.

> *I have seen it go right, and that relies heavily on the person supplying the UPG building trust as a nonmanipulative, flexible negotiator who checks his or her sources and signal clarity before jumping in with "but the Gods told me." I've personally found it works better to foster a relationship with a few key members of said group who believe in UPG and trust your ability to discern and dissect what your guides (and Gods) are trying to say in a nonbiased and humble way.*
>
> *I also keep a healthy relationship with my own cynicism. I frequently refer to my own guides as my "imaginary friends," especially when dealing with groups or people who do not*

necessary ascribe to the same thoughts, ideas, and practices as I. They still know what I mean, but it removes that trump card feeling of the Gods Say So. After all, many times UPG is for personal spiritual growth and not really meant to be applied as a new standard of practice for everyone who works with said Deity.

—Del, U.S. Pagan

Another point that seems to make a difference in whether groups are able to smoothly assess and integrate personal gnosis is their willingness to reach out to other groups and people, and ask about their reasoning for integrating or refusing UPG. While no Neo-Pagan tradition is required to adopt the practices of any other tradition, when we become too isolated, we lose out on the hard work done by others. We end up reinventing wheels that could have been easily provided by a simple phone call or e-mail. While the religious beliefs or approaches of other groups may not be for you, those congregants may have valuable experiences with a particular spiritual activity and may have come to a deeper understanding of it, which might have been missed by the people pushing it in your group—especially if it is fairly recent gnosis for them. In addition, practitioners in other groups may specialize in information regarding your question and may have references and resources that you don't.

If group members aren't sure how to handle someone's gnosis, they need to call up those people in the group or out of it who are knowledgeable about the subject. By this, I mean that Joe Smith, who knows very little about the theology of Judaism, who never goes to Temple, and who doesn't honor the Sabbath, has infinitely less right and position to discuss and evaluate a person's Judaic-inspired gnosis than a rabbi. If the person who developed the gnosis was studying Kabbalah, he or she should go to a Kabbalistic scholar to evaluate the gnosis, as not all rabbis are Kabbalists. The authority should

> have a combination of knowledge of the subject matter, respect in the general and specialist community, and learnedness in the applicable lore—including other gnoses.
>
> The gnosis should be discussed and debated, tested and evaluated—but even if there can be no corroboration, the gnosis should remain respected so long as it is consistent with the general teachings. Odin's penchant for purple thongs may neither be contained in the lore nor lie among the general knowledge of those who know and serve Odin, and perhaps he's even told Sara Asatru to buy him yellow V-strings with butterflies on them. The gnosis should remain respected until it can be proven otherwise, even if it's only honored by me. Maybe he decided he likes my purple thongs and Sara's yellow butterfly V-strings; even Gods like variety. Who wants to wear the same underwear every day? BORING. But I may need to be significantly less tied to the knowledge that Odin wears a purple thong and sings in the shower than I am to the idea that Odin knows the spells of life and learned them on the Tree. Really, is the color of his thong so significant? (Besides, everyone knows he goes commando.)
>
> —Aleksa, U.S. Pagan

When things cannot be decided by discussion, it may be best to ask the elders, priests, priestesses, or spiritual leaders to cast a deciding vote. These leaders should have a record of modeling good skills in conflict resolution and disagreeing with respect and courtesy. You may find that the leaders you most trust to judge the issue are ones who have been seen, in the past, to act from both humility and conviction. If they have been able to hold staunchly and visibly to their own code, while openly acknowledging that it is possible that they could be wrong and would alter that code—but only with a huge body of evidence to the contrary—they may be seen as trustworthy enough to make that decision for everyone else.

The Pagan groups that we've spoken to who are actively building in ways to judge gnosis seem to be either groups with a mix of both Reconstructionists (or former Reconstructionists) and general eclectic Pagans—"Reconstructionists, Revivalists, and Revolutionaries!" as one member of Ár nDraíocht Féin, the largest Pagan Druidic group in the U.S., told us—or newer initiatory mystery groups working with spiritualism, possession, and constant attempts at communication with Gods or spirits that require a high level of accuracy in order to keep things safe. In each case, a high percentage of people came to the group not just from different non-Pagan faiths but with existing experience in other Pagan denominations. It may be that the assembling of people who already had deep and varying understandings of Paganism from their own perspectives made it more necessary to come up with a way of sensitively judging each others' gnosis, or the group would simply splinter and fly apart. Sometimes it is under pressure that elements either break or become diamonds.

> *Our grove includes various different pantheons in its highday throughout the year. I am often in charge of the Midsummer ritual, in which we use a Gaulish pantheon. Because there is no extant Gaulish mythology, I am responsible for creating a myth for that particular rite. I have used my own personal gnosis to do this. I have cultivated the presence of the Gaulish Gods Taranos and Artaion, who have become my patrons. Each year, I have increased in my understanding in working with them, and in 2006, the gnosis that one could say I received from them allowed us to do a tremendously successful public magick working. Our Seer has done the same for the annual Imbolc rite in working with Brigidh, and these seem to be the most popular and best-loved rites of the year.*
> **—Julian Greene, ADF Pagan**

> *In ADF, there is no effort (nor any need, that I can see) to judge the validity of UPG. I think it can be assumed that everyone's UPG is basically valid as UPG. To accept it as more*

than that, however, requires comparison with facts, traditions, and others' experiences. If it is found to be reasonably consistent with these, then it may gain a bit more weight, and over time it may even accrue into tradition, becoming PCPG. For example, in ADF rituals, we call in a Deity to fill a role called the "gatekeeper." We have characteristics and traditions associated with this ritual role. A hunch that a certain Deity may make a good gatekeeper may begin as UPG. That choice may gain weight through comparison with facts: if rites with that Deity as gatekeeper always seem to go awry, that's evidence against it; if they go well, that's evidence for it. The choice may gain more weight if ancient traditions link that Deity with gates, travel between worlds, and so forth. It may gain still more weight if others have used that Deity as a gatekeeper with good results. In this way, UPG can become meaningful beyond the individual and can become tradition.

The Deity Manannan has become tradition in this way for Gaelic rites, while Oghma was experimented with but is no longer used much today. This has gained weight by being supported by the following facts: (1) it has consistently worked well over time in many different rituals; (2) it is consistent with historical Gaelic traditions depicting Manannan's character; and (3) it is consistent with a large number of other ADF members' experiences. The gnosis "Manannan makes a good gatekeeper" therefore seems a good candidate for PCPG status. At the same time, the door is always open for other Deities to be experimented with, though they must go through the same process to become something worthy of being called "tradition."

ADF is proud to have one dogma and one only, called the Doctrine of Archdruidic Fallibility. This states that the archdruid can always be wrong. By extension, we can all be wrong sometimes. We are mortals with limitations, and so the question of validity will always be an ongoing discussion.

We can only come to a certain degree of consensus, and that happens in ADF through discussion, debate, and (sometimes) general agreement.

—Brandon, U.S. ADF Pagan

Another important piece of the puzzle, according to the groups we spoke to, was having a preexisting atmosphere where cooperation and teamwork were valued, and where the social "code" emphasized that honesty would be met with appreciation, even when disagreements took place, but that it would be tempered with courtesy. Honesty and courtesy have always been uncomfortable bedfellows, and it is very easy for one of them to kick the other out of bed. They need to be equally valued in the culture of a particular group if that group intends to grow past a tiny, isolated gathering of friends and not splinter apart. People need to be encouraged to speak from a place of consideration for others, but at the same time, people's variant truths must not be met with such scorn and ridicule that they feel forced to remain silent at all times, even at the after-ritual potluck. Few things are sadder to us than when we speak up about something controversial and are shouted down by the loudest voices in the room, and then afterward people timidly come up to thank us for speaking up, because they're afraid to do it themselves.

The main issue, I think is the manner in which these matters are discussed. If one can stick to critiques of an argument that are well stated and completely expressed, rather than personal attacks and sound bites, then these matters can be handled quite easily and without too much difficulty. Frequent expressions of appreciation and admiration for one another, I think, also help to lessen the difficulties involved—as long as everyone feels validated (even if not agreed with) and appreciated, then differences of opinion can exist peacefully. We've succeeded fairly well with this thus far in the Ekklesía, and any dissent or upset over this has not been voiced publicly. Just as I try to emphasize that "this works for me, but it may not for you," I also often say, "Please voice your opinions, positive or negative, on this matter," and in all honesty I rarely get either, but when either one does emerge, those opinions have been handled quite calmly and equitably for the most part.

—P. Sufenas Virius Lupus, Hellenic Pagan

The best experience I had with a gnosis going right for a group was following a pathworking with the Companionship of the Amber Chalice on the contours and patterns of the local land. One member was told by our group "contact" that we should walk the path of Brighton's underground river, the Wellesbourne, which flows on a short course from the north of the city and out to sea next to Brighton Pier. (We are on the south coast of England, so it flows into the Channel.) The source of the Wellesbourne is about seven miles to the northwest, and for the last mile or so it is joined by an equal tributary from the northeast, so our group, then consisting of six, divided with three of us walking one route and three the other. We met at a place called the Level, where the two watercourses join, and then walked the rest of the way together, finishing with a short meditation on the beach followed by a celebratory meal.

Some of us did approach this exercise more seriously than others—the group I was with included the member who had received the message, and we conducted the walk "mindfully," no stopping for snacks or talking about matters not related to the local land and the river. The other group treated it more as a "fun" exercise and needed some persuading to complete the task with a meditation (which had been part of the instruction) before stopping for refreshment! But we did all feel in retrospect that it was a powerful exercise, and I personally have felt very aware of and connected to the flow of the river through the city ever since. In fact, I think that the character of Brighton (as an easygoing, bohemian city where alternative cultures and lifestyles are accepted and celebrated) owes much to this underground watercourse, which cleanses and refreshes the city and discourages stagnation and hidebound conservatism.

—Rose Alba, U.K. Pagan

18

THE ROCKY ROAD TO INTRAFAITH DIALOGUE

As you share your gnosis with others, you will quickly discover that some believe you are divinely inspired and some think you aren't. As others share their gnosis with you, you will find yourself accepting some messages and questioning others. Despite the best efforts of great theologians and scholars, we have not yet achieved universal consensus on the nature of the Divine or on appropriate ways to interact with the Gods. After several thousand years of what the Theosophists called "World Teachers," we have yet to achieve a universally accepted World Religion. If Jesus, Buddha, and Muhammad didn't do it, chances are you won't either.

Here's the good news: nobody expects you to convert the masses—and that includes your Gods. For the most part, Deities are more concerned with behavior than with belief. They don't worry so much about what the masses think or feel as with what they *do*. The reality of particular Gods and their presence are of vital importance to those mystics who work with them. For the mystics who don't have such a relationship, and for those not called to work face-to-face with the Gods, it is much less pressing. Warriors like Ogou and Thor have more respect for courageous atheists than devout cowards. Compassionate Gods such as Kwan Yin are more concerned with your kindness to your fellow human beings than with your theology. It's perfectly fine for most to see their Gods as role models rather than objects of worship.

So long as you present your gnosis to the best of your ability, it will reach those who need to hear. Even those who do not accept it as divinely inspired might well get something out of it. Your words may provide them with food for thought or cause them to explore aspects of your Deity that they might not have considered before. The gnosis may percolate in their subconscious and influence their behavior for the better. Even the very act of rejecting your words may do them good if it forces them to defend their own beliefs and clarify (for themselves or for others) their own thoughts on the Divine.

We may choose not to engage with someone else's personal gnosis, but it may be more difficult for us to wholly disengage from the people who are espousing said gnosis. If we are going to work together as a spiritual community, we need to find ways of dealing with each other, if only socially, and of handling theological disagreements. We are all well aware of dysfunctional interfaith and intrafaith encounters, from the Crusades to suicide bombing. Unfortunately, we are still in the process of developing more productive ways to discuss theological differences and engage in dialogue aimed at mutual understanding and coexistence rather than refutation and conversion.

DIALOGUE, DISAGREEMENT, AND PROSELYTIZING

It is foolish, generally speaking, for a philosopher to set fire to another philosopher in Smithfield Market because they do not agree in their theory of the universe. That was done very frequently in the last decadence of the Middle Ages, and it failed altogether in its object. But there is one thing that is infinitely more absurd and unpractical than burning a man for his philosophy. This is the habit of saying that his philosophy does not matter, and this is done universally in the twentieth century, in the decadence of the great revolutionary

> period. . . . *A man's opinion on tram cars matters; his*
> *opinion on Botticelli matters; his opinion on all things does*
> *not matter. He may turn over and explore a million objects,*
> *but he must not find that strange object, the universe; for*
> *if he does he will have a religion, and be lost. Everything*
> *matters—except everything.*
>
> **—Gilbert K. Chesterton**[1]

Many who have come to their new spiritual path from Christianity—
and Neo-Paganism is by and large a religion of converts—have a great
distaste for anything that smacks of proselytizing. To them, saying "I
am right and you are wrong" is akin to proclaiming "If you don't repent,
you're going to burn in hell." Those who disagree with someone else's
spiritual beliefs, or even ask too many uncomfortable questions, are
scorned as intolerant "fundies." "Acceptance of opinions" and "tolerance
of diversity" are all-important, even if couched in smug, condescending
passive-aggression. Discussion is reduced to bland platitudes about how
we are all special snowflakes, and everything we say and believe should
be cherished as valuable. Instead of honest and critical discussion, we
get pats on the head and gold stars for our efforts.

Discussion involves an exchange of ideas and discourse about their
ramifications. It may get intense, even heated at times, but this is fine
so long as everyone remains respectful and the questions focus on ideas
rather than individuals. Smiling, nodding, and saying "Everyone's
truths are true for them, and every belief is just as good as every other
belief" is not interfaith discussion. Rather, it is a way of avoiding questions about the substance and foundation of your beliefs and about the
level of your commitment. Instead of sparking conversation, it shuts it
down or reduces it to polite superficialities.

Disagreement need not involve proselytizing. It may actually be a
good way of establishing boundaries and setting forth the differences
between your respective beliefs. No Orthodox rabbi will accept that G-d
has a son or that the Qur'an is an improved version of the Torah. That
doesn't mean that he cannot have cordial relations with local Christian

or Muslim leaders or that they cannot engage in honest and sincere dialogue about each other's beliefs. They might wish to understand each other so they could help defuse difficulties between their congregations. They might check in when they've heard some inflammatory "fact" on the Internet. ("So could you explain *jihad* for me, Imam? Then maybe I can shut this putz up once and for all.") Or they might just be curious—if you're spiritually inclined enough to become a member of the clergy, chances are you're interested in talking shop with others in the industry.

This kind of discourse has been going on among representatives of mainstream religious denominations for centuries. They are not afraid to ask each other tough questions, nor do they expect their colleagues to agree with them on every theological point. Many of them have learned to engage in dialogue without the specter of conversion raising its ugly head; they can find value in other religions without feeling the need to become adherents and can recognize that value without denigrating their own faith. Certainly we find groups within these faiths that are skeptical of and even openly hostile to ecumenical efforts, but as their communities and neighborhoods grow more diverse, they have become increasingly marginalized. We are moving, slowly, into a world of civil interfaith interactions, whether everyone likes it or not.

A cursory glance suggests that Neo-Paganism is considerably more tolerant than many of these traditions, yet a look at the demographics of American Neo-Paganism indicates that we may have a long way to go. As a movement, American Neo-Paganism remains overwhelmingly white, college educated, middle class, and politically liberal. There is less political, economic, and ethnic diversity at an average Pagan gathering than at a typical mosque. All too often, "tolerance" has been extended only to people who do not challenge preconceptions, make waves in the community, or insist on "playing the race card" by pointing out uncomfortable facts. Christian-bashing is rampant in Neo-Paganism, something we must overcome as a community if we are to participate in interfaith dialogue. At the very least, we can start by learning tolerance and appreciation for differences in *intrafaith* discussions. We've all seen it done badly; let's prove that we can do better.

If we are going to engage with gnosis in our greater community, we need to learn how to deal with theological differences. We have to move beyond tolerance into inclusion. Instead of the bland sameness of a "melting pot" in which all beliefs are boiled down into an inoffensive mush, we must recognize the value of diversity and difference. However, if we are going to learn how to deal with the beliefs of others, we must first figure out just what we ourselves believe.

GOOD FENCES AND GOOD NEIGHBORS

One of the ways I've tried to bridge the gap of understanding is by saying something like, "Look, in my experience the Gods are real and do interact with human beings, sometimes very dramatically. You don't have to share my belief, but you should know that this is where I'm coming from."

If they persist in talking down to me or trying to get me to admit I'm wrong, then I respond with something like, "Thanks, but I'm secure in my faith and I don't feel inclined to change my point of view." As I said above, it isn't my job to hand-hold people, and if my refusal to adopt their worldview threatens them, it's their issue, not mine.

—Elizabeth Vongvisith,
U.S. Northern Tradition Pagan

If we are going to have discussions about faith, it may be wise to start not with finding common ground but instead by determining the places where our views are irreconcilably different. This allows us to establish boundary markers between our beliefs. If I am a hard polytheist who believes in the existence of many Gods, and you are an atheist who believes in none, that is an insurmountable gap. We may be able to discuss the reasons why we each came to our respective conclusions, but chances are that neither will be able to sway the other. And that is perfectly fine, as this is a discussion and not a debate. We're not trying to score points or win converts, but rather to understand each other's position more clearly, so that we can better extrapolate and understand each other's future actions and needs.

This process of defining these boundaries can be painful for many people. When you state your beliefs, you run the risk of encountering disagreement. People might tell you that you are mistaken, silly, even crazy. Those who grew up in dysfunctional environments may have learned that their opinion doesn't matter. Trying to get your group to come up with a joint statement of belief can be like nailing custard to a wall. Disagreements can arise, and feelings can be hurt. It's difficult to avoid the notion that you're arguing over a variation of how many angels can dance on the head of a pin. Because we can't confirm these answers in the same way we can confirm a mathematical proof or a scientific experiment, at the end of the day it all comes down to one strongly held opinion against another. There's a reason that many etiquette experts advise steering clear of discussions about politics or religion at family gatherings.

Perhaps more intimidating is that in setting these boundaries we must define our beliefs. Most of us would rather hold on to the soothing aspects of our personal mythologies and gloss over the more challenging features. If we accept that the Gods are real, then we must engage with their less flattering aspects. If the stories about Zeus the Sky Father and wise ruler are true, what about the tales that paint him as a serial rapist? How does Ogou the brave warrior relate to Ogou the savage killer who swims in rivers of blood? If we decide the Gods are our own creations, then why are we spending all this time and energy on our imaginary friends? Wouldn't we be better off admitting that the Universe is a soulless, mechanistic place, wherein injustices go unpunished and evil is often rewarded, instead of wasting our time with fairy tales? These are not easy questions for which we can find pat answers, but they are questions we cannot avoid if we want our spirituality to be something more than an entertaining diversion.

Nobody can "prove" that the Gods exist independently, that they are all human creations, that they are all emanations of Spirit, or that they are all silly myths holding us back from Progress and Science. But we can take our beliefs and draw them out to their logical conclusions, then examine the differences between presupposition A and presupposition B. We can point to the reasons we have arrived at our respective conclusions and point to flaws or problems we see with the other person's conclusions. In response, the other person might point out places where we have misunderstood his or her beliefs or point out issues he or she had with ours. This is an integral part of any honest interfaith or intrafaith dialogue: if beliefs are worth holding, they are worth defending. Yet, we *can* disagree on theological issues without resorting to violence, whether physical or verbal; there are upright, moral people to be found in all faith communities. You can accept the person, or the group, without accepting the gnosis. (This, of course, works both ways. A group might think you're a perfectly charming person who has a great deal to offer without accepting your UPG as valid.) Time will show who was right and who was wrong—or time will lead to different denominations that respect each other but that disagree on articles of doctrine.

Articles of faith need not be commandments written in stone, but they can be very useful as guidelines for prospective members and as informational statements for curious nonmembers. These can be as simple as "We honor the Olympians and believe the Gods we serve are the same Gods who were served in ancient Greece," or "We find power, wisdom, and strength in the divine and heroic archetypes of pre-Christian northern Europe," or even "We consider the nature of the Gods to be a mystery and welcome all who wish to reverently and respectfully explore that mystery." By putting your beliefs into writing, you provide a focal point for your future spiritual work and let people know how you approach your Gods.

INCLUSION AND EXCLUSION

As you continue working with personal gnosis and incorporating it into your group, some of you may find that it draws you closer to your Gods. Others may grow increasingly cynical, and some may even begin treating your gnosis with scorn or open contempt. This is often a reaction born out of fear. The idea that the Gods might intervene in the daily lives of their worshippers can be terrifying. Ridicule can be a less discomforting response than accepting a message and all its ramifications. At other times, an unenthusiastic reaction may denote a healthy skepticism with roots in previous negative experiences. After being burned by hucksters claiming divine justification, people may find it very difficult indeed to trust those who say they are speaking with Deities. But regardless of the motivations, gnosis can rip a group apart in a spectacularly messy fashion.

If you are skeptical about the contents of some of or all of the gnosis being presented to your group, you may first want to ask yourself how the truth or falsity of this gnosis affects you. Do you think it is actively harmful or merely silly? Are you afraid other groups might ostracize you or marginalize your organization as fluffy, kooky, or any of the other adjectives frequently thrown about in Pagan flame wars? Is it interfering with your relationship with the other members who have accepted it? Why do you think it is or might be false? The more clearly you can answer these questions for yourself, the more clearly you can raise your objections before the group.

When you speak out, you should express your feelings in an honest but polite fashion. Explain the reasons for your concern; be critical of ideas and actions but try to avoid attacking people. ("I disagree with statement X" is good. "You're a bunch of delusional idiots" is bad.) If your problem is that you reject out of hand the idea of conversations between humans and Gods, then you have hit one of those boundary markers we discussed earlier. It's unlikely that you and your group will be able to achieve consensus on the question. Alternately, if you are open to the possibility but doubtful about the gnosis your group is accepting, you should be clear about what parts of the message bother you and why. If your group members close ranks and treat honest questions with hostility, then there's a problem with their behavior no matter where the messages in question originate. If they are willing to discuss the issue, but you are unable to resolve your differences, you need to consider your options.

If you have a friendly working relationship and can agree to disagree, you may be able to continue as a member no matter how you feel about the gnosis. Many who attend mainstream churches do so for the social benefits and the feeling of community. So long as you can treat the rest of the congregation with respect, this may work for you as well. If you are unable to do so, or if your group insists that all members accept these revelations as a condition of continued membership, then your wisest course of action may be a polite departure.

DO THE GODS NEED YOUR DEFENSE?

Today, words like *reverence* and *respect* make many people uncomfortable. Kneeling before the Gods is groveling in fear, while condemning disrespect of the Gods is bigotry and intolerance. The ranting of online trolls is "free speech" that must be protected by law, and holy scriptures of any religion are silly superstitions that can be mocked at will. Yet historically in many cultures, blasphemy was a far more serious crime than murder. The drunken thug who slew his friend in a tavern brawl killed an individual, while the blasphemer threatened the very underpinnings of the society.

On the other hand, if we believe the Gods are real, should we consider the possibility that they may find certain words or actions to be intolerable insults? On rare occasions when we engage them in conversation, we may be told that certain people or groups have offended them. This does not mean we are to bomb their homes, send them threatening messages, or act out in any of the other ways people have responded to what they perceived as "blasphemy." At most, it may mean that we are told to dissociate from a particular group or to avoid a person who persists in treating our Gods with disrespect. It may also mean that we are called to defend our Gods, but we need to think hard about how we are to do that.

As we pointed out in previous chapters, if you slant your divine message in such a way that it will not be accepted by its intended audience—and especially if the distracting slant is coming from your own anger or contempt, righteous or otherwise—you have dishonored the message. If it was really entrusted to you, you owe it to the Gods to think about how it will be received and do your best to present it in as clean and nonjudgmental a way as possible. If you intend for this message to last for decades or even centuries, and perhaps be added to the common canon of Pagan writings, it would behoove you to be careful of (or perhaps omit entirely) any references to specific individuals or groups who you consider to be "offending the Gods." Remember that sixty years from now, that will be considered a quaint historical quarrel that has little bearing on contemporary worship . . . and you want to be remembered for your message, not your infighting. Simply speak the truth about your beliefs as you understand them, and leave it at that.

This may make you unpopular in some quarters. To be a speaker for the Gods is never an easy task, and it is not to be undertaken lightly. We advise divination, meditation, and prayer when charged with such a duty. It is vital that you make sure you are speaking by divine command, not out of personal indignation or self-righteousness. But if you are going to share the words of your Gods with the world, don't be surprised if some of those words cause hard feelings. You can present the words as politely and as fairly as you can, but be advised that the Gods have a way of pushing the required buttons no matter how much you sugarcoat their message.

If you or your group members have found yourselves on the receiving end of one of these condemnations, you may have responded with defensive anger. You may have thought your critic was being judgmental and overly harsh; you may have suggested that he or she grow a sense of humor and get a life. But you may be well-served to consider those words yet again, especially if they still sting the way unvarnished truth often does. Sometimes the most valuable lessons we receive from the Gods are the most difficult. Ego projections tend to puff up your vanity, and divine contacts are quick to deflate that ego when it gets in the way of the tasks set before you. Probably the best option is for you to breathe, put aside the issue, and check again in six months or more. If you find that you were wrong, there's a great deal of honor in admitting it, because it will encourage others to do the same in their own time.

Acceptance of gnosis can bind us together as believers. But even if we reject gnosis and those who bring it, we still owe responsibilities of hospitality and courtesy. In the Hellenic world, *philoxenia* (friendship to the stranger) laid moral and material obligations on hosts when travelers came to their house, and on the guests who accepted their hospitality. Similar traditions can be found in areas as disparate as northern Europe and the Arabian Desert. Those who do not worship as we do may not be our spiritual kinfolk, but we nevertheless are required to treat them with the respect and consideration due any stranger who comes in peace. Courtesy is more than vapid pleasantries, and "inclusion" can happen only when we take seriously those we seek to include. If that involves debate and disagreement, then let us debate as comrades and disagree as friends.

EPILOGUE

The Future of Peer-Corroborated
Personal Gnosis

Chuang-tzu and a friend were walking on a bridge over a river. Chuang-tzu looked down and exclaimed with a smile, "Look how happy the fish are splashing in the stream!" His friend said, "You are not a fish, how do you know they are happy?" Chuang-tzu grinned back and said, "You are not me, how you do know that I do not know that the fish are happy?"[1]

If you look closely at the history of most—if not all—mainstream religions, you will see a highway behind them littered with the discarded and suppressed ideas of past idealists, mystics, and random subgroups. Some of these concepts and practices were discarded for good reason—for example, they promoted or justified the abuse of humans by other humans. We may all be glad to get rid of those spiritual beliefs, but those make up only a small percentage of the total. Most of the rest either vanished because their proponents died and the fruit of their divine connection was lost, or because it was deliberately suppressed by existing religious edifices whose people were determined not to give believers a choice in their beliefs.

In Neo-Paganism, we pride ourselves on freedom of thought,

sometimes to the overcompensation point—we may reject practices that are associated in our minds with religious constriction, even when they are not constricting in and of themselves. On the other hand, we are a widely varied demographic with attitudes that range from (as we've indicated in multiple areas in this book) "Just let everyone do what they want, and don't analyze it" to "There's our way and then there's the wrong way, and there's no discussing it." What these two stances have in common is that they both thrive on a lack of open, thoughtful discussion. We've historically shied from those discussions because we don't want to have to disagree with each other . . . mostly because we have so few models of courteous, thoughtful, and even appreciative religious disagreement. After a thousand years of watching people slaughter, beat down, and vilify each other over theological differences, we are like children of a dysfunctional family whose understanding of how to deal with conflict in a relationship is limited to either smiling denial or screaming, vicious battery.

Yet, of all religious persuasions, it seems to us that Pagans have one of the best chances for learning otherwise, even if we did grow up in a world of dysfunctional models. We live in an era when such things can be questioned. In most of the Western world, at least, we do have freedom of religion and speech to an extent that people a couple of centuries ago could never have conceptualized. We live in an era when it is no longer acceptable to kill your neighbors to eliminate their differing gnosis. Technology has made communication of ideas fast and pervasive. And with modern technology, a message that once might have taken centuries to spread now can be broadcast worldwide with a few keystrokes.

In addition, our variability of ideas and practices means that in order to survive in cooperation with each other, we must in self-defense step beyond the mistakes of the other faiths that have risen before us. In a very real way, they made those bloody mistakes for us, so that we don't have to repeat them. It is in the best interests of everyone in the Pagan demographic to think, very hard, about the issues raised in this book and figure out a compassionate way to handle them before we fall into those past errors. (And for small groups in this demographic who would prefer to remain isolated and learn nothing from any other group, we quote Benjamin Franklin: If we do not hang together, we will most assuredly all hang separately.) We'd like to see the Pagan demographic as a proving ground to show that it is possible for human beings to explore these touchy subjects together and still be kind to each other.

> *I agree that discussion and close examination of personal gnosis and shared gnosis is vital within communities. These insights may be useful for the community, or they may have nothing whatsoever to do with it. They may later be found to be firmly within the tradition when further research is undertaken, and that corroboration is a very exciting feeling.*
>
> *I do not, however, think that people should be shouted down and silenced for expressing opinions that fall outside of a tradition's mainstream. Mystics are always outside the mainstream of a tradition; there is no religion that I'm aware of where every member was a mystic. Outlying voices have almost always been regarded with suspicion because of their potential challenge to established authority and orthodoxy.*
>
> *If people are not comfortable discussing the results of their meditations and their visionary work, they are not likely to be able to connect with others getting the same or similar results. Nor is it likely that they'll just stumble across corroborating facts from the scholarly end of the tradition. I see discussions about personal gnosis as a necessary part of collaboration within a community and a way of sorting the wheat from the chaff. I see it as a necessary part of the growth and maturation of a community. Without these discussions, the community can only stagnate.*
>
> **—Erynn Rowan Laurie,**
> **U.S. Celtic Reconstructionist Pagan**

The message that we hold out at the end of this book is one of hope. We can, as a demographic, learn to share our personal gnosis in ways that are thoughtful and do not castigate the beliefs of others, but merely offer an alternative. We can learn to receive other people's gnosis equally thoughtfully, and not react to disagreements from a place of fear and insecurity. Let us say it one more time, clearly: If even one person in your spiritual group, in your tradition, or in your entire demographic is forced into silence about his or her relationship with the Gods because that person rightly fears hostility and contempt, you are failing. We won't say *you have failed,* because the problem is eminently redeemable. We just need to act like the mature adults who we claim to be, even in the face of the one topic that is most often banned at the dinner table.

Back at the beginning of this book, we defined the term *peer-corroborated personal gnosis,* and it is to this term that we return now. We believe that Pagans can figure out a system to upgrade more UPG to PCPG, because our faiths and our nascent values are a good test site for this experiment in spiritual connection. We also believe that once we've managed it, we will have something very special to offer to the world, and to those who will come after us. This term also implies that we can, if we try, learn more of the mysteries than we know today. Certainly our ancestors worked hard to study the mysteries and the beings that stand behind the veil; our religion exists today due to their hard work. What new understanding of the mysteries will we leave the Pagans of the future? It's something we'd all better start working on now.

> *Personal gnosis lives in a fun, shifting balance/dance with tradition and structure. It's like good poetry. Excellent poetry is made up of inspiration, talent, "that wild, silky part of ourselves without which no poem can live." (Quoted from* A Poetry Handbook, *by Mary Oliver, greatest living poet in the United States.) But if it stops there, a poem is inaccessible, often ridiculous, full of mess, an inspired but unrealized dream. The other half of a truly excellent poem is work—form, structure, discipline, knowledge. It's knowing how a good poem works—sound, rhetoric, passion, word choice— and the ability to apply that knowledge in order to take that raw beauty and shape it into something brilliant, readable,*

shareable, something that possesses both strength and grace. Of course, poetry without the wild, silky parts is boring. So, absolutely, I would give up everything for those delicious, sweet revelations from the core of my blood, the ancestors, the Gods (Io Dionysos! Io Euoi!)—but I know that they cannot exist in a way that is useful and authentic, connected and rich, unless they are grounded in and balanced by structure and tradition.

—Ruby Sara, U.S. Neo-Pagan

NOTES

INTRODUCTION: RECLAIMING OUR GODS, RECONSTRUCTING OUR FAITH

1. Ambrose Bierce, *The Unabridged Devil's Dictionary,* eds. David Shultz and S. T. Joshi (Athens: University of Georgia Press, 2001), 108.
2. Gabi Greve, "Sujinsama, the God of Water," Darumasan-Japan, http://groups.yahoo.com/group/Darumasan-Japan/message/496 (accessed September 20, 2011).
3. C. S. Lewis, *The Essential C.S. Lewis,* ed. Lyle Dorsett (New York: Simon and Schuster, 1996), 40.
4. Aleister Crowley, *Liber 777 vel Prolegomena Symbolica ad Systemam Skeptico-Mysticæ viæ Explicandæ Fundamentum Hieroglyphicum Sanctisimorum Scientæ Summæ* (York Beach, Maine: Weiser, 1986), ii.
5. Friedrich Nietzsche, *The Birth of Tragedy out of the Spirit of Music* (1872; Ian Johnston translation, 2009), Johnstonia, http://records.viu.ca/~johnstoi/nietzsche/tragedy_all.htm (accessed September 12, 2011).
6. Ibid.

CHAPTER 4. LEGENDS, LORE, AND LIVING FAITH: ON PRIMARY SOURCES AND HOLY WRIT

1. Syed Mumtaz Ali, "Sama Mystical Music," Deen Islam Western Sufi Resource Guide, 2000, www.deenislam.co.uk/mix/sama.html (accessed November 27, 2011).
2. Shukavak N. Dasa, "A Hindu Primer: Do Hindus Worship Idols?" Sri

Devasthenam Sanskrit Religious Center, 2007, www.sanskrit.org/www/Hindu Primer/idols.html (accessed November 27, 2011).

3. Tracey R. Rich, "Yiddish Language and Culture," Judaism 101, 2004–11, www.jewfaq.org/yiddish.htm (accessed November 25, 2011).

4. Anya Kless, "Samael, God of the Left Hand," Fruit of Pain, February 11, 2011, http://fruitofpain.wordpress.com/2011/02/11/samael-god-of-the-left-hand (accessed November 30, 2011).

5. Kinjou Ten, "Otakukin," Temple of the Ota'Kin, 2002, http://otakukin.otherkin.net (accessed November 28, 2011).

6. L. Allen and D. Woolsey, "Tië eldaliéva: the Elven Path," Tië eldaliéva: The Hidden Realm, 2005–2007, www.lassiquendi.com/TheHiddenRealm (accessed November 28, 2011).

7. Colin Clark, *My Week with Marilyn* (New York: Weinstein Books, 2011), 58.

8. Duane Varan, "Television, Culture and State: New Forums for Negotiating Identity in the Pacific," *Continuum: The Australian Journal of Media and Culture* 8, no. 2 (1994), http://wwwmcc.murdoch.edu.au/ReadingRoom/8.2/Varan.html (accessed December 5, 2011).

9. Ibid.

10. Vikas Basaj, "In India, the Golden Age of Television Is Now," *New York Times,* February 11, 2007, www.nytimes.com/2007/02/11/business/yourmoney/11india.html (accessed December 6, 2011).

11. Helen A. Berger, "Are Solitaries the Future of Paganism?" Patheos Pagan Portal, August 23, 2010, www.patheos.com/Resources/Additional-Resources/Solitaries-The-Future-Of-Paganism?print'1 (accessed December 6, 2011).

CHAPTER 5.
DELUSIONS, LIES, AND SKEPTICISM

1. Chuck Fager, "Fraud: Greater Ministries Leaders Get Lengthy Prison Terms," Christianity Today, October 1, 2001, www.christianitytoday.com/ct/2001/october1/15.21.html (accessed January 1, 2012).

2. Doreen Valiente, "Charge of the Goddess" (written in the mid-1950s), The Doreen Valiente Foundation, http://doreenvaliente.org/doreen-valientes-poems/poem-the-charge-of-the-goddess (accessed January 2, 2012).

3. Jason R. Cohen, "Fwd: [LR] I Do Not Want to Live," Latter_Rain, May 25, 2011, http://groups.yahoo.com/group/Latter_Rain/message/48790 (accessed January 2, 2012).

4. Joshuah Bearman, "Heaven's Gate: The Sequel," *LA Weekly,* March 21, 2007, http://web.archive.org/web/20070701033109/http://www.laweekly.com/general/features/heavens-gate-the-sequel/15930/ (accessed January 2, 2012).

5. Chris Nelson, "A Brief History of the Apocalypse: The Early Days: 2800 BC–1700 AD," A Brief History of the Apocalypse, 2011, www.abhota.info/end1.htm (accessed January 2, 2012).

6. B. A. Robinson, "Predictions of the End of the World by Jehovah's Witnesses," Ontario Consultants on Religious Tolerance, 2003, www.religioustolerance.org/witness8.htm (accessed January 2, 2012).

7. Watch Tower Bible and Tract Society of Pennsylvania, "Our History and Organization," Jehovah's Witnesses Official Media Website, www.jw-media.org/aboutjw/article41.htm#membership (accessed January 2, 2012).

8. Patricia Cohen, "Reason Seen More as Weapon Than Path to Truth," *New York Times,* June 14, 2011, www.nytimes.com/2011/06/15/arts/people-argue-just-to-win-scholars-assert.html?_r=2&pagewanted=all (accessed January 2, 2012).

CHAPTER 6. SO WHO CAN BE A MYSTIC?

1. C. S. Lewis, *Till We Have Faces: A Myth Retold* (New York: Houghton Mifflin Harcourt, 1980), 249.

2. Richard S. Epstein, *Keeping Boundaries* (Arlington, Va.: American Psychiatric Publications, 1994), 54–55.

3. Lynne McTaggart, *The Intention Experiment* (New York: Simon and Schuster, 2008), 78.

4. Sudhir Kakar, "Ramakrishna and the Mystical Experience" in *The Annual of Psychoanalysis,* eds. Jerome Winer and Benjamin Garber (London: Routledge, 1992), 225.

5. Tobin Hart and Amy Waddell, "Spiritual Issues in Counseling and Psychotherapy: Toward Assessment and Treatment," http://66.160.135.235/acrobat/hart_and_waddell.pdf (accessed June 11, 2009).

6. Beverly Engel, *Loving Him without Losing You: How to Stop Disappearing and Start Being Yourself* (New York: John Wiley and Sons, 2000), 43–44.

7. Ernest Hartmann, "Paths to Peace," Tufts University, November 21, 2003, www. tufts.edu/~ehartm01/Boundaries%20and%20peace.doc (accessed June 11, 2009).

8. Evelyn Underhill, "Mysticism and Psychology," part one, section III in *Mysticism: A Study in Nature and Development of Spiritual Consciousness,* Christian Classics Ethereal Library, www.ccel.org/ccel/underhill/mysti cism.iii.iii.html (accessed June 12, 2009).

9. Jess Byron Hollenbeck, *Mysticism: Experience, Response and Empowerment* (University Park, Pa.: Penn State University Press, 1996), 422.

10. Hazrat Inayat Khan, "The Mystic's Nature," in *Philosophy, Psychology and Mysticism,* Wahiduddin's Web, http://wahiduddin.net/mv2/XI/XI_III_17. htm (accessed June 12, 2009).

11. Louis Proal, *Passion and Criminality in France: A Legal and Literary Study,* trans. A. R. Allinson (Paris: Charles Carrington, 1901), 425.

12. Saint Teresa of Avila, chap. XXIX in *Autobiography,* Catholic First, www .catholicfirst.com/thefaith/catholicclassics/stteresa/life/teresaofavila07 .html#CHAPTER XXIX (accessed June 15, 2009).

CHAPTER 7. JUDGING THE MESSAGE BY YOURSELF: THE PROCESS OF DISCERNMENT, PART I

1. Saint Anselm of Canterbury, chap. I in *Proslogium,* trans. Sidney Norton Deane (1903), Christian Classics Ethereal Library, www.ccel.org/ccel/ anselm/basic_works.iii.ii.html (accessed December 26, 2011).

2. Rabbi Nechemia Coopersmith, "Does Belief in God Require a Leap of Faith?" Kiruv.com, June 30, 2008, http://oldsite.kiruv.com/SSI/art icleToPrint.asp?PageURL=/teachingMaterials/Shmooze/Faith_and_ Knowledge0.xml&teaser=Does+belief+in+God+require+a+leap+of+faith %3F. (accessed September 27, 2012).

3. John M. Riddle, *Contraception and Abortion from the Ancient World to the Renaissance* (Cambridge, Mass.: Harvard University Press, 1992), 25–26.

CHAPTER 8. MAD WISDOM: MENTAL ILLNESS AND PERSONAL GNOSIS

1. Sally Clay, "Old & Crazy," Zangmo Blue Thundercloud, 1996, www.sal lyclay.net/Z.text/Old.html (accessed December 29, 2011).

CHAPTER 9. SIGNAL CLARITY:
HEARING THE DIVINE VOICE

1. Galina Krasskova, "On Prayer: A Heathen Perspective," Patheos, December 15, 2010, www.patheos.com/Resources/Additional-Resources/On-Prayer-A-Heathen-Perspective-Galina-Krasskova.html?print=1 (accessed January 1, 2012).

2. Greek Orthodox Metropolitan Diocese of Atlanta, "The Jesus Prayer," 2009, www.orthodoxprayer.org/Jesus Prayer.html (accessed January 1, 2012).

3. Bhagavad Gita, trans. S. Radhakrishnan (Hammersmith, U.K.: Harper-Thorsons, 1995), verses 6.10–14.

4. Mickey Hart, *Drumming at the Edge of Magic* (New York: HarperCollins, 1990), 118–19.

5. Ibid.

6. Penny Petrone, *Northern Voices: Inuit Writing in English* (Toronto: University of Toronto Books, 1992), 116–17.

7. Dairy Council of California, "Portion Distortion: Serving Sizes Are Growing," Meals Matter, 2011, www.mealsmatter.org/Articles-And-Resources/Healthy-Living-Articles/Portion-Distortion.aspx (accessed December 30, 2011).

8. Peter Berresford Ellis, "A Hunger for Justice," Irish Democrat, 2006, www.irishdemocrat.co.uk/features/a-hunger-for-justice (accessed December 31, 2011).

9. Paul Reps, ed., *Zen Flesh, Zen Bones* (London: Penguin Books, 1982), 43.

10. Osho. "The Seeker Has to Be Silent, Then God Speaks," Osho Teachings, Osho Discourses, 2010, www.oshoteachings.com/osho-the-seeker-has-to-be-silent-then-god-speaks/ (accessed December 25, 2011).

11. Simon Holloway, "Thoughts from the Silence: A Vipassana Review," Davar Akher, December 26, 2010, http://benabuya.com/2010/12/26/thoughts-from-the-silence-a-vipassana-review/ (accessed December 25, 2011).

12. Ibid.

13. The Russian Primary Chronicle, trans. and eds. Samuel Hazzard Cross and Olgerd P. Sherbowitz-Wetzor (Cambridge, Mass.: Medieval Academy of America, 1953). Available at University of Toronto, www.utoronto.ca/elul/English/218/PVL-selections.pdf (accessed September 28, 2012).

14. Albert Hofmann, "The Discovery of LSD and Subsequent Investigations on Naturally Occurring Hallucinogens," chap. 7 in *Discoveries in Biological Psychiatry,* eds. Frank J. Ayd, Jr., and Barry Blackwell (Philadelphia: J. B. Lippincott, 1970). Available at Psychedelic Library, www.psychedelic -library.org/hofmann.htm (accessed December 29, 2011).

15. Blynn Garland Bunney, William E. Bunney, Jr., and Arvid Carlsson, "Schizophrenia and Glutamate: An Update," *Psychopharmacology: The Fourth Generation of Progress, 2000,* www.acnp.org/g4/gn401000116/ch114.html (accessed December 30, 2011).

16. Ben Paynter, "The Big Business of Synthetic Highs," *Bloomberg Businessweek,* June 16, 2011, www.businessweek.com/magazine/content/11_26/b4234058348635.htm (accessed December 30, 2011).

17. Danny Nemu, "U.K. Ayahuasca Prosecution Concludes with a Verdict of Guilty," Bia Labate, August 8, 2011, www.bialabate.net/news/uk-ayahuasca-prosecution-concludes-with-a-verdict-of-guilty (accessed December 30, 2011).

18. liftyourskinnyfists, "the Void, the Hospital and the Cops: experience with Amanitas—A. muscaria (ID 51941)," Erowid.org, June 15, 2006, www.erowid.org/experiences/exp.php?ID=51941.

CHAPTER 11. SILENCE AND FAITH

1. Carole Zaleski, "The Dark Night of Mother Teresa," *First Things,* May 2003, www.firstthings.com/article/2007/08/the-dark-night-of-mother-teresa-42 (accessed December 23, 2011).

2. Elizabeth Lev, "Mother Teresa Endured God's Silence," *Catholic Insight,* October 2007, http://catholicinsight.com/online/features/printer_752.shtml (accessed December 23, 2011).

CHAPTER 12. NEO-PAGANISM AND ITS ATTITUDES

1. Galina Krasskova, "Race, Gender, and the Problem of Ergi in Modern Heathenry," in *Essays in Modern Heathenry II* (Hubbardston, Mass.: Asphodel Press, 2012), 60–61.

2. Personal communication. Conversation with Gythia (Priestess) Elizabeth Vongvisith.

CHAPTER 13. HISTORICAL PRECEDENTS:
GNOSIS IN ANCIENT TIMES

1. Peter Gray, "Play Makes Us Human V: Why Hunter-Gatherers' Work Is Play," *Psychology Today,* July 2, 2009, www.psychologytoday.com/print/30523 (accessed January 8, 2012).

2. Roberte N. Hayamon, "Shamanism in Siberia: From Partnership in Supernature to Counter-power in Society," in *Shamanism, History and the State* (Ann Arbor: University of Michigan Press, 1996), 80–81.

3. Sandra Scham, "The World's First Temple," *Archaeology* 61, no. 6 (November–December 2008), www.archaeology.org/0811/abstracts/turkey.html (accessed January 8, 2012).

4. M. Charlesworth, "Introduction," in *Religion in Aboriginal Australia: An Anthology,* 2nd ed., ed. M. Charlesworth, D. Bell, H. Morphy, and K. Maddock (Saint Lucia, Australia: University of Queensland Press, 1992). Available at International Theology Reading List, http://theology1.tripod.com/readings/charlesworth.htm (accessed January 9, 2012).

5. John Zerzan, "Agriculture: Demon Engine of Civilization," The Anthropik Network, 1998, http://rewild.info/anthropik/library/zerzan/demon-engine-of-civilization/index.html (accessed January 9, 2012).

6. Dua-Khety, "The Instruction of Dua-Khety" (Adolf Erman translation, 1927), Kibbutz Reshafim, www.reshafim.org.il/ad/egypt/texts/instructions_of_kheti.htm (accessed January 9, 2012).

7. John Aberth, *From the Brink of the Apocalypse: Confronting War, Famine, Plague and Death in the Later Middle Ages* (London: Routledge, 2000), 13–14.

8. Ross Kraemer, "Ecstasy and Possession: The Attraction of Women to the Cult of Dionysos," *Harvard Theological Review* 72, no. 1 (1979): 78.

9. Robin Waterfield, *Why Socrates Died: Dispelling the Myths* (New York: W. W. Norton, 2009), 26–44.

10. Anthony Spalinger, "The Limitations of Formal Ancient Egyptian Religion," *Journal of Near Eastern Studies* 57, no. 4 (1988): 252.

11. Giovanni de Plano Carpini, "The Destruction of Kiev" (1246), University of Toronto Research Repository, https://tspace.library.utoronto.ca/citd/RussianHeritage/4.PEAS/4.L/12.III.5.html (accessed January 10, 2012).

12. Anne Llewellyn Barstow, "Joan of Arc and Female Mysticism," *Journal of Feminist Studies in Religion* 1, no. 2 (Fall 1985): 33–36.

13. Giorgio de Santillana, *The Crime of Galileo* (Chicago: University of Chicago Press, 1955), 310.

14. Galileo Gallilei, *Dialogue Concerning the Two Chief World Systems, Ptolemaic and Copernican*, trans. Stillman Drake (Berkeley and Los Angeles: University of California Press, 1967), 103.

15. Isaac Newton, "Twelve Articles on Religion," Keynes Ms. 8, King's College, Cambridge, U.K., The Newton Project, www.newtonproject. sussex.ac.uk/view/texts/normalized/THEM00008 (accessed January 12, 2012).

16. Guy Debord, *La société du spectacle* (1967; Kenaz Filan translation, 2012). Original available at http://sami.is.free.fr/Oeuvres/debord_societe_spec tacle_1.html (accessed January 12, 2012).

17. Malaclypse the Younger [Gregory Hill], *The Principia Discordia or, How I Found the Goddess and What I Did To Her When I Found Her, Wherein Is Explained Absolutely Everything Worth Knowing About Absolutely Anything (Fourth Edition)* (1970). Available at Principia Discordia, http://principi adiscordia.com/book/6.php (accessed January 13, 2012).

CHAPTER 15. COMMUNITY DIVINATION: THE PROCESS OF DISCERNMENT, PART 3

1. Robert Ferguson, *The Vikings: A History* (New York: Viking Adult, 2009), 109.

2. William G. Sinnigen and Arthur E. R. Boak, *A History of Rome to A.D. 565,* 6th ed. (New York: Macmillan, 1977), 92.

3. Max Maven, *Book of Fortunetelling* (New York: Prentice-Hall, 1992), 3.

4. Iona Opie and Moira Tatum, *A Dictionary of Superstition* (Oxford: Oxford University Press, 1992), 88.

5. Henry James Forman, *The Story of Prophecy* (New York: Farrar and Rinehart, 1936), 36.

6. Ibid., 38.

7. Maven, *Book of Fortunetelling,* 138.

8. Forman, Story of Prophecy, 41.

CHAPTER 18.
THE ROCKY ROAD TO INTRAFAITH DIALOGUE

1. Gilbert K. Chesterton, "Introductory Reports on the Importance of Orthodoxy," chap. I in *Heretics* (New York: John Lane, 1905). Available at Christian Classics Ethereal Library, www.ccel.org/ccel/chesterton/heretics .iv.html (accessed January 4, 2012).

EPILOGUE: THE FUTURE OF PEER-CORROBORATED
PERSONAL GNOSIS

1. Burton Watson, trans., *Basic Writings of Chuang-tzu* (New York: Columbia University Press, 2003), 110.

INDEX

Books of Related Interest

Drawing Down the Spirits
The Traditions and Techniques of Spirit Possession
by Kenaz Filan and Raven Kaldera

Neolithic Shamanism
Spirit Work in the Norse Tradition
by Raven Kaldera and Galina Krasskova

Pagan Astrology
Spell-Casting, Love Magic, and Shamanic Stargazing
by Raven Kaldera

New Orleans Voodoo Handbook
by Kenaz Filan

How to Create Sacred Water
A Guide to Rituals and Practices
by Kathryn W. Ravenwood

Shamanic Breathwork
Journeying beyond the Limits of the Self
by Linda Star Wolf

Barbarian Rites
The Spiritual World of the Vikings and the Germanic Tribes
by Hans-Peter Hasenfratz, Ph.D.

Alchemical Healing
A Guide to Spiritual, Physical, and Transformational Medicine
by Nicki Scully

INNER TRADITIONS • BEAR & COMPANY
P.O. Box 388
Rochester, VT 05767
1-800-246-8648
www.InnerTraditions.com

Or contact your local bookseller